"Not every reader of this book needs to be an investor in search of practical advice. Almost anybody curious about the relationship between the behavior of economics, the performance of firms and the ups and downs of the stockmarket will find something of interest here."

—*The Economist*

"*The Warren Buffett Way* is accessible to average readers because Mr. Hagstrom reduces the billionaire's techniques to some easily understandable tenets. For those willing to study fundamentals, the book demonstrates the rewards that can come down the road."

—*The Dallas Morning News*

"Forget the skepticism. Author Robert G. Hagstrom has done investors a service by systematically analyzing and describing the great investor's methods . . . Hagstrom reveals the basic simplicity of Buffett's thinking."

—*Investor's Digest of Canada*

"Simply the most important new stock book of the 1990s, to date. If you think you know all about Warren Buffett, you have a lot to learn from this book. I can't say enough good things about it, so I won't say much more than *read it.*"

—Kenneth L. Fisher, *Forbes*

"Warren Buffett is surely the Greatest Investor of the century—not so much because he built a great fortune within a free market as because he has shared his important thinking with us and has openly demonstrated the sagacity and courage so vital to success. Berkshire Hathaway has been my largest, longest investment. Warren has been my best teacher."

—Charles D. Ellis
Managing Partner
Greenwich Associates

"Warren Buffett is often characterized simply as a 'value investor' or a 'Ben Graham disciple.' Hagstrom fills in the rest of the story with some immensely practical pointers on pondering the market."

—Martin S. Fridson
Managing Director
Merrill Lynch

The Warren Buffett Way

Investment Strategies
of the
World's Greatest
Investor

ROBERT G. HAGSTROM, JR.

JOHN WILEY & SONS, INC.

New York • Chichester • Brisbane • Toronto • Singapore

To Maggie, my best friend and my wife,
whose love and support
makes all things possible for me.

Copyright © 1995, 1994 by Robert G. Hagstrom, Jr.
Published by John Wiley & Sons, Inc.

First Wiley mass market edition published 1997.

Library of Congress Cataloging-in-Publication Data:

Hagstrom, Robert G., 1956-
    The Warren Buffett way: investment strategies of the world's
    greatest investor / Robert G. Hagstrom.
        p.   cm.
    includes index.
    ISBN 0-471-04460-1 (cloth ed.)   ISBN 0-471-13298-5 (paper ed.)
    ISBN 0-471-17750-4 (mass market)
    1. Buffett, Warren.   2. Capitalists and financiers–United States–
Biography.   3. Investments–United States.   I. Title.
HG172.B84H34   1994
332.6–dc20   94-20586

Printed in the United States Of America

10 9 8 7 6 5 4 3

FOREWORD

ONE WEEKDAY EVENING early in 1989 I was home when the telephone rang. Our middle daughter, Annie, then eleven, was first to the phone. She told me that Warren Buffett was calling. I was convinced this had to be a prank. The caller started by saying, "This is Warren Buffett from Omaha [as if I might confuse him with some other Warren Buffett]. I just finished your book, I loved it, and I would like to quote one of your sentences in the Berkshire annual report. I have always wanted to do a book, but I never have gotten around to it." He spoke very rapidly with lots of enthusiasm and must have said forty words in fifteen or twenty seconds, including a couple of laughs and chuckles. I instantly agreed to his request and I think we talked for five or ten minutes. I remember he closed by saying, "If you ever visit Omaha and don't come by and see me, your name will be mud in Nebraska."

Clearly not wanting my name to be mud in Nebraska, I took him up on his offer about six months later. Warren Buffett gave me a personal tour of every square foot of the office (which did not take long, as the whole operation could fit inside less than half of a tennis court), and I said hello to all eleven employees. There was not a computer or a stock quotation machine to be found.

After about an hour we went to a local restaurant where I followed his lead and had a terrific steak and my first cherry Coke in thirty years. We talked about jobs we had as children, baseball, and bridge, and exchanged stories about companies in which we had held investments in the past. Warren discussed or answered questions about each stock and operation that Berkshire (he never called his company Berkshire Hathaway) owned.

Why has Warren Buffett been the best investor in history? What is he like as an individual, a shareholder, a manager, and an owner of entire companies? What is so unique about the Berkshire

Hathaway annual report, why does he donate so much effort to it, and what can someone learn from it? To attempt to answer those questions, I talked with him directly, and reread the last five annual reports and his earliest reports as chairman (the 1971 and 1972 reports each had only two pages of text). In addition, I had discussions with nine individuals that have been actively involved with Warren Buffett in varied relationships and from different viewpoints during the past four to over thirty years: Jack Byrne, Robert Denham, Don Keough, Carol Loomis, Tom Murphy, Charlie Munger, Carl Reichardt, Frank Rooney, and Seth Schofield.

In terms of his personal qualities, the responses were quite consistent. Warren Buffett is, first of all, very content. He loves everything he does, dealing with people and reading mass quantities of annual and quarterly reports and numerous newspapers and periodicals. As an investor he has discipline, patience, flexibility, courage, confidence, and decisiveness. He is always searching for investments where risk is eliminated or minimized. In addition, he is very adept at probability and as an oddsmaker. I believe this ability comes from an inherent love of simple math computations, his devotion and active participation in the game of bridge, and his long experience in underwriting and accepting high levels of risk in insurance and in reinsurance. He is willing to take risks where the odds of total loss are low and upside rewards are substantial. He lists his failures and mistakes and does not apologize. He enjoys kidding himself and compliments his associates in objective terms.

Warren Buffett is a great student of business and a wonderful listener, and able to determine the key elements of a company or a complex issue with high speed and precision. He can make a decision not to invest in something in as little as two minutes and conclude that it is time to make a major purchase in just a few days of research. He is always prepared, for as he has said in an annual report, "Noah did not start building the Ark when it was raining."

As a manager he almost never calls a division head or the chief executive of a company but is delighted at any time of the day or night for them to call him to report something or seek counsel. After investing in a stock or purchasing an entire operation, he becomes a cheerleader and sounding board: "At Berkshire we don't tell 400% hitters how to swing," using an analogy to baseball management.

Two examples of Warren Buffett's willingness to learn and

adapt himself are public speaking and computer usage. In the 1950s Warren invested $100 in a Dale Carnegie course "not to prevent my knees from knocking when public speaking but to do public speaking while my knees are knocking." At the Berkshire annual meeting in front of more than 2,000 people, Warren Buffett sits on a stage with Charlie Munger, and, without notes, lectures and responds to questions in a fashion that would please Will Rogers, Ben Graham, King Solomon, Phil Fisher, David Letterman, and Billy Crystal. To be able to play more bridge, early in 1994 Warren learned how to use a computer so he could join a network where you can play with other individuals from their locations all over the country. Perhaps in the near future he will begin to use some of the hundreds of data retrieval and information services on companies that are available on computers today for investment research.

Warren Buffett stresses that the critical investment factor is determining the intrinsic value of a business and paying a fair or bargain price. He doesn't care what the general stock market has done recently or will do in the future. He purchased over $1 billion of Coca-Cola in 1988 and 1989 after the stock had risen over fivefold the prior six years and over five-hundredfold the previous sixty years. He made four times his money in three years and plans to make a lot more the next five, ten, and twenty years with Coke. In 1976 he purchased a very major position in GEICO when the stock had declined from $61 to $2 and the general perception was that the stock was definitely going to zero.

How can the average investor employ Warren Buffett's methods? Warren Buffett never invests in businesses he cannot understand or that are outside his "Circle of Competence." All investors can, over time, obtain and intensify their "Circle of Competence" in an industry where they are professionally involved or in some sector of business they enjoy researching. One does not have to be correct very many times in a lifetime as Warren states that twelve investment decisions in his forty year career have made all the difference.

Risk can be reduced greatly by concentrating on only a few holdings if it forces investors to be more careful and thorough in their research. Normally more than 75 percent of Berkshire's common stock holdings are represented by only five different securities. One of the principles demonstrated clearly several times in this book is to buy great businesses when they are having a temporary problem or when the stock market declines and creates bargain prices for outstanding franchises. Stop trying to predict the direction of the stock market, the economy, interest rates, or elections, and stop wasting money on individuals that do this for a living. Study the facts and the financial condition, value the company's future outlook, and purchase when everything is in your favor. Many people invest in a way similar to playing poker all night without ever looking at their cards.

Very few investors would have had the knowledge and courage to purchase GEICO at $2.00 or Wells Fargo or General Dynamics when they were depressed as there were numerous learned people saying those companies were in substantial trouble. However, Warren Buffett's purchase of Capital Cities/ABC, Gillette, Washington Post, Affiliated Publications, Freddie Mac, or Coca-Cola (which have produced over $6 billion of profits for Berkshire Hathaway, or 60 percent of the $10 billion of shareholders' equity) were all well-run companies with strong histories of profitability, and were dominant business franchises.

In addition to his own shareholders, Warren Buffett uses the Berkshire annual report to help the general public become better investors. On both sides of his family he descended from newspaper editors, and his Aunt Alice was a public school teacher for more than thirty years. Warren Buffett enjoys both teaching and writing about business in general and investing in particular. He taught on a volunteer basis when he was twenty-one at the University of Nebraska in Omaha. In 1955, when he was working in New York City, he taught an adult education course on the stock market at Scarsdale High School. For ten years in the late 1960s and 1970s he gave a free lecture course at Creighton University. In 1977 he served on a committee headed by Al Sommer, Jr., to advise the Securities and Exchange Commission on corporate disclosure. After that involvement, the scale of the Berkshire annual report changed dramatically with the 1977 report written in late 1977 and early 1978. The format became more similar to the partnership reports he produced from 1956 to 1969.

Since the early 1980s, the Berkshire annual reports have informed shareholders of the performance of the holdings of the company and new investments, updated the status of the insurance and the reinsurance industry, and (since 1982) have listed acquisition criteria about businesses Berkshire would like to purchase. The report is generously laced with examples, analogies, stories, and metaphors containing the do's and don'ts of proper investing in stocks.

Warren Buffett has established a high standard for the future performance of Berkshire by setting an objective of growing intrinsic value by 15 percent a year over the long term, something few people, and no one from 1956 to 1993 besides himself, have ever done. He has stated it will be a difficult standard to maintain due to the much larger size of the company, but there are always opportunities around and Berkshire keeps lots of cash ready to invest and it grows every year. His confidence is somewhat underlined by the final nine words of the June 1993 annual report on page 60: "Berkshire has not declared a cash dividend since 1967."

Warren Buffett has stated that he has always wanted to write a book on investing. Hopefully that will happen some day. However, until that event, his annual reports are filling that function in a fashion somewhat similar to the nineteenth-century authors who wrote in serial form: Edgar Allen Poe, William Makepeace Thackery, and Charles Dickens. The Berkshire Hathaway annual reports from 1977 through 1993 are seventeen chapters of that book. And also in the interim we now have *The Warren Buffett Way,* in which Robert Hagstrom outlines Buffett's career and presents examples of how his investment technique and methods evolved as well as the important individuals in that process. The book also details the key investment decisions that produced Buffett's unmatched record of performance. Finally, it contains the thinking and the philosophy of an investor that consistently made money using the tools available to every citizen no matter their level of wealth.

PETER S. LYNCH

PREFACE

WARREN BUFFETT is an amazing man. Not only has he become our country's leading investment authority, his performance record, which dates back over four decades, is unparalleled. Buffett's personal net worth is currently well over $10 billion, a direct result of his investment savvy. Yet his personal style and temperament are not what you would expect of a typical billionaire. The company he directs, Berkshire Hathaway, is headquartered not in New York but in Omaha, Nebraska. Buffett drives his own car and does his own taxes. He is gracious, kind, and honest. He is also enormously intelligent, quick, and intuitive. A man of great warmth and genuine charm, Buffett has captured the fancy of the media and of investors large and small.

The original edition of this book enjoyed remarkable success, and as its author that is, of course, gratifying. But I know, without question, that the success of the book is really a testament to Warren Buffett. In a period when investment markets appear more puzzling than sensible, it is not surprising that investors all over the world have become keenly interested in Buffett's investment approach and ideas.

The buy-and-hold investment strategy that is at the core of Buffett's approach appeals intuitively to people. The concept of buying a good business and holding this investment for several years, thus achieving returns commensurate with the economics of the business, is simple and straightforward. Investors can easily understand and appreciate the mechanics of this approach. Warren Buffett's attraction is twofold. One, he is the designated representative of the buy-and-hold approach and, two, he also happened to become a billionaire by practicing this style of investing.

I believe *The Warren Buffett Way* describes a simple approach. There are no computer programs to learn, no two-inch thick investment banking manuals to decipher. Whether you are financially able to purchase 10 percent of a company or merely one hundred shares, *The Warren Buffett Way* can help you achieve profitable investment returns. But do not judge yourself against Warren Buffett. His brilliance, his resources, his intuitive powers, his experience accumulated during four decades of simultaneously owning and investing in businesses all make it improbable that you can imitate his returns. Instead, compare your results against your peer group, whether that group includes growth mutual funds, index funds, or the market in general.

To be successful you must be willing to study and learn about your companies, and have the emotional fortitude to disregard short-term changes in the market. If you are in need of constant affirmation, particularly from the stock market, the probability of benefiting from *The Warren Buffett Way* is diminished. But if you can think for yourself, apply relatively simple methods, and have the courage of your convictions, the chance for profit is greatly increased.

NEW FOR THE PAPERBACK EDITION

In the year since the original edition of *The Warren Buffett Way* was published, quite a lot has happened to Warren Buffett and Berkshire Hathaway. As such, the text has been updated to reflect Buffett's latest investments.

The most notable event that has recently occurred is the well-publicized purchase of Capital Cities/ABC by the Walt Disney Company. This merger, which is the second-largest corporate takeover ever, makes Buffett one of the largest shareholders of the Walt Disney Company. The Disney–Cap Cities merger is explained and analyzed in Chapter Eight, "A Few More Good Stocks." This chapter is entirely new to the paperback edition and also analyzes four other recent Buffett purchases including Gannett Company, PNC Bank, Salomon Incorporated, and American Express Company. The previous edition's concluding chapter, "An Unreasonable Man," is now Chapter Nine.

Throughout this paperback edition we have made editorial changes and updated tables when appropriate. Notably, the valuation tables in the Appendix now use the term *owner earnings* as described in the book in place of the more confusing term *cash flow.* We have also identified *k* in the tables as the discount rate, which often corresponds to the thirty-year U.S. Treasury bond. However, as you will see, Buffett sometimes adjusts the discount rate higher than bond yields particularly during periods when interest rates are cyclically low.

Even with these updates, the principles outlined in the book have remained the same. "That's why we call them principles," Buffett once quipped.

I have an obligation to disclose that I am now portfolio manager of a mutual fund called the Focus Trust. This fund is being managed based on the same tenets outlined in this book. As such, the fund owns several of the stocks discussed in this book. Four stocks in particular, The American Express Company, Capital Cities/ABC, The Walt Disney Company, and Gannett, are recent purchases of the Fund and may be purchased by the fund soon after this paperback edition appears. To ensure complete disclosure, I have also mentioned this fact by using a footnote throughout Chapter Eight.

WRITING THIS BOOK

In 1984, while training to be an investment broker with a brokerage firm, I was asked to read a Berkshire Hathaway annual report. This was my first exposure to Warren Buffett. Like most people who read Berkshire's annual reports, I was instantly impressed with the clarity of Buffett's writings. As a young professional during the 1980s, my head was always spinning trying to keep up with the stock market, the economy, and the constant buying and selling of securities. Yet each time I read a story about Warren Buffett or an article written by him, his rational voice seemed to rise above the market's chaos. It was this calming influence that inspired me to write this book.

I had never met Warren Buffett before writing this book, and I did not consult with him while developing it. Although, consultation surely would have been an added bonus, I was fortunate to be able to draw from his own extensive writings on the subject of investing dating back well over two decades. Through the book I have employed extensive quotes from Berkshire Hathaway's annual reports, specifically the chairman's letters. Mr. Buffett granted permission to use this copyrighted material, but only after he had an opportunity to review the book. However, this permission in no way implies that Mr. Buffett cooperated on the book or that he made available to me secrets or strategies that are not already available from his writings. Almost everything Mr. Buffett does is public, but it is loosely noted. What was needed, in my opinion, and what would be valuable to investors, was a thorough examination of his thoughts and strategies aligned with the purchases that Berkshire made over the years, all compiled in one source.

The principal challenge I faced in writing the book was to prove or disprove Buffett's confession that "what (I) do is not beyond anybody else's competence." Some critics argue that, despite his success, Warren Buffett's idiosyncrasies prevent his investment approach from being widely adopted. I disagree. Mr. Buffett *is* idiosyncratic—it is a source of his success; but I will argue that his methodology, once understood, is applicable to both individual and institutional investors alike. It is the goal of this book to help investors employ the strategies that I believe made Warren Buffett successful.

In order for investors to adapt Buffett's approach it was necessary first to provide an outline of his tenets, or concepts. In this regard, I believe the book has succeeded. But I want to emphasize that even if you follow all the tenets outlined in the book, it is not likely that you will generate a 23 percent average annual gain over the next thirty years. Even Mr. Buffett admits the possibility of Berkshire repeating this performance is remote. However, I do believe that if you follow these tenets you will stand a better chance of outperforming the market.

ACKNOWLEDGMENTS

I am very fortunate that numerous friends and associates took the time and energy to help me develop this book. First, I would like to thank both of my partners, John Lloyd and Virginia Leith, who supported this project from its beginning. I am especially grateful to Virginia, who suffered through reading the entire original manuscript as well as many revisions and has made countless valuable comments. Thanks also to Kelly Anne Kelly, Carol Greening, and Cindy Yeager, who keep our firm running smoothly.

Several people have read parts of the manuscript and/or made valuable suggestions. I would like to thank Burton J. Gray and Charles D. Ellis for their earliest words of encouragement. Thanks also to Peter Gibbons-Neff and Jack Gregg. Louis DiSilvestro and Charles DeVinney, at Marshall and Stevens, were particularly helpful with valuation issues. Thanks to Robert Coleman, at Combined Capital Management, who shared his valuable time entertaining lengthy discussions about Warren Buffett. I am also indebted to William H. Miller III, president of Legg Mason Fund Advisor, who has been a friend and intellectual coach for many years.

I owe a great deal to a valued friend, Charles E. Haldeman, Jr., at Cooke & Bieler. Ed took the time to read the entire manuscript and generously made several suggestions that greatly improved this work.

Stewart Davis and Mary Melaugh of Symmetrix Corporation, in Lexington, Massachusetts, completed an exhaustive search on several topics in this book. The thoroughness of their research gave me confidence that little was left uncovered.

I am particularly grateful to John Fitzgerald and Linda Penfold for their assistance at Standard & Poor's Compustat. Both John and Linda provided valuable financial research and graphs.

My relationship with John Wiley & Sons has been pleasurable. I wish to thank Myles Thompson, finance editor, who championed this book from its earliest proposal. Thanks also to Michael Cohn who took the time to help a first-time writer.

I want to express my deep appreciation to Maggie Stuckey who worked tirelessly fine-tuning the book. Her care and thoughtful suggestions made this book measurably better and I will always be grateful to her.

Thanks also to Warren Buffett. Not only for his teachings but for allowing me to use his copyrighted material. It is next to impossible to improve on what Mr. Buffett has already said. The book is better for having been allowed to use his written words rather than subjecting you to reading a second-best paraphrase.

Without a doubt, I would have never started this book, much less been able to finish, without the love and care of my family. My parents, Bob and Ruth Hagstrom, never wavered in their support of my ventures. Their patience allowed me to find my own path. My sons, Robert and John, were a great help sitting on their father's lap helping him type the manuscript. My daughter Kimmy was a greater help baby-sitting her brothers while I corrected the mistakes made while they sat on my lap. Kimmy pulled extra duty in the past several months, and I appreciate and love her all the more for that. Lastly, and most important, I want to thank my wonderful wife, Maggie. On the first day I told her I was going to write this book, she smiled and convinced me that it could be done. Over the months she managed our family while I had the luxury of time to work. Maggie gave me the unending love and encouragement that helped bring this book to a successful completion.

ROBERT G. HAGSTROM, JR.

Philadelphia, Pennsylvania
September 1995

CONTENTS

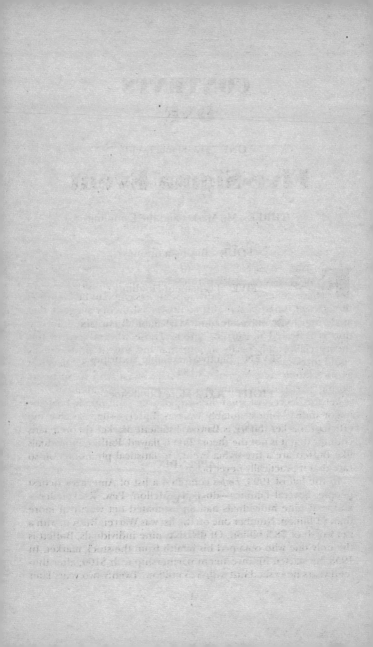

ONE

Five-Sigma Event

FOR YEARS ACADEMICIANS and investment professionals have debated the validity of what has come to be known as the *efficient market theory*. This controversial theory suggests that analyzing stocks is a waste of time because all available information is reflected in current prices. Those who adhere to this theory claim, only partly in jest, that investment professionals could throw darts at a page of stock quotes and pick winners just as successfully as a seasoned financial analyst who spent hours poring over the latest annual report or quarterly statement.

Yet the success of some individuals who continually beat the major indices—most notably Warren Buffett—suggests that the efficient market theory is flawed. Efficient market theoreticians counter that it is not the theory that is flawed. Rather, individuals like Buffett are a five-sigma event,[1] a statistical phenomenon so rare that it practically never occurs.

In the fall of 1993, *Forbes* compiled a list of America's richest people. Several families—du Pont, Mellon, Pew, Rockefeller—and sixty-nine individuals had an estimated net worth of more than $1 billion. Number one on the list was Warren Buffett, with a net worth of $8.3 billion. Of the sixty-nine individuals, Buffett is the only one who obtained his wealth from the stock market. In 1956, he started his investment partnership with $100; after thirteen years he cashed out with $25 million. Twenty-two years later

1

he had amassed the largest individual fortune in the United States. But to fully appreciate Buffett, you have to go beyond the dollars and performance accolades.

PERSONAL HISTORY AND INVESTMENT BEGINNINGS

Warren Edward Buffett was born August 30, 1930, in Omaha, Nebraska. He is the son of Howard and Leila Buffett. Howard Buffett, a long-time resident of Omaha, was a local stockbroker and Republican congressman. As a boy, Warren Buffett was fascinated with numbers. He easily could keep track of mathematical calculations in his head. At age eight, Buffett began reading his father's books on the stock market. When he was eleven, he marked the board at Harris Upham where his father was a broker. That same year he bought his first shares of stock, Cities Service Preferred.

When Buffett lived in Washington, D.C., while his father served in Congress, his interests turned entrepreneurial. At age thirteen, Buffett worked two paper routes, delivering the *Washington Post* and the Washington *Times-Herald*. With his savings, he acquired reconditioned pinball machines for $25 each and placed them in local barbershops. Soon Buffett owned seven machines and was taking home $50 a week. Later, with a high school friend, Buffett bought a 1934 Rolls Royce for $350 and rented it out for $35 a day. By the time he graduated from high school at sixteen, Buffett had saved $6,000.

While in his senior year at the University of Nebraska, Buffett read Benjamin Graham's classic book, *The Intelligent Investor*. This treatise on investing so influenced Buffett that, after receiving his college degree, he left his hometown of Omaha and traveled to New York to study with Ben Graham at the Columbia Graduate Business School. Graham preached the importance of understanding a company's intrinsic value. He believed that investors who accurately calculated this value and bought shares below it were better off. This mathematical approach appealed to Buffett's sense of numbers.

After graduating from Columbia with a master's degree in economics, Buffett returned to Omaha to serve a brief stint in his father's brokerage firm. During this period, Buffett stayed in contact with his former teacher by writing to him about various investment ideas. In 1954, at Graham's invitation, Buffett moved to New York and joined the Graham–Newman Corporation. During his tenure at Graham–Newman, Buffett became fully immersed in his mentor's investment approach. In addition to Buffett, Graham also hired Walter Schloss, Tom Knapp, and Bill Ruane. Schloss went on to manage money at WSJ Ltd. Partners for twenty-eight years. Knapp, a Princeton chemistry major, was a founding partner in Tweedy, Browne Partnerships, and Ruane started the Sequoia Fund.

In 1956, Graham–Newman disbanded. Graham, then sixty-one, decided to retire. Buffett returned to Omaha. Armed with the knowledge he had acquired from Graham, and with the financial backing of family and friends, Buffett began a limited investment partnership. He was twenty-five years old.

The partnership began with seven limited partners who together contributed $105,000. Buffett, the general partner, started with one hundred dollars. The limited partners received 6 percent annually on their investment and 75 percent of the profits above this bogey. Buffett earned the other 25 percent. Over the next thirteen years, Buffett compounded money at an annual rate of 29.5 percent.[2] This was no easy task. Although the Dow Jones Industrial Average declined in price five different years in that thirteen-year period, Buffett's partnership never had a down year.

Buffett promised his partners that "our investments will be chosen on the basis of value not popularity" and that the partnership "will attempt to reduce permanently capital loss (not short-term quotational loss) to a minimum."[3] During the partnership, Buffett not only bought minority positions but controlling interests in several public and private companies. In 1961 he bought Dempster Mill Manufacturing Company, a farm equipment manufacturer, and in 1962 he began purchasing shares in an ailing textile company called Berkshire Hathaway.

As Buffett's reputation became more widely known, more people asked him to manage their money. As more investors came in, more partnerships were formed, until Buffett decided in 1962 to reorganize everything into a single partnership. That year, he moved the partnership office from his home to Kiewit Plaza in Omaha, where his office remains today. By 1965, the partnership's assets had grown to $26 million.

In 1969, Buffett decided to end the investment partnership. He

3

found the market highly speculative and worthwhile values increasingly scarce. During the late 1960s, the stock market was dominated by highly priced growth stocks. The "nifty fifty" were on the tip of every investor's tongue. Stocks like Avon, IBM, Polaroid, and Xerox were trading at fifty to one hundred times earnings. Buffett mailed a letter to his partners confessing that he was out of step with the current market environment. "On one point, however, I am clear," he said. "I will not abandon a previous approach whose logic I understand, although I find it difficult to apply, even though it may mean foregoing large and apparently easy profits to embrace an approach which I don't fully understand, have not practiced successfully and which possibly could lead to substantial permanent loss of capital."[4]

At the beginning of the partnership, Buffett had set a goal of outperforming the Dow by an average of ten percentage points each year. Between 1957 and 1969, he did beat the Dow—not by ten percentage points a year but by twenty-two! (See Figure 1.1.) When the partnership disbanded, investors received their portions. Some investors were given an education in municipal bonds and others were directed to a money manager. The only individual that Buffett recommended was Bill Ruane, his old classmate at Columbia. Ruane agreed to manage some of the partners'

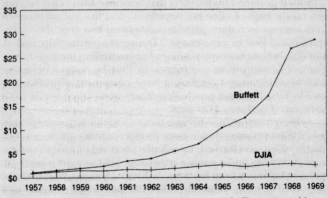

Figure 1.1. Cumulative value of dollars invested, Buffett partnership vs. Dow Jones Industrial Average.

money and thus was born the Sequoia Fund. Other members of the partnership, including Buffett, invested their proportional interests in Berkshire Hathaway. Buffett's share of the partnership had grown to $25 million, and that was enough to give him control of Berkshire Hathaway. During the next two decades, both Buffett's and Berkshire's wealth soared.

THE EARLY DAYS OF BERKSHIRE HATHAWAY

The original company, Berkshire Cotton Manufacturing, was incorporated in 1889. Forty years later, Berkshire combined operations with several other textile mills, resulting in one of New England's largest industrial companies. During this period, Berkshire produced approximately 25 percent of the country's cotton needs and absorbed 1 percent of New England's electrical capacity. In 1955, Berkshire merged with Hathaway Manufacturing and the name was subsequently changed to Berkshire Hathaway.

Unfortunately, the years following the merger were dismal. In less than ten years, stockholder's equity dropped by half and loss from operations exceeded $10 million. Despite these miserable results, the Buffett partnership took control of Berkshire Hathaway in 1965. During the next twenty years, Buffett, along with Ken Chace who managed the textile group, labored intensely to turn around the New England textile mills. Results were disappointing. Returns on equity struggled to reach double digits.

By the late 1970s, shareholders of Berkshire Hathaway began to question the wisdom of retaining an investment in textiles. Buffett made no attempt to hide the difficulties, but on several occasions explained his thinking: the textile mills were the largest employer in their area; the work force was an older age group that possessed relatively nontransferable skills; management had shown a high degree of enthusiasm; the unions were being reasonable; and, lastly, Buffett believed that some profits could be attained in the textile business. However, he made it clear that he expected the textile group to earn positive returns on modest capital expenditures. "I won't close down a business of sub-normal profitability merely to add a fraction of a point to our corporate returns," said Buffett. "I also feel it inappropriate for even an exceptionally profitable company to fund an operation once it appears to have unending losses in prospect. Adam Smith would disagree with my first proposition and Karl Marx would disagree with my second; the middle ground," he explained, "is the only position that leaves me comfortable."[5]

As Berkshire Hathaway entered the 1980s, Buffett was coming to grips with certain realities. First, the very nature of the textile business made high returns on equity improbable. Textiles are commodities and commodities by definition have a difficult time differentiating their products from those of their competitors. The foreign competition, employing a cheaper labor force, was squeezing profit margins. Second, in order to stay competitive, the textile mills would require significant capital improvements— a prospect that is frightening in an inflationary environment and disastrous if the business returns are anemic.

Buffett was faced with a difficult choice. If he made large capital contributions to the textile division in order to remain competitive, Berkshire Hathaway would be left with poor returns on what was becoming an expanding capital base. If he did not reinvest, Berkshire's textile mills would become less competitive with other domestic textile manufacturers. Whether Berkshire reinvested or not, foreign competition continued to have an advantage by employing a cheaper labor force.

By 1980, the annual report revealed ominous clues for the future of the textile group. That year, the group lost its prestigious lead-off position in the Chairman's Letter. By the next year, textiles were not discussed in the Letter at all. Then, the inevitable: in July of 1985, Buffett closed the books on the textile group, thus ending a business that began some one hundred years earlier.

Despite the misfortunes of the textile group, the experience was not a complete failure. First, Buffett learned a valuable lesson about corporate turnarounds: they seldom succeed. Second, the textile group did generate enough capital in the earlier years to buy an insurance company and that is a much brighter story.

INSURANCE OPERATIONS

In March of 1967, Berkshire Hathaway purchased, for $8.6 million, the outstanding stock of two insurance companies headquartered in Omaha: National Indemnity Company and National Fire

& Marine Insurance Company. It was the beginning of Berkshire Hathaway's phenomenal success story.

To appreciate the phenomenon, it is important to recognize the true value of owning an insurance company. Insurance companies are sometimes good investments, sometimes not. They are, however, always terrific investment vehicles. Policyholders, in paying premiums, provide a constant stream of cash; insurance companies invest this cash until claims are filed. Because of the uncertainty of when claims will occur, insurance companies opt to invest in liquid marketable securities—primarily stocks and bonds. Thus Warren Buffett had acquired not only two modestly healthy companies, but a cast-iron vehicle for managing investments.

In 1967, National Indemnity and National Fire & Marine Insurance had a bond portfolio worth more than $24.7 million and stock portfolio worth $7.2 million. In two years, the combined stock and bond portfolio of the insurance companies approached $42 million. This was a handsome portfolio for a seasoned stock picker like Buffett. He had already experienced some limited success managing the textile company's security portfolio. When Buffett took control of Berkshire in 1965, the corporation had $2.9 million in marketable securities. By the end of the first year, Buffett enlarged the securities account to $5.4 million. In 1967, the dollar return from investing was three times the return of the entire textile division, which had ten times the equity base of the common stock portfolio.

It has been argued that when Buffett entered the insurance business and exited the textile business, he merely exchanged one commodity company for another. Insurance companies, like textiles, are selling a product that is indistinguishable. Insurance policies are standardized and can be copied by anyone. There are no trademarks, patents, advantages in location, or raw materials that distinguish insurance companies. It is easy to get licensed, and insurance rates are an open book. Often the most distinguishable attribute of an insurance company is its personnel. The efforts of individual managers have enormous impact on an insurance company's performance.

In the late 1960s insurance was a profitable business. At year end 1967, National Indemnity had a net income of $1.6 million on $16.8 million in premiums earned. By 1968, while net income rose to $2.2 million, premiums earned increased to $20 million.

Buffett's early success in insurance led him to expand aggressively into this group. During the 1970s, he purchased three and organized five other insurance companies.

Despite this positive momentum, by the late 1970s, Buffett was beginning to have some concerns. Certain factors beyond his immediate control were beginning to affect the cost side of the equation. Although the consumer price index was rising 3 percent annually, medical and auto repair costs were rising three times faster. Furthermore, the damages awarded to plaintiffs in court cases, damages that insurance companies had to pay, were increasing at an alarming rate. Buffett estimated that total costs were rising approximately 1 percent per month; unless insurance rates rose equally, profit margins would begin to shrink.

But rates were not rising; they were dropping. In a commodity business, low pricing is used to gain market share. The problem, Buffett learned, was that some companies were willing to sell insurance policies below the cost of doing business rather than risk losing market share. They apparently were betting that insurance rates would improve so they could recapture profits and offset earlier underwriting losses. Buffett's common sense prevented him from extending Berkshire's insurance operations into unprofitable territory. Buffett believed that most insurers would not stop writing unprofitable policies until there was a huge catastrophe, natural or financial.

Unwilling to compete on price basis, Buffett instead sought to distinguish Berkshire's insurance companies in two other ways. First, by its financial strength. Today, Berkshire's net worth ranks second only to State Farm in the property casualty industry. Additionally, Berkshire's investment portfolio (its *float*) compared to premium volume is three times the industry average.

The second method of differentiation involved Buffett's total indifference to the level of insurance volume written by Berkshire. In any given year, according to Buffett, he was willing to write five times as much business as the year before, or only one-fifth as much. His hope was to always write large volumes of business but only at prices that make sense. If prices were low, he was quite content to do very little business. This underwriting philosophy was instilled at National Indemnity by the founder of the company, Jack Ringwalt. Since that time, Buffett said, Berkshire has never wavered from this underwriting discipline.

Berkshire's dramatic change in insurance volume was not caused by Berkshire itself, explained Buffett, but by the "here today, gone tomorrow" behavior of other insurance companies. When competing insurance companies rushed to offer prices below expected costs, customers left Berkshire. However, when insurance companies vanished from the marketplace because they were frightened by recent losses, Berkshire, noted Buffett, stood by as a constant supplier of insurance, but only at prices that made sense. Buffett's approach is likened to a stabilizer for the insurance industry. "We add huge capacity when capacity is short and become less competitive only when capacity is abundant. Of course we don't follow this policy in the interests of stabilization," he said, "we follow it because we believe it to be the most sensible and profitable course of business."[6]

In the 1990s, brutal price competition, continual underwriting losses, and poor investment results combine to produce a shaky picture for the insurance industry as a whole. Buffett continually lectures that financial soundness and fiscal responsibility will make a significant difference for Berkshire Hathaway. Berkshire's superior financial strength has distinguished its insurance operations from the rest of the industry. In a sense, the financial integrity that Buffett has imposed on Berkshire's insurance companies has created a franchise in what is otherwise a commodity business.

To be sure, Berkshire's insurance companies experienced pain over the last ten years, and Buffett suffered his fair share of insurance mistakes. But his investment expertise and common sense business practices have placed shareholders of Berkshire Hathaway in an enviable position.

NONINSURANCE BUSINESSES

Berkshire Hathaway, Inc., is best understood as a holding company. In addition to the insurance companies, it also owns a newspaper, a candy company, a furniture store, a jewelry store, an encyclopedia publisher, a vacuum cleaner business, and a company that manufactures and distributes uniforms.

The story of how Buffett came to acquire these diverse businesses is interesting in itself. Perhaps more to the point, the stories collectively give us a valuable insight into Buffett's way of looking at companies. It will come as little surprise that he used the same yardstick to evaluate companies for possible acquisitions as for additions to the Berkshire Hathaway stock portfolio. And there is another factor. As we will see later, owning these companies also provided Buffett with direct hands-on experience that was to become critical in later stock acquisitions.

Blue Chip Stamps

Shortly after purchasing Berkshire Hathaway, Buffett began buying stock in a holding company called Diversified Retailing. It owned a Baltimore department store called Hochschild-Kohn and Associated Retail Stores, a chain of seventy-five women's apparel stores. Like the textile mills, Buffett was able to buy the company at less than book value and, additionally, the people managing the business were, in Buffett's words, "first class." Unfortunately, like the textile mills, a bargain purchase price and top management did not save Buffett from inheriting a difficult business. Three years after Berkshire merged with Diversified Retailing, Buffett sold Hochschild-Kohn. In 1987, he sold Associated Stores. Both businesses were sold because of declining economics. But just as the textile mills allowed Buffett the opportunity to capitalize on the insurance business, the purchase of Diversified Retailing allowed Berkshire the opportunity to control three new businesses.

In addition to department stores, Diversified Retailing owned a company called Blue Chip Stamps, which provided supermarkets and gasoline stations with trading stamps to give their customers. Stamps were collected into books and in turn exchanged for merchandise. To purchase the merchandise, the supermarkets and gasoline stations created a pool of money, or float, which Blue Chip Stamps managed. In the late 1960s Blue Chip Stamps had a float of more than $60 million in unredeemed stamps. This float ultimately allowed Buffett to purchase other businesses including a candy company, a newspaper, and a savings and loan.

Berkshire Hathaway, through its subsidiaries, began purchasing stock in Blue Chip Stamps in the late 1960s. Buffett himself had also bought Blue Chip Stamps stock. After Diversified Retailing and Berkshire Hathaway merged, Berkshire Hathaway became the majority owner of Blue Chip Stamps. Finally, in 1983, Berkshire acquired the balance of Blue Chip Stamps in a merger between the two companies.

See's Candy Shops

In January 1972, Blue Chip Stamps purchased See's Candy Shops, a West Coast manufacturer and retailer of boxed chocolates. The asking price for the company was $40 million. See's had $10 million in cash so the net price was actually $30 million. Buffett offered $25 million and the sellers accepted.

See's long-term record of performance was the responsibility of Chuck Huggins, who had managed See's since Blue Chip Stamps' purchase. Today, Huggins manages 225 candy shops and oversees the production and distribution of 27 million pounds of candy each year. In 1993, See's had revenues of $201 million and returned to Berkshire $24.3 million in net operating earnings. This is an excellent result considering that chocolate consumption in the United States is stagnant. See's success is based on two essential ingredients, product quality and customer service.

In 1982, Buffett was offered $125 million to sell See's—five times the 1972 purchase price. Buffett decided to pass. A wise decision. Over the last eleven years, See's has returned to Berkshire $212 million—cash—in after-tax earnings. During that same period, See's required $44 million in capital expenditures, roughly equal to the $39 million that it depreciated and amortized.

Buffalo News

Like See's, the *Buffalo News* was added to Berkshire Hathaway's fold via Blue Chip Stamps. In 1977, Blue Chip bought the *Buffalo News* for $33 million from the estate of Mrs. Edward H. Butler, Jr. As a boy, Buffett and a childhood friend published a horse racing tip sheet called the *Stable Boy Selections*. At that time he could only dream of owning a major metropolitan newspaper. Today, Buffett trumpets the success of the *Buffalo News* like a proud father boasting the success of an offspring, and there is substantial reason to feel proud.

Penetration rate and news hole are two statistics that help measure the success of the newspaper. The penetration rate, or percentage of local households that purchase the newspaper each day, ranks the *News* as the number one major metropolitan newspaper in its market. The *news hole*, the portion of the newspaper devoted to news rather than advertising, reached 52.3 percent in 1990. That makes the *News* the most "news-rich" paper in the country.

The relationship between news hole and profits is inexorably linked. A newspaper with a high news hole will attract a wider cross section of readers, thereby increasing the penetration rate. The higher penetration rate makes a newspaper a valuable advertising vehicle for businesses. Furthermore, because the *News* has kept costs down, it can afford to publish a newspaper with half the pages devoted to news.

Much of the success of the *News* comes from the stewardship of Murray Light, editor, and Stan Lipsey, publisher. Both have been with the *News* since the Blue Chip Stamps purchase of the paper and the subsequent merger with Berkshire Hathaway. Stan Lipsey and Murray Light can take a bow for making the *Buffalo News* the stalwart of the newspaper industry.

A SEARCH FOR NEW COMPANIES

Starting in 1982, Buffett began to place advertisements in Berkshire's annual reports seeking businesses that might be for sale. Specifically, he was looking for companies with consistent earnings power of at least $10 million after tax. Furthermore he wanted companies that were able to achieve good returns on equity without using much debt. The business had to be simple and understandable. If it involved high technology, he admittedly would not understand the company. Finally, Buffett wanted companies that were able to provide their own management; he did not want to supply it.

In Berkshire's 1990 annual report, Buffett shared a letter he had sent to someone who was considering selling his family business. It is interesting for what it reveals of Buffett's thinking.

Buffett pointed out in the letter that Berkshire does not have an acquisition department or a staff of MBA-trained business managers. When Buffett buys a company, he does not supply the management. The business that Buffett purchases operates with an extraordinary degree of freedom and is usually managed by the same family members who managed the business before the Berkshire purchase. In fact, Buffett typically requires that the people who were responsible for successfully managing the business remain with the company. Because of tax matters, Berkshire purchases a majority stake in the company so it can consolidate the earnings. The previous owners frequently retain a minority stake in the company. The only areas that Buffett controls are capital allocation and compensation of the top managers. Outside these two areas, managers are free to operate as they see fit. As Buffett remarked, some managers choose to discuss the business environment with him and others do not. It is a matter of personalities.

After a sale, Buffett wrote to the prospective seller, you will be no richer than before; you will merely have a different type of wealth. You will exchange a percent of a closely held business for a lot of cash. The cash will ultimately be put into stocks and bonds, which you will understand less well than the original business.

Because family members of closely held businesses often have conflicting demands on assets, the type of business relationship that Berkshire offers is ideal. The owners are able to redeploy the wealth among the family members and at the same time retain a portion of a business they have long cherished. Buffett gets a great company, a proportional share of the company's earnings, and a management team with a proven track record.

From the advertisements in Berkshire's annual reports, a menagerie of companies has been purchased. In 1993, combined sales for the noninsurance operations were $2.0 billion; Berkshire's share of the net after tax earnings was $176 million—37 percent of Berkshire's total 1993 operating earnings.

Nebraska Furniture Mart

The Nebraska Furniture Mart (NFM), a single-store operation in Omaha, is the largest home-furnishing store in the country. In 1983, Berkshire Hathaway purchased 90 percent of NFM, leaving 10 percent with the family members who were retained to manage the business. Louie Blumkin remained president and his three sons—Ron, Irv, and Steve—contributed to the company's success. The matriarch of the family and chairman of the board was Rose Blumkin, Louie's mother. Mrs. Blumkin, warmly referred to as Mrs. B, began NFM in 1937 with $500 in capital. When Buffett bought NFM, Mrs. B was ninety years old and was still working seven days a week.

From day one, Mrs. B's marketing strategy was "sell cheap and tell the truth." When Buffett purchased NFM, it was generating $100 million in annual sales while operating from a 200,000-square-foot store. Ten years after the acquisition, annual sales had grown to $209 million and Berkshire's share of after-tax profits had grown to $78 million.

The interesting thing is, NFM sales have grown faster than the population of Omaha. When NFM's annual sales were $44 million, Buffett said, it appeared that the company was capturing all of the business in Omaha. So how does NFM continue to grow? By growing its marketing area. A few years ago a Des Moines consumer report identified NFM as the third-favorite in the city out of a group of twenty furniture retailers—except that it isn't in the city; it's 130 miles away in Omaha.

Borsheim's

Soon after Mrs. B immigrated from Russia, her parents and five brothers and sisters followed. One of her sisters, Rebecca, married Louis Friedman and together they purchased a small jewelry store in Omaha, Nebraska, in 1948. Mr. Friedman's son, Ike, joined the family business in 1950, followed eventually by Ike's son and two sons-in-law.

What worked for the Blumkins in the furniture business worked for the Friedmans in the jewelry trade: sell cheap and tell the truth. Like the Furniture Mart, the Borsheim's jewelry store has one large location. For this reason, Borsheim's expense ratios are several points lower than most competitors. Borsheim's generates high sales volume and strong buying power. With an eye on expenses and store traffic that reaches 4,000 strong on seasonal buying days, the Friedmans have a recipe for success.

Like the Nebraska Furniture Mart, Borsheim's has been able to widen its market share beyond Omaha. Some customers travel hundreds of miles to shop at Borsheim's. The company also has a strong mail order business, which helps keep operating costs low—18 percent of sales, compared to 40 percent of sales for most competitors. Wal-Mart has 15 percent operating costs and what works for diapers, explains Buffett, works with diamonds. By keeping costs low, Borsheim's is able to sell at low prices and expand its market share. According to Buffett, Borsheim's store in Omaha does more jewelry business than any other store in the country, except for Tiffany's in New York City.

The Fechheimer Brothers Company

In January 1986, Bob Heldman, chairman of Fechheimer Brothers and a longtime shareholder of Berkshire Hathaway, wrote Buffett a letter. He had read Berkshire's business advertisements and thought Fechheimer met Buffett's preconditions. Buffett and Heldman met in Omaha and by summertime, Buffett had added another business.

Fechheimer manufactures and distributes uniforms. The company traces its roots all the way back to 1842, and the Heldman family has been involved since 1941. Like the Blumkins and the Friedmans, the Heldmans are a multigenerational working family. Brothers Bob and George Heldman and their sons—Gary, Roger, and Fred—are in the business. The Heldman family wished to continue running the business but there was a greater need to redeploy the wealth of the business. Receiving cash from Berkshire and still retaining a partial ownership in the company was ideal.

To this date, Buffett has never visited Fechheimer's headquarters in Cincinnati, nor has he toured any of its plants. The economics of the business were solid and the Heldmans had supplied the company with the management's next generation. Buffett paid $46 million for 84 percent of the capital stock in 1986. During the next six years, sales grew from $75 million to $122 million and capital expenditures averaged less than $2 million annually. During this period, Fechheimer has returned to Berkshire $49 million in after-tax profits, earning on average 14 percent of beginning shareholders equity.

The Scott & Fetzer Company

The Scott & Fetzer Company (Scott Fetzer) owns several leading products including Kirby vacuum cleaners; World Book Encyclopedias (including Child Craft and Early Learning); Wayne furnace burners, sump, utility, and sewage pumps; and Campbell Hausfeld air compressors, air tools, and painting systems. The company is headquartered in Westlake, Ohio, and is managed by Ralph Schey.

When Berkshire bought Scott Fetzer, the company had seventeen operating businesses that contributed $700 million in annual sales. Buffett divided the company into three divisions—Kirby Vacuum Cleaners, World Book, and Scott Fetzer Manufacturing Group—all managed by Ralph Schey.

Buffett paid $315 million in cash for Scott Fetzer's businesses in January 1986, making it one of Berkshire's largest business acquisitions. Since that time, this purchase has exceeded his own optimistic expectations. Today, Scott Fetzer's three divisions account for approximately 35 percent of Berkshire's noninsurance operating earnings.

In 1992, Scott Fetzer earned a record $110 million in pretax earnings. What is incredible, noted Buffett, is the company achieved these earnings while employing $116 million in equity capital and very little in leverage. Scott Fetzer's return on equity, Buffett figured, would easily place it among the top 1 percent of the Fortune 500. Over the last seven years, the company has been able to reduce its investment in both fixed assets and inventory. Scott Fetzer has distributed more than 100 percent of its earnings back to Berkshire Hathaway while simultaneously increasing its own earnings. Berkshire Hathaway has profited enormously by the Scott Fetzer acquisition and one of the main reasons, Buffett confided, is Ralph Schey.

H. H. Brown

In July of 1991, Berkshire purchased for cash the H. H. Brown Shoe Company, which manufactures, imports, and markets footwear. In 1992, it generated $25 million in pretax profits.

At best, Buffett said, the shoe business is a difficult one; to be successful, a shoe company requires the services of outstanding managers. Fortunately for Berkshire Hathaway, part of the purchase price for H. H. Brown included Frank Rooney.

In 1929, an entrepreneur by the name of Ray Hefferman bought H. H. Brown for $10,000. Not long after, Frank Rooney married Hefferman's daughter. On the wedding day, he was told by his new father-in-law that he should abandon any thought of working at H. H. Brown. Frank went to work instead for Melville Shoe Company and eventually became chief executive officer of its successor, Melville Corporation. When Ray Hefferman, at age ninety, fell ill, he finally asked Frank to manage H. H. Brown. After Ray Hefferman's death, the Hefferman family decided to sell the shoe business. Enter Berkshire Hathaway.

Buffett decided to buy H. H. Brown, in spite of shoes being a tough business, because of three factors. First, the company was demonstrably profitable. Second, Frank Rooney agreed to continue managing the business. Third, H. H. Brown had a very unusual compensation system that, according to Buffett, "warmed my heart." Each year, the key managers of H. H. Brown are paid a base salary of $7,800 plus a percentage of the profits calculated after capital reinvestment. This, noted Buffett, makes the managers acutely aware that the equity capital is not cost-free. Too often, he said, managers are compensated regardless of profits, losses, and capital reinvestment. At H. H. Brown, the managers truly walk in the same shoes as the owners.

Dexter Shoe

It is Buffett's preference to purchase companies for cash. However, he will on occasion issue stock in Berkshire Hathaway in exchange for ownership in a company, but only when Berkshire receives as much in intrinsic value as it gives up. In the fall of 1993, Berkshire expanded its investment in the shoe business by agreeing to purchase Dexter Shoe Company for $420 million in Berkshire Hathaway stock—25,221 shares.

Dexter Shoe Company, based in Maine, is the country's largest independently owned footwear manufacturer. Because of Berkshire's success with H. H. Brown, Buffett was familiar with the shoe business. Buffett confided that Dexter Shoe was the type of company Berkshire appreciated. The company had a long and profitable track record. Its shoes, asserted Buffett, represented a unique franchise. Dexter's New England footwear includes its well-known moccasin and boat shoes. Lastly, Buffett shared management's philosophy of focusing on longer-term corporate goals. Buffett admitted that he would have purchased Dexter for cash or for stock. It was Dexter's owners who wanted Berkshire Hathaway stock.

CHARLIE

Any dissertation on Warren Buffett and Berkshire Hathaway would be incomplete without acknowledging Charles T. Munger. Charles Munger, Charlie to the readers of Berkshire's annual reports, is vice chairman of Berkshire Hathaway. He is also, in Buffett's eyes, Berkshire's comanaging partner.

Their friendship began more than thirty years ago. Charlie is a native of Omaha but, unlike Buffett, his education was in legal, not business, matters. After graduating from Harvard Law School, Charlie started a law firm in Los Angeles called Munger Tolles & Olson. During a visit to Omaha in 1960, Charlie and Buffett met and the conversation naturally turned to investing. Buffett tried to persuade Charlie that the road to riches was investing, not law. Buffett's arguments were convincing because soon thereafter, Charlie established an investment partnership similar to Buffett's investment partnership.

From 1962 through 1975, Charlie managed an investment partnership with stellar success. Despite the 1973–1974 bear market, his partnership achieved a 19.8 percent average annual compounded return—far better than the Dow Jones Industrial Average's 5.0 percent return during this same period (see Figure 1.2). Charlie's portfolio was concentrated in fewer but larger stock positions, and so results were more volatile. Nonetheless, his approach was similar to Buffett's in that they both sought to purchase some discount to underlying value.

One of Charlie's partnership investments was Blue Chip Stamps. Like Buffett, Charlie began buying stock in Blue Chip Stamps in the late 1960s; eventually, he became chairman of the board of Blue Chip Stamps. His responsibilities included managing Blue Chip Stamps's portfolio of securities, which were used to offset stamp redemption liabilities.

Through the 1960s and 1970s, Charlie and Buffett kept in contact. Their relationship was formalized in 1978 when Diversified Retailing merged with Berkshire Hathaway. At that time, Charlie

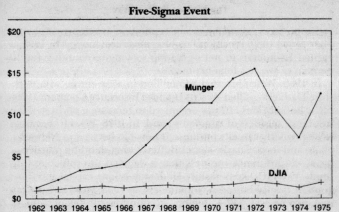

Figure 1.2. Cumulative value of dollars invested, Munger partnership vs. Dow Jones Industrial Average.

became a member of Berkshire Hathaway's board; when Berkshire and Blue Chip Stamps merged, he became vice chairman. During Blue Chip's peak earnings years, Buffett and Charlie not only acquired See's Candy Shops and the *Buffalo News*, in 1973 they acquired 80 percent of Wesco Financial Corporation.

Wesco Financial Corporation

While Charlie was chairman of Blue Chip Stamps, Louis Vincenti was chief executive officer of Wesco Financial. After Blue Chip Stamps and Berkshire Hathaway merged, Vincenti, then seventy-seven years old, retired and Charlie became chairman and chief executive of Wesco. The company has three major subsidiaries: Precision Steel, Wesco-Financial Insurance Company, and Mutual Savings and Loan.

Precision Steel, located in Franklin Park, Illinois, was purchased by Wesco Financial in 1979 for $15 million. At first glance, Precision Steel looks like another indistinguishable commodity company. But, this company has built a reputation for providing specialized grades of strip steel. Their prices are reasonable and the technical service is superb. During periods of short supply,

Precision Steel gained a national reputation as a dependable supplier. Since 1980, Precision Steel has never lost money. In 1993, it earned $2 million in net operating income, accounting for 10 percent of Wesco's total net income.

In 1985, Wesco invested $45 million in a coventure with Berkshire Hathaway, called Wesco-Financial Insurance Company (Wes-FIC). Initially, Wes-FIC was organized to reinsure a portion of the insurance business of Fireman's Fund. In 1988, Wes-FIC began to write property casualty business; it now has licenses in Nebraska, Utah, and Iowa. Charlie shares Buffett's long-standing practice of bypassing insurance business that is deemed unprofitable. Currently, Wes-FIC, like Berkshire Hathaway, is long capital and short good insurance business. Nonetheless, in 1993, Wes-FIC's operating income was $12.4 million, accounting for 60 percent of Wesco's total net income.

Although Charlie comments on the insurance business each year in Wesco's annual report to shareholders, insurance is clearly Buffett's passion. Charlie's passion is the savings and loan business.

Charlie's involvement with Mutual Savings and Loan dates back twenty years. During this period, he has endured a reckless industry sabotaged by people with poor judgment and sometimes criminal actions, and overseen by understaffed, underfinanced regulators. The experience is frightfully similar to Buffett's encounter with the insurance industry.

When the savings and loan disaster was beginning to show itself, few were willing or able to take evasive action in order to circumvent the obvious financial perils. Charlie Munger had the courage to reverse course and take Mutual Savings in a new direction. Between 1979 and 1985, because of the high cost of savings and the uncertainty of future interest rates, Mutual Savings made no new loans. In 1980, Charlie sold fifteen branch offices, leaving only the corporate headquarters and a single branch office in a shopping mall across the street. He also sold $307 million in savings accounts and a equal amount of its highest yielding mortgages. What remained were the lowest yielding mortgages with the shortest maturities.

In short, after seeing the danger flags, Charlie lightened his load, battened down the hatches, and prepared to sail into a hurricane. In 1981, despite lower operating profits, Mutual Savings had the highest ratio of shareholders equity to total interest bearing liabilities of any mature savings and loan. Mutual Savings also had a higher portion of assets invested in short-term cash equivalents, intermediate tax-free bonds, and utility preferred stocks, producing a tax equivalent yield almost twice the typical savings and loan mortgage portfolio.

"Bartles and Jaymes"

During the last three decades, the friendship between Charlie and Buffett has flourished. Buffett himself refers to the two of them as Berkshire's version of "Bartles and Jaymes." At Berkshire's annual meeting, they sit in straight-back chairs on the stage of the Orpheum Theater answering shareholders' questions. A few years ago, Buffett sheepishly announced that he bought a corporate jet, much to Charlie's chagrin. Charlie felt the idea of a corporate jet was so extravagant, he wanted to name the plane "The Aberration." Buffett joked that Charlie's idea of luxury travel was an air conditioned bus. The truth is, Charlie does travel by plane, but reserves his seats in coach class. Unable to compromise on the use of a corporate jet, Charlie and Buffett decided to name the plane "The Indefensible."

Charlie's frugality does not end with his choice of travel. Each year, Charlie writes Wesco's annual report. So as not to employ financial public relations people, Charlie does not use color graphics or charts. Frequently he uses the same descriptive phrases in his reports year after year, changing only the numbers. Unlike Buffett, Charlie does include a photograph (in black and white) of Wesco's corporate headquarters in the annual report, but for many years he used the same one, until shareholders teased him for using a picture so old it included automobiles from the 1960s. Charlie finally broke down and ordered a new photo—still black and white—of Wesco's corporate headquarters. The only difference he could see, Charlie mildly commented, was that the trees in front of the building had grown. Fortunately for Wesco's shareholders, their investment has grown, too, over the years. When Berkshire acquired Wesco in 1973, the price of Wesco's stock was $6. By the end of 1993, it had reached $129. Excluding the payment of a modest dividend over the years, rate of return on Wesco's stock since 1973 is 16.6 percent.

In 1991, Ken Chace retired and Buffett's wife, Susan, was nominated to fill the vacancy on Berkshire Hathaway's board. Mrs. Buffett is the second-largest shareholder of Berkshire Hathaway and if she outlives Buffett, she will inherit his shares of Berkshire stock. In the event of Buffett's death, Berkshire's shareholders can take solace in two facts. First, none of Buffett's stock will have to be sold and Mrs. Buffett has been instructed not to sell any of Berkshire's subsidiaries simply for a flattering price. Second, and more important, Buffett has asked Charlie to assume total responsibility for managing Berkshire Hathaway. In addition, Buffett humorously explained to his shareholders, "Upon my death Berkshire's earnings will immediately increase by one million dollars—Charlie will sell the corporate jet the next day, ignoring my wish to be buried with 'The Indefensible.'"

Both Charlie and Buffett possess an uncompromising attitude toward commonsense business principles. Like Buffett, who endured poor returns in the insurance industry and for a time refused to write policies, Charlie refused to make loans when confronted with an unruly savings and loan industry. Both exhibit managerial qualities necessary to run high-quality businesses. Berkshire Hathaway's shareholders are blessed in having managing partners who look after their interest and help them make money in all economic environments. With Buffett's policy on mandatory retirement—he does not believe in it—Berkshire's shareholders will continue to benefit, not from one mind but two, long into the future.

THE MAN AND HIS COMPANY

Warren Buffett is not easy to describe. Physically he is unremarkable, with looks often described as grandfatherly. Intellectually he is considered a genius, yet his down-to-earth relationship with people is truly uncomplicated. He is simple, straightforward, forthright, and honest. He displays an engaging combination of sophisticated dry wit and cornball humor. He has a profound reverence for those things logical and a foul distaste for imbecility. He embraces the simple and avoids the complicated.

Reading the annual reports, one is struck by how comfortable Buffett is quoting the Bible, John Maynard Keynes, or Mae West. Of course the operable word is "reading." Each report is sixty to seventy pages of dense information: no pictures, no color graphics, no charts. Those who are disciplined enough to start on page one and continue uninterrupted are rewarded with a healthy dose of financial acumen, folksy humor, and unabashed honesty. Buffett is very candid in his reporting. He emphasizes both the pluses and the minuses of Berkshire's businesses. He believes that people who own stock in Berkshire Hathaway are owners of the company, and he tells them as much as he would like to be told if he were in their shoes.

The company that Buffett directs, Berkshire Hathaway, is the embodiment of his personality, his business philosophy, and his own unique style. Looking at Berkshire, we can see Buffett's key principles in operation. All the qualities that Buffett looks for in companies—qualities that unfold in the chapters that follow—are displayed in his company. And here, too, we see the Buffett Way reflected in some unusual and refreshing corporate policies. Two examples: the charity designation program and the compensation program.

Executive compensation has become a source of heated debate between shareholders and management. Annual salaries of senior management can easily exceed one million dollars. In addition to these lofty salaries, executives of publicly traded companies are customarily rewarded with fixed-price stock options, often tied to corporate earnings but very seldom tied to the executive's actual job performance.

When stock options are passed out indiscriminately, says Buffett, managers with below average performance are rewarded equally as well as managers who have had excellent performance. In Buffett's mind, even if your team wins the pennant you do not pay a .350 hitter the same as a .150 hitter.

At Berkshire, Buffett uses a compensation system that rewards managers for performance. The reward is not tied to the size of the enterprise, the individual's age, or Berkshire's overall profits. As far as Buffett is concerned, good unit performance should be rewarded whether Berkshire's stock price rises or falls. Instead, executives are compensated based on their success at meeting performance goals keyed to their area of responsibility. Some managers are rewarded for increasing sales, others for reducing expenses or curtailing capital expenditures. At the end of the year, Buffett does not hand out stock options—he writes checks. Some are quite large. Managers can use the cash as they please. Many purchase Berkshire stock, thereby ultimately taking the same risks as the owners.

Buffett allows managerial rewards to be substantial. Mike Goldberg, who runs the insurance operations, was paid $2.6 million in 1992. But when the insurance business endured tough times, he earned his base salary of $100,000. Buffett's own salary plus bonus is $100,000 each year. Undoubtedly he is the lowest paid Fortune 500 chief executive in the country. Of course he owns 475,000 shares of stock, but Berkshire does not pay a dividend. To this day, he is the only billionaire who does his own taxes.

Perhaps nothing so typifies Buffett's unique way of doing things as Berkshire's method of distributing charitable donations. It is called the shareholder designation program. Shareholders, based on the proportional number of shares they own, can designate the recipients of Berkshire's charitable contributions. With most corporations it is the senior officers and board members who select the charities that will benefit from corporate contributions. Often they choose their own favorite charities, and shareholders—whose money is being given—have no input on this decision. This goes against Buffett's grain. "When A takes money from B to give to C," he says, "and A is a legislator, the process is called taxation. But when A is an officer or director of a corporation, it is called philanthropy."[7]

At Berkshire, the shareholder names the charity and Berkshire writes the check. In 1981, the first year of this program, Berkshire distributed $1.7 million to 675 charities. Over the next twelve years, Berkshire contributed $60 million to thousands of charities. In 1993 alone, shareholders of Berkshire Hathaway donated $9.4 million to 3,110 charities.

It is but one small measure of Berkshire's phenomenal financial success. When Buffett took control of Berkshire, the corporate net worth was $22 million. Twenty-nine years later, it has grown to $10.4 billion. It is Buffett's goal to increase the book value of Berkshire Hathaway at a 15 percent annual rate—well above the return achieved by the average American company. Since 1964, Berkshire's book value per share has grown from $19 to $8,854. On a year-by-year basis, Berkshire's returns have at times been volatile; changes in the stock market and thus the underlying stocks that Berkshire owns create wide swings in per-share value (see Table 1.1). But the compounded annual rate is

Table 1.1   Berkshire's Corporate Performance vs. the S&P 500

| Year | Annual Percentage Change | | |
	In Per-Share Book Value of Berkshire (1)	In S&P 500 with Dividends Included (2)	Relative Results (1)–(2)
1965	23.8	10.0	13.8
1966	20.3	(11.7)	32.0
1967	11.0	30.9	(19.9)
1968	19.0	11.0	8.0
1969	16.2	(8.4)	24.6
1970	12.0	3.9	8.1
1971	16.4	14.6	1.8
1972	21.7	18.9	2.8
1973	4.7	(14.8)	19.5
1974	5.5	(26.4)	31.9
1975	21.9	37.2	(15.3)
1976	59.3	23.6	35.7
1977	31.9	(7.4)	39.3
1978	24.0	6.4	17.6
1979	35.7	18.2	17.5
1980	19.3	32.3	(13.0)
1981	31.4	(5.0)	36.4
1982	40.0	21.4	18.6
1983	32.3	22.4	9.9
1984	13.6	6.1	7.5
1985	48.2	31.6	16.6
1986	26.1	18.6	7.5
1987	19.5	5.1	14.4
1988	20.1	16.6	3.5
1989	44.4	31.7	12.7
1990	7.4	(3.1)	10.5
1991	39.6	30.5	9.1
1992	20.3	7.6	12.7
1993	14.3	10.1	4.2
1994	13.9	1.3	12.6

Source: Berkshire Hathaway 1993 Annual Report.

Notes: Data are for calendar years with these exceptions: 1965 and 1966, year ended 9/30; 1967, 15 months ended 12/31.

Starting in 1979, accounting rules required insurance companies to value the equity securities they hold at market rather than at the lower of cost or market, which was previously the requirement. In this table, Berkshire's results through 1978 have been restated to conform to the changed rules.

23.3 percent—exceeding Buffett's goal of 15 percent and far outdistancing the gain in the Standard & Poor's 500 Index. This relative performance is all the more impressive when you consider that Berkshire is penalized by both income and capital gains taxes and the Standard & Poor's 500 returns are pretax.

Berkshire Hathaway, Inc., is complex but not complicated. It owns several businesses—the insurance companies and the other businesses described in this chapter, plus other minor subsidiaries not described due to space limitations—and, using the income stream from insurance premiums, it also buys shares in publicly traded companies. Running through it all is Warren Buffett's down-to-earth way of looking at business: whether it be a business he's considering buying outright, a business he's evaluating for stock purchase, or the management of his own company. Those who would aspire to a measure of Buffett's success could do far worse than adopt his philosophy.

TWO

The Two Wise Men

THE EDUCATION OF Warren Buffett is best understood as a synthesis of two distinct investment philosophies from the minds of two legendary figures, Benjamin Graham and Philip Fisher. "I'm 15 percent Fisher," Buffett said, "and 85 percent Benjamin Graham."[1] It is not surprising that Graham's influence over Buffett is broad. Buffett was first an interested reader of Graham, then student, then employee, then collaborator, and finally his peer. Graham molded Buffett's untrained mind. However, those who consider Buffett to be the singular product of Graham's teachings are ignoring the influence of another towering financial mind, Philip Fisher.

After Buffett read Fisher's book, *Common Stocks and Uncommon Profits* (Harper & Brothers, 1958), he sought out the writer. "When I met him (Fisher), I was as impressed by the man as by his ideas," said Buffett. "Much like Ben Graham, Fisher was unassuming, generous in spirit and an extraordinary teacher." Although Graham's and Fisher's investment approach differ, Buffett noted, they "parallel in the investment world."[2]

BENJAMIN GRAHAM

Graham is considered the dean of financial analysis. He was awarded that distinction because "before him there was no (finan-

27

cial analysis) profession and after him they began to call it that."[3] Graham's two most celebrated works are *Security Analysis*, coauthored with David Dodd and originally published in 1934, shortly after the 1929 stock market crash and in the depths of the nation's worst depression; and *The Intelligent Investor*, originally published in 1949. While other academicians sought to explain this economic phenomenon, Graham helped people regain their financial footing and proceed with a profitable course of action.

Graham was born in London on May 9, 1894. His parents moved to New York when he was an infant. Graham's earliest education was at Boy's High in Brooklyn. At age twenty, he received a bachelor of science degree from Columbia University and was elected to Phi Beta Kappa. Graham was fluent in Greek and Latin and held interests in both mathematics and philosophy. Despite his nonbusiness education, he began a career on Wall Street. He started as a messenger at the brokerage firm of Newburger, Henderson & Loeb, posting bond and stock prices on a blackboard for $12 a week. From messenger, he rose to writing research reports and, soon thereafter, was awarded a partnership in the firm. By 1919, he was earning an annual salary of $600,000; he was twenty-five years old. In 1926, Graham formed an investment partnership with Jerome Newman. It was this partnership that hired Buffett some thirty years later. Graham–Newman survived the 1929 crash, the depression, World War II, and the Korean War before it dissolved in 1956.

From 1928 through 1956, while at Graham–Newman, Graham taught night courses in finance at Columbia. Few people know that Graham was financially ruined by the 1929 crash. For the second time in his life—the first being when his father died, leaving the family financially unprotected—Graham set about to rebuild his fortune. The haven of academia allowed Graham the opportunity for reflection and reevaluation. With the counsel of David Dodd, also a professor at Columbia, Graham produced a complete dissertation on conservative investing.

Security Analysis first appeared in 1934. Between them, Graham and Dodd had more than fifteen years of investment experience. It took them four years to complete the book. When *Security Analysis* was first published, Louis Rich of *The New York Times* wrote, "It is a full-bodied mature, meticulous and wholly meritorious outgrowth of scholarly probing and practical sagacity. If this influence should ever exert itself, it will come about by causing the mind of the investor to dwell upon securities rather than upon the market."[4]

In the first edition, Graham and Dodd dedicated significant attention to corporate abuses. Prior to the securities acts of 1933 and 1934, corporate information was misleading and totally inadequate. Most industrial companies refused to divulge sales information, and the valuation of assets was frequently suspicious. Corporate misinformation was used to manipulate the prices of securities, both in initial public offerings and in the aftermarkets. After the securities acts, corporate reforms were slow but deliberate. By the time the third edition of the book appeared in 1951, references to corporate abuses were eliminated, and in its place Graham and Dodd addressed the problems of stockholder–management relations. These problems centered on management's competence and the policy on dividends.

The essence of *Security Analysis* is that a well-chosen, diversified portfolio of common stocks, based on reasonable prices, can be a sound investment. Step by careful step, Graham helped the investor see the logic of his approach.

The first problem that Graham had to contend with was the lack of a single, universal definition for investment. Quoting Justice Brandeis, Graham pointed out that "investment is a word of many meanings." And the issue does not turn on whether the item is a stock (and therefore speculative by definition) or a bond (and therefore an investment). The purchase of a poorly secured bond cannot be considered an investment just because it is a bond. Neither can a stock with a price per share of less than its net current assets be considered a speculation just because it is a stock. The decision to purchase a security with borrowed money in hopes of making a quick profit is speculation, regardless of whether it is a bond or stock. Here, Graham said, intention more than character will determine whether the security is an investment or a speculation.

Considering the complexities of the issue, Graham proposed his own definition. "An investment operation is one which, upon thorough analysis, promises safety of principal and a satisfactory return. Operations not meeting these requirements are speculative."[5] Graham preferred to speak of investment as an operation that precluded the purchase of a single issue. Early on, Graham recommended diversifying investments to reduce risk.

The "thorough analysis" that he insisted upon was explained as "the careful study of available facts with the attempt to draw conclusions therefrom based on established principles and sound logic."[6] Graham went further by describing analysis as a three-step function: descriptive, critical, and selective.

In the descriptive phase, the analyst gathers all the facts outstanding and presents them in an intelligent manner. In the critical phase, the analyst is concerned with the merits of the standards used to communicate information. Ultimately, the analyst is interested in the fair representation of the facts. In the selective phase, the analyst passes judgment on the attractiveness or unattractiveness of the security in question.

For a security to be considered an investment, said Graham, there must be some degree of safety of principal and a satisfactory rate of return. Graham explained that safety is not absolute. Rather, the investment should be considered safe from loss under reasonable conditions. Graham did admit that a most unusual or improbable occurrence can put a safe bond into default. Satisfactory return includes not only income but price appreciation. Graham noted that "satisfactory" is a subjective term. He does say that *return* can be any amount, however low, as long as the investor acts with a degree of intelligence and adheres to the full definition of investment. An individual who conducts a thorough financial analysis based on sound logic, indicating a reasonable rate of return without compromising safety of principal, would be considered, by Graham's definition, an investor, not a speculator.

Had it not been for the bond market's poor performance, Graham's definition of investing might have been overlooked. But when, between 1929 and 1932, the Dow Jones Bond Average declined from 97.70 to 65.78, bonds could not mindlessly be considered pure investments. Like stocks, bonds not only lost considerable value but many issuers went bankrupt. Therefore, what was needed was a process that could distinguish the investment characteristics of both stocks and bonds from their speculative counterparts.

Throughout Graham's life he was disturbed by the issues of investment and speculation. Toward the end of his life, Graham watched with dismay as institutional investors embraced actions that were clearly speculative. Shortly after the 1973–1974 bear market, Graham was invited to attend a conference of money managers hosted by Donaldson, Lufkin, and Jenrette. As Graham sat at the conference roundtable, he was shocked by what was being admitted by his professional peer group. "I could not comprehend," said Graham, "how the management of money by institutions had degenerated from sound investment to this rat race of trying to get the highest possible return in the shortest period."[7]

Graham's second contribution—after distinguishing between investment and speculation—was a methodology whereby the purchase of common stocks would qualify as an investment. Before *Security Analysis*, little had been accomplished using a quantitative approach to selecting stocks. Prior to 1929, listed common stocks were primarily railroads. Industrial and utility companies were a small portion of the overall list of stocks. Banks and insurance companies, the favorites of wealthy speculators, were unlisted stocks. Those companies, primarily railroads, that arguably had investment value traded at a price that was close to their par value. These companies were backed by real capital value.

As the country entered the bull market of the 1920s, the general disposition of all stocks, including industrials, began to improve. Prosperity fueled further investment, most notably in real estate. Despite the short-lived Florida real estate boom in 1925, followed by the Florida real estate bust of 1926, commercial banks and investment banking firms continued to recommend real estate. Real estate investment spurred investment activity and, ultimately, business activity. This link continued to fan the flames of optimism. As Graham noted, uncontrolled optimism can lead to mania, and one of the chief characteristics of mania is its inability to recall the lessons of history.

Looking back, Graham identified three forces that he felt were responsible for the stock market crash. First was the manipulation of stocks by the exchanges and investment firms. Each day, brokers were told which issues to "move" and what to say to generate excitement about the stock. Second was bank policy to lend money for the purpose of buying stocks. Banks loaned money to speculators, who in turn anxiously awaited the latest hot tip from Wall Street. Bank lending for securities purchases rose from $1 billion in 1921 to $8.5 billion in 1929. Since the loans were backed by the value of stocks, when the Crash occurred, like a house of cards, everything tumbled down. Today, there are security laws to protect individuals from brokerage fraud, and the practice of buying securities on margin is greatly curtailed, compared to the 1920s. But the one area that could not be legislated, yet in Graham's mind was just as responsible for the Crash, was excessive optimism—the third force.

The danger of 1929 was not that speculation tried to masquerade as investing but rather that investing fashioned itself into speculation. Graham noted that historical optimism was rampant. Encouraged by the past, investors projected an era of continued growth and prosperity. The buyers of stocks began to lose their sense of proportion about price. Graham said people were paying prices for stocks without any sense of mathematical expectation. Stocks were worth any price that the optimistic market quoted, he said. It was at the height of this insanity that the line between speculation and investment blurred.

When the full impact of the stock market crash was felt, common stocks were once again labeled speculations. As the Depression began, the whole concept of common-stock investing was an anathema. However, noted Graham, investment philosophies change with psychological states. After World War II, confidence in common stocks rose once again. When Graham wrote the third edition of *Security Analysis* between 1949 and 1951, he acknowledged that common stocks had become an instrumental part of an investor's portfolio.

In the twenty years following the stock market crash, numerous academic studies analyzing the different approaches to common stock investing appeared. Graham himself described three approaches: the cross-section approach, the anticipation approach, and the margin of safety approach.

The cross-section approach would be today's equivalent of index investing. As Graham noted, selectivity was exchanged for diversification. An investor would purchase equal amounts of the thirty industrial companies of the Dow Jones Index and benefit equally as well as those selected companies. Graham pointed out that there was no certainty that Wall Street could accomplish results that were better than this index.

The anticipation approach was subdivided into the short-term selectivity and the growth stock approaches. Short-term selectivity is an approach where individuals seek to profit from companies that have the most favorable outlook over the near term, usually six months to a year. Wall Street expends much energy forecasting the economic prospects—including sales volume, costs, and earnings—that a company can expect to achieve. The fallacy of this approach, according to Graham, was that sales and earnings are often volatile and the anticipation of near-term economic prospects could easily be discounted in the stock price. Lastly, and more fundamentally, Graham charged that the value of an investment is not what it will earn this month or next, nor what next quarter's sales volume will be, but what that investment can expect to return to an investor over a long period of time. Decisions based on short-term data are too often superficial and temporary. Not surprising, because of its emphasis on change and transaction, the short-term selectivity approach is the dominant approach on Wall Street.

Growth stocks, simplistically defined, are companies that grow sales and earnings at rates above those of the average business. Graham used the National Investors Corporation definition, which identified growth companies as companies whose earnings move from cycle to cycle. The difficulties of succeeding with the growth-stock approach, explained Graham, centered on the investor's ability to identify growth companies and then to ascertain what degree the current share price already discounted the growth potential of the company.

Each company has what is called a *life cycle* of profits. In the early development stage, a company's revenues accelerate and earnings begin to materialize. During the rapid expansion stage, revenues continue to grow, profit margins expand, and there is a sharp increase in earnings. When a company enters the mature-growth stage, revenues begin to slow, and so do earnings. In the last stage, stabilization-decline, revenues drop, and both profit margins and earnings decline.

Growth investors, according to Graham, face a dilemma. If they select a company that is in the rapid-expansion stage, they may find the success of the company is temporary. Because the company has not endured years of testing, the company's profits may soon evaporate. On the other hand, a company in the mature-growth stage may be in a more advanced stage, soon to enter a stabilization-decline period when earnings begin to shrink. The ability to pinpoint a company on its life cycle has, for decades, perplexed financial analysts.

If we assume that the investor has accurately pinpointed a

growth company, what price should the investor pay? Obviously, if it is well known that a company is in a period of prosperity, its share price will be relatively high. Graham asked, How are we to know whether or not the price is too high? The answer is difficult to determine and, furthermore, even if it could be accurately determined, the investor immediately faces a new risk—that the company will grow more slowly than anticipated. If this occurs, the investor would have paid too much and the market likely will then price the shares lower.

If the analyst, in Graham's words, is optimistic about the company's future growth and further believes that the company will be a suitable addition to the portfolio, the analyst has two techniques for purchase: purchase shares of the company when the overall market is trading at a low price (which generally occurs during some type of correction, usually a bear market), or purchase the stock when it trades below its intrinsic value, although the overall market is not substantially cheap. In either technique, Graham said, a "margin of safety" is present in the purchase price.

Buying securities only at market lows leads to some difficulties. First, it entices the investor to develop some formula that indicates at which points the market is expensive and at which points the market is cheap. The investor, Graham explained, becomes hostage to predicting market turns, a process that is far from certain. Second, when the market is fairly valued, investors are unable to profitably purchase common stocks. However, waiting for a market correction before purchasing stocks may become tiring and is, in the end, futile.

Graham suggested that an investor's energies would be better used by identifying undervalued securities, regardless of the overall market price level. For this strategy to work systematically, Graham admitted, investors need a method or technique to identify undervalued stocks. The goal of the analyst is to develop the ability to recommend stocks that are selling below their calculated value. The idea of buying undervalued securities regardless of market levels was a novel idea in the 1930s and 1940s. It was Graham's goal to outline such a strategy.

Graham reduced the concept of sound investing to a motto he called the "margin of safety." This motto sought to unite all securities, stocks, and bonds in a singular approach to investing. If, for example, an analyst reviewed the operating history of a company and discovered that, on average, for the last five years, the company was able to earn annually five times its fixed charges, then a company's bonds, said Graham, possessed a margin of safety. Graham did not expect the investor to accurately determine the company's future income. Instead, he figured that if the margin between earnings and fixed charges was large enough, the investor would be protected from an unexpected decline in the company's income.

Establishing a margin-of-safety concept for bonds was not too difficult. The real test was Graham's ability to adapt the concept for common stocks. Graham reasoned that a margin of safety existed for common stocks if the price of the stock was below its intrinsic value. Obviously, for the concept to work, analysts needed a technique for determining a company's intrinsic value. Graham's definition of intrinsic value, as it appeared in *Security Analysis*, was "that value which is determined by the facts." These facts included a company's assets, its earnings and dividends, and any future definite prospects. Graham admitted that the single most important factor in determining a company's value was its future earnings power. Simplistically, a company's intrinsic value could be found by estimating the earnings of the company and multiplying those by an appropriate capitalization factor. This factor, or multiplier, was influenced by the company's stability of earnings, assets, dividend policy, and financial health.

Using the intrinsic-value approach, Graham said, was limited by an analyst's imprecise calculations for a company's economic future. Graham was concerned that an analyst's projections could be easily negated by a host of potential future factors. Sales volume, pricing, and expenses are difficult to forecast, thus making the application of a multiplier that much more complex. Not to be dissuaded, Graham did suggest that the margin of safety could work successfully in three areas. First, it worked well with stable securities such as bonds and preferred stocks. Second, it could be used in comparative analysis. Third, Graham figured that if the spread between the price of a company and the intrinsic value of a company was large enough, the margin-of-safety concept could be used to select stocks.

Graham asked readers to accept the idea that intrinsic value is an elusive concept. It is distinct from the market's quotation price. Originally, intrinsic value was thought to be the same as a company's book value, or the sum of its real assets minus obligations. This notion led to the early belief that intrinsic value was definite. However, analysts came to know that the value of a company was not only its net real assets but, additionally, the value of the earnings these assets produced. Graham proposed that it was not essential to determine a company's exact intrinsic value but, instead, accept an approximate measure or range of value. To establish a margin of safety, the analyst simply needs an approximate value that is considerably higher or lower than its market price.

Financial analysis is not an exact science, Graham said. There are certain quantitative factors—including balance sheets, income statements, earnings and dividends, assets and liabilities—that do lend themselves to thorough analysis. There are also qualitative factors that are not easily analyzed but are nonetheless essential ingredients in a company's intrinsic value. The two qualitative factors that are customarily addressed are "management capability" and the "nature of the business."

Graham, generally, had misgivings about the emphasis placed on qualitative factors. Opinions about management and the nature of a business are not easily measurable, and that which is difficult to measure, reasoned Graham, could be badly measured. It was not that Graham believed these qualitative factors had no value. Rather, when investors placed too much emphasis on these elusive concepts, the potential for disappointment increased. Optimism over qualitative factors often found its way to a higher multiplier. Graham's experience led him to believe that to the extent investors moved away from hard assets and toward intangibles, such as management capability and the nature of a business, they invited potentially risky ways of thinking.

Make sure of your ground, Graham said. Start with net asset values as the fundamental departure point. If you bought assets, your downside was limited to the liquidation value of those assets. Nobody, reasoned Graham, can bail you out of optimistic growth projections if those projections are unfilled. If a company was perceived to be an attractive business, possessing superb management who predicted high future earnings, it would no doubt attract a growing number of stock buyers. "So they (investors) will buy it," said Graham, "and in doing so they will bid up the price and hence the price to earnings ratio. As more and more investors become enamored with the promised return, the price lifts free from underlying value and floats freely upward, creating a bubble that expands beautifully until finally it must burst."[8]

If the greatest amount of a company's intrinsic value is measured in the quality of management, the nature of the business, and optimistic growth projections, there is little margin of safety, Graham said. If, on the other hand, a greater amount of a company's intrinsic value is the sum of measurable, quantitative factors, Graham figured that the investor's downside was more limited. Fixed assets are measurable. Dividends are measurable. Current earnings as well as historical earnings are measurable. Each of these factors can be demonstrated by figures and become a source of logic referenced by actual experience.

Graham said that having a good memory was his one burden. It was the memory of being financially deprived twice in a lifetime that led him to embrace an investment approach that stressed downside protection versus upside potential. There are two rules of investing, Graham said. The first rule is, Don't lose. The second rule is, Don't forget rule number one. This "don't lose" philosophy steered Graham toward two common stock selection approaches that, when applied, adhered to the margin of safety. The first approach was buying a company for less than two-thirds of its net asset value. The second approach was focusing on low price-to-earnings ratio stocks.

Buying a stock for a price that is less than two-thirds of its net assets fit neatly into Graham's sense of the present and satisfied his desire for some mathematical expectation. Graham gave no weight to a company's plant, property, and equipment. Furthermore, he deducted all of the company's short- and long-term liabilities. What remained was the net current assets. If the stock price was below this per-share value, Graham reasoned that a margin of safety existed. Therefore, a purchase was warranted. Graham considered this to be a foolproof method of investing. He did clarify that the results were based on the probable outcome of a group of stocks (diversification), not on the basis of individual results. Such stocks were pervasive at bear market bottoms and more scarce during bull markets.

Acknowledging that waiting for a market correction before making an investment may be unreasonable, Graham set out to design a second approach to buying stocks. He focused on stocks that were down in price and sold at a low price-to-earnings ratio.

Additionally, the company must have some net asset value. In other words, the company must owe less than it is worth. Throughout his career, Graham worked with several variations of this approach. Shortly before his death, Graham was revising the fifth edition of *Security Analysis* with Sidney Cottle. At that time, Graham was analyzing the financial results of stocks that were purchased based on a ten-year, low price-to-earnings multiple, a stock price that was equal to half its previous market high and, of course, a net asset value. Graham tested stocks back to 1961 and found the results very promising.

Both approaches—buying a stock for less than two-thirds of net asset value and buying stocks with low price-to-earnings multiples—had a common occurrence. The stocks that Graham selected, based on these methods, were deeply out of favor with the market. Some macro- or microevent caused the market to price these stocks below their value. Graham felt strongly that these stocks, priced "unjustifiably low," were attractive purchases.

Graham's conviction rested on certain assumptions. First, he believed that the market frequently mispriced stocks. This mispricing was most often caused by the human emotions of fear and greed. At the height of optimism, greed moved stocks beyond their intrinsic value, creating an overpriced market. At other times, fear moved prices below intrinsic value, creating an undervalued market. The second assumption was based on the statistical phenomenon "reversion to the mean," although Graham did not use that term. More eloquently, he quoted Horace who said, "Many shall be restored that now are fallen, and many shall fall that now are in honor." However stated, Graham believed that an investor could profit from the corrective forces of an inefficient market.

PHILIP FISHER

While Graham was writing *Security Analysis*, Philip Fisher was beginning his career as an investment counselor. After attending the Stanford University Graduate School of Business Administration, Fisher began work as an analyst at the Anglo London & Paris National Bank in San Francisco. In less than two years, he was made head of the bank's statistical department. It was from this perch that he witnessed the 1929 stock market crash. Then, after a brief career with a local brokerage house, Fisher decided to start his own investment counseling firm. On March 1, 1931, Fisher & Company began soliciting clients.

Starting an investment counseling firm in the early 1930s might have appeared unwise. However, Fisher found out, much to his surprise, that he had two advantages. First, every investor, with any money after the stock market crash, was probably unhappy with his or her present broker. Second, businesspeople, in the midst of the Depression, had plenty of time to sit and talk with Fisher. At Stanford, one of Fisher's business classes had required him to accompany his professor on periodic visits to companies in the San Francisco area. The professor engaged business managers in a series of discussions about their companies. Driving back to Stanford, Fisher and his professor talked endlessly about the companies and managers they visited. "That hour each week, Fisher says, was the most useful training he ever received."[9] It was these experiences, Fisher noted, that led him to believe that superior profits could be made by (1) investing in companies with above average potential and (2) by aligning oneself with the most capable management. To isolate these exceptional companies, Fisher developed a "point system" that qualified a company by the characteristics of its business and its management.

The characteristic of a business that most impressed Fisher was a company's ability to grow sales and profits over the years at rates greater than the industry average.[10] In order to do so, Fisher believed that a company needed to possess "products or services with sufficient market potential to make possible a sizable increase in sales for at least several years."[11] Fisher was not so much concerned with consistent annual increases in sales. Rather, he judged a company's success over a period of several years. He was aware that changes in the business cycle would have a material effect on sales and earnings. However, Fisher identified companies that, decade by decade, showed promise of above-average growth. According to Fisher, the two types of companies that could expect to achieve above-average growth were companies that, were (1) "fortunate and able" and were (2) "fortunate because they are able."

Aluminum Company of America was an example, Fisher said, of a company that was "fortunate and able." The company was "able" because the founders of the company were people of great ability. Alcoa's management foresaw the commercial uses for their product and worked aggressively to capitalize the aluminum market to increase sales. The company was also "fortunate," Fisher said, because events outside management's immediate control were having a positive impact on the company and its market. The swift development of airborne transportation was rapidly increasing sales of aluminum. Because of the aviation industry, Alcoa was benefiting far more than management originally envisioned.

Du Pont was a company, according to Fisher, that was "fortunate because it was able." If Du Pont had stayed with its original product, blasting powder, the company would have fared as well as most typical mining companies. But because management capitalized on the knowledge it had gained through the manufacturing of gunpowder, Du Pont was able to launch new products, including nylon, cellophane, and Lucite. These products created their own markets, producing billions of dollars in sales for Du Pont.

A company's research and development efforts, Fisher noted, contribute mightily to the sustainability of the company's above-average growth in sales. Obviously, Fisher explained, neither Du Pont nor Alcoa would have succeeded over the long term without a significant commitment to research and development. Even nontechnical businesses, he noted, need a dedicated research effort to produce better products and more efficient services.

In addition to research and development, Fisher also examined a company's sales organization. According to him, a company could develop outstanding products and services, but unless they were "expertly merchandised," the research and development effort would never translate into revenues. It is the responsibility of the sales organization to help customers understand the benefits of a company's products and services. A sales organization, Fisher explained, should also monitor its customer's buying habits and be able to spot changes in a customer's needs. The sales organization, according to Fisher, becomes the invaluable link between the marketplace and the research and development unit.

However, market potential alone is insufficient. Fisher believed that, even though capable of producing above-average sales growth, a company was an inappropriate investment if it was unable to generate profits for shareholders. "All the sales growth in the world won't produce the right type of investment vehicle if, over the years, profits do not grow correspondingly," he said.[12]

Accordingly, Fisher examined a company's profit margins, its dedication to maintaining and improving profit margins, and, finally, its cost analysis and accounting controls.

Fisher believed that superior investment returns were never obtained by investing in marginal companies. Those companies often produce adequate profits during expansion periods but see their profits decline rapidly during difficult economic times. For this reason, Fisher sought companies that were not only the lowest-cost producer of products or services but were dedicated to remaining so. A company with a low breakeven point, or a correspondingly high profit margin, is better able to withstand depressed economic environments. Ultimately it can drive out weaker competitors thereby strengthening its own market position. No company, Fisher said, will be able to sustain its profitability unless it is able to break down the costs of doing business while simultaneously understanding the cost of each step in the manufacturing process. In order to do so, he explained, a company must instill adequate accounting controls and cost analysis. This cost information, Fisher noted, enables a company to direct its resources to those products or services with the highest economic potential. Furthermore, accounting controls will help identify snags in a company's operations. These snags, or inefficiencies, act as an early warning device aimed at protecting the company's overall profitability.

Fisher's sensitivity about a company's profitability was linked with another concern, which he identified as the ability of a company to grow in the future without requiring equity financing. If a company is only able to grow by issuing equity, he said, the larger number of shares outstanding will cancel out any benefit that stockholders might realize from the company's growth. A company with high profit margins, he explained, is better able to generate funds internally. These funds can be used to sustain its growth without diluting existing shareholder's ownership, a situation caused by equity financing. In addition, a company that is able to maintain adequate cost controls over its fixed assets and working capital needs is better able to manage its cash needs and avoid equity financing.

Fisher was aware that superior companies possess not only above-average business characteristics but, equally as important, are directed by individuals who possess above-average management capabilities. These managers, he said, are determined to develop new products and services that will continue to spur sales growth long after current products or services are largely exploited. Many companies, Fisher noted, have adequate growth prospects from existing lines of products and services that will sustain these companies for several years, but few have policies in place to ensure consistent gains for ten to twenty years. "Management must have a viable policy," he said, "for attaining these ends with all the willingness to subordinate immediate profits for the greater long-range gains that this concept requires."[13] Subordinating immediate profits, he explained, should not be confused with sacrificing immediate profits. The above-average manager simultaneously has the ability to implement the company's long-range plans while focusing on the daily operations of the company.

In addition to this ability, Fisher asked, does the business have a management of unquestionable integrity and honesty? Do the managers behave as if they are trustees for the stockholders, or does it appear as if management is only concerned with its own well-being? One way to determine management's intention, Fisher confided, is to observe how management communicates with its shareholders. All businesses, good and bad, will experience a period of unexpected difficulties. Commonly, when business is good, management talks freely; but when business declines, does management talk openly about the company's difficulties or does it clam up? How management responds to business difficulties, Fisher noted, tells a lot about itself.

For a business to be successful, he argued, management must develop good working relations with all of its employees. Employees, he explained, should genuinely feel that their company is a good place to work. Blue-collar employees should feel that they are treated with respect and decency. Executive employees should feel that promotion is based on ability, not favoritism. Also, Fisher asked, what is the depth of management? Has the chief executive officer a talented team, and is he able to delegate authority to run parts of the business?

Finally, Fisher examined the peculiarity of a company, that is, its business and management aspects plus how it compares to other businesses in the same industry. In this search, Fisher tried to uncover clues that might lead him to understand the superiority of a company in relation to its competitors. Fisher argued that reading only the financial reports of a company is not enough to justify an investment. The essential step in prudent investing is to uncover as much about a company as possible from those individuals who are familiar with the company. Admittedly, Fisher was attempting a catch-all inquiry. He called this random inquiry "scuttlebutt." Today we might call it the business grapevine. If handled properly, Fisher claimed, scuttlebutt will provide substantial clues that will enable the investor to identify outstanding investments.

Fisher's scuttlebutt investigation led him to interview customers and vendors. He sought out former employees as well as consultants who had worked for the company. Fisher contacted research scientists in universities, government employees, and trade association executives. He also interviewed competitors. Although executives may sometimes hesitate to disclose too much about their own company, Fisher noted, they never lack an opinion about their competitors. "It is amazing," Fisher said, "what an accurate picture of the relative points of strength and weaknesses of each company in an industry can be obtained from a representative cross section of the opinions of those who in one way or another are concerned with any particular company."[14]

Most investors are unwilling to commit the time and energy Fisher required to understand a company. Developing a scuttlebutt network and arranging interviews is time consuming; replicating the scuttlebutt process for each company can be exhausting. Fisher reduced his workload by reducing the number of companies he owned. According to Fisher, he would rather own a few outstanding companies than a larger number of average businesses. Generally, his portfolios included fewer than ten companies, and often three to four companies represented 75 percent of his equity portfolio.

Fisher believed that to be successful, investors needed to do but a few things well. This included investing in companies that were within the investor's circle of competence. Fisher said earlier mistakes were "to project my skill beyond the limits of experience. I began investing outside the industries which I believed I thoroughly understood, in completely different spheres of activity; situations where I did not have comparable background knowledge."[15]

IN COMPARISON

The differences between Graham and Fisher are apparent. Graham, the quantitative analyst, emphasized only those factors that could be measured: fixed assets, current earnings, and dividends. Graham's investigative research included only corporate filings and annual reports. Unlike Fisher, Graham did no interviewing of customers, competitors, or managers. He was only interested in developing an investment approach that could easily and safely be adapted by the average investor. In order to limit risk, Graham counseled investors to fully diversify their portfolio holdings.

Fisher's approach to investing can be viewed as the antithesis of Graham. Fisher, the qualitative analyst, emphasized those factors that he believed increased the value of a company: future prospects and management capability. Whereas Graham was interested in purchasing only cheap stocks, Fisher was interested in purchasing companies that had the potential to increase their intrinsic value over the long term. Unlike Graham, Fisher would go to great lengths, including conducting extensive interviews, to uncover bits of information that might improve his selection process. Finally, in contrast to Graham, Fisher preferred to concentrate his portfolio holdings and include only a few stocks.

Warren Buffett believes that these two different doctrines "parallel in the investment world." His investment approach has been to combine a qualitative understanding of the business and its management, taught by Fisher, with a quantitative understanding of price and value, taught by Graham.

SYNTHESIS

Shortly after Graham's death in 1976, Buffett became the designated steward of Graham's value approach to investing. Indeed, Buffett's name became synonymous with value investing.[16] This appointment appeared logical. He was the most famous of Graham's dedicated students, and Buffett himself never missed an opportunity to acknowledge the intellectual debt he owed to Graham. Even today, Buffett considers Graham to be the one individual, after his father, who had the most influence on his investment life.[17] How, then, does Buffett reconcile his intellectual indebtedness to Graham with stock purchases such as American Express (1964), The Washington Post Company (1973), GEICO (1978), Capital Cities/ABC (1986), The Coca-Cola Company (1988), and Wells Fargo & Company (1990)? None of these companies passed Graham's strict financial test for purchase, yet Buffett made significant investments in all of them.

In his earlier purchases, Buffett exhibited unquestioning dedication to Graham's approach. Searching for companies that were selling for less than their net working capital, Buffett bought an anthracite company, a street railway company, and a windmill company. Soon Buffett began to realize that a few stocks he had purchased using Graham's strict quantitative guidelines were becoming unprofitable investments. While he was working at Graham–Newman, Buffett's research led him to dig deeper into a company's financial reports in hopes of understanding what was causing a company's stock price to languish. What Buffett learned was that several companies that he had bought at a cheap price (hence they met Graham's test for purchase) were cheap because their underlying businesses were suffering.

As early as 1965, Buffett was becoming aware that Graham's strategy of buying cheap stocks was not ideal.[18] According to Buffett, Graham's value approach was to buy a stock so low in price that some "hiccup" in the company's business would allow investors to sell their shares at higher prices. Buffett called this strategy the "cigar butt" approach to investing. Walking down the street, an investor eyes a cigar butt lying on the ground and picks it up for one last puff. Although it's a lousy smoke, its bargain price makes the puff all the more worthwhile. For Graham's strategy to consistently work, Buffett argued, someone must play the role of liquidator. If not a liquidator, then some other investor must be willing to purchase shares of your company, forcing the price of the stock upward.

As Buffett explained, if you paid $8 million for a company whose assets are worth $10 million, you will profit handsomely if the assets are sold on a timely basis. However, if the underlying economics of the business are poor and it takes ten years to sell the business, your total return is likely to be below average. "Time is the friend of the wonderful business," Buffett learned, "the enemy of mediocre."[19] Unless he could facilitate the liquidation of his poorly performing companies and profit from the difference between his purchase price and the market value of the assets of a company, his performance would replicate the poor economics of the underlying business.

From his earliest investment mistakes, Buffett began moving away from Graham's strict teachings. "I evolved," he admitted, but "I didn't go from ape to human or human to ape in a nice even manner."[20] He was beginning to appreciate the qualitative nature of certain companies, compared to the quantitative aspects of others, but he still found himself searching for bargains. "My punishment," he confessed, "was an education in the economics of short-line farm implementation manufacturers (Dempster Mill Manufacturing), third-place department stores (Hochschild-Kohn), and New England textile manufacturers (Berkshire Hathaway)."[21] Buffett, attempting to explain his dilemma, quoted Keynes: "The difficulty lies not in the new ideas but in escaping from the old ones." Buffett's evolution was delayed, he admitted, because what Graham taught him was so valuable to him.

Even today, Buffett continues to embrace Graham's primary idea, the theory of the margin of safety. "Forty-two years after reading that," Buffett noted, "I still think those are the right three words."[22] What Buffett learned from Graham was that successful investing involved the purchase of stocks when the market price of those stocks was at a significant discount to the underlying business value.

In 1984, speaking before students at Columbia University to mark the fiftieth anniversary celebration of *Security Analysis*, Buffett explained that there is a group of successful investors who acknowledge Ben Graham as their common intellectual patriarch.[23] Graham provided the theory of margin of safety, but each student, noted Buffett, has developed different ways to apply this theory to determine a company's business value. However, the common theme is that they are all searching for some discrepancy between the value of a business and the price of the securities of that business. Individuals who are confused by Buffett's recent purchases fail to separate theory and methodology. Buffett clearly embraces Graham's margin of safety theory, but he has steadfastly moved away from Graham's methodology. According to Buffett, the last time it was easy to profit from Graham's methodology was in 1973–1974.

As early as 1969, Buffett was studying Fisher's writings. But it was Charlie Munger who was most responsible for moving Buffett toward Fisher's thinking. Charlie, in a sense, was the embodiment of Fisher's qualitative theories. Charlie had a keen appreciation of the value of a better business. Both See's Candy Shops and Buffalo News were tangible examples of good businesses available at reasonable prices. Charlie educated Buffett about the wisdom of paying up for a good business.

Ben Graham, the East Coast academician, represents the low-risk quantitative approach to investing. Fisher, the West Coast entrepreneur, represents a higher-risk qualitative approach to investing. It is interesting that Buffett, who has combined the quantitative attributes of Graham with the qualitative attributes of Fisher, has settled in Nebraska, midway between the coasts.

From Fisher, Buffett learned that the type of business purchased matters a lot. He also learned that management can affect the value of the underlying business, hence management's attributes needed to be studied as well. Fisher counseled that in order to become fully informed about a business, an investor had to investigate all aspects of the company and its competitors. From Fisher, Buffett learned the value of scuttlebutt. Throughout the years, Buffett has developed an extensive network of contacts who assist him in evaluating different businesses.

Finally, Fisher taught Buffett not to overstress diversification. According to Fisher, investors have been misled, believing that putting their eggs in several baskets reduces risk. The disadvantage of purchasing too many stocks is that it becomes impossible to watch all the eggs in all the different baskets. Investors run the risk of putting too little in a company that they are more familiar with and too much in a company that they are unfamiliar with. According to Fisher, buying a company without a thorough understanding of the business may be more risky than having limited diversification.

Graham did not think about businesses. Nor did he ponder the capabilities of management. He limited his research investigation to corporate filings and annual reports. If there was a mathematical probability of making money because the share price was less than the assets of the company, Graham purchased the company, regardless of its business or its management. In order to increase the probability of success, Graham chose to purchase as many of these statistical equations as possible. This thinking is the polar opposite of Fisher's. If Graham's teachings were limited to these precepts, Buffett would have little regard for him. But the margin of safety theory that Graham emphasized is so important to Buffett that all other current weaknesses of Graham's methodology can be overlooked.

In addition to the margin of safety theory, which became the intellectual framework for Buffett's thinking, Graham helped Buffett appreciate the folly of following stock market fluctuations. Stocks have an investment characteristic and a speculative characteristic, Graham taught Buffett. The margin of safety helps explain a stock's investment characteristic. The speculative characteristics of a stock are a consequence of people's fear and greed. These emotions, present in most investors, cause stock prices to gyrate far above and below a company's intrinsic value. Graham taught Buffett that if he could insulate himself from the emotional whirlwinds of the stock market, he had the opportunity to exploit the irrational behavior of other investors, who purchased stocks based on emotion, not logic. Buffett learned from Graham how to think independently. If you have reached a logical conclusion based on sound judgment, Graham counseled Buffett, do not be dissuaded just because others may disagree. "You are neither right nor wrong because the crowd disagrees with you," wrote Graham. "You are right because your data and reasoning are right."[24]

Buffett's dedication to both Graham and Fisher is understandable. Graham gave Buffett the intellectual basis for investing, the margin of safety, and helped Buffett learn to master his emotions in order to take advantage of market fluctuations. Fisher gave Buffett an updated, workable methodology that enabled him to identify good long-term investments. The frequent confusion surrounding Buffett's investment actions is easily understood when people acknowledge that Buffett is the synthesis of both Graham's and Fisher's philosophy.

"It is not enough to have good intelligence," wrote Descartes, "the principle thing is to apply it well." It is the application that separates Buffett from other investment managers. A number of his peers are highly intelligent, disciplined, and dedicated. Buffett stands above them all because of his formidable ability to implement his strategies.

THREE

Mr. Market and
the Lemmings

WHEN WARREN BUFFETT began his investment partnership in 1956, his father counseled him to wait before making any purchases. At 200, the Dow Jones Industrial Average was too high, he said. Buffett, who started with $100, figures that, had he listened to his father, that is all he would have today. Instead, despite the general market level, he began investing the partnership's funds. Even at his young age, he quickly grasped the difference between purchasing individual stocks and speculating about the direction of the general market. Whereas purchasing companies requires certain accounting and mathematical skills, managing market fluctuations requires investors to master their emotions. Throughout his investment career, Buffett has been able to disengage himself from the emotional forces of the stock market.

THE STOCK MARKET

Despite computer programs and black boxes, it is still people who make markets. Because emotions are stronger than reason, fear and greed move stock prices above and below a company's intrin-

49

sic value. Investor sentiment has a more pronounced impact on stock prices than a company's fundamentals. When people are greedy or scared, Buffett says, they often will buy or sell stocks at foolish prices. Buffett recognized early on that the long-term value of his stock holdings was determined by the economic progress of the businesses, not daily market quotations. Over the long term, common stock prices have a remarkable relationship to the underlying economic value of the business, he said. As a company's economic value increases over time, so too will the price of the shares of the business. If, on the other hand, the company falters, the stock price will reflect this. Of course, over shorter periods, Buffett learned that the price of stocks will move above or below its business value, dependent more on emotions than economics.

The Temperament of an Investor

Ben Graham taught Buffett that the basic difference between investors and speculators lies in their attitudes toward stock pricing. The speculator, noted Graham, tries to anticipate and profit from price changes. On the contrary, the investor seeks only to acquire companies at reasonable prices. Graham told Buffett that the successful investor is often the individual who has achieved a certain temperament. Graham figured that an investor's worst enemy was not the stock market but oneself. Despite superior abilities in mathematics, finance, and accounting, individuals who could not master their emotions were ill suited to profit from the investment process. Graham helped his students recognize the folly of the stock market fluctuations by sharing an allegory he titled "Mr. Market." Buffett, in Berkshire's 1987 annual report, shared Graham's story with his shareholders.

To understand the irrationality of stock prices, imagine that you and Mr. Market are partners in a private business. Each day without fail, Mr. Market quotes a price at which he is willing to either buy your interest or sell you his. The business that you both own is fortunate to have stable economic characteristics, but Mr. Market's quotes are anything but. For you see, Mr. Market is emotionally unstable. Some days, Mr. Market is cheerful and can only see brighter days ahead. On these days, he quotes a very high price for shares in your business. At other times, Mr. Market is discouraged and, seeing nothing but trouble ahead, quotes a very low price for your shares in the business.

Mr. Market has another endearing characteristic, said Graham. He does not mind being snubbed. If Mr. Market's quotes are ignored, he will be back again tomorrow with a new quote. Graham warned his students that it is Mr. Market's pocketbook, not his wisdom, that is useful. If Mr. Market shows up in a foolish mood, you are free to ignore him or take advantage of him, but it will be disastrous if you fall under his influence.

Buffett reminded his shareholders that to be successful, one needs good business judgment and the ability to protect oneself from the emotional whirlwind that Mr. Market unleashes. Buffett confessed that, to remain insulated from the silliness of the market, he often kept Graham's allegory in mind.

Forecasting

Graham said, "The farther one gets away from Wall Street, the more skepticism one will find as to the pretensions of stock-market forecasting or timing."[1] Since Omaha is a good distance from New York, it is not surprising that Buffett gives zero credence to market predictions. Buffett cannot predict short-term market movements and does not believe that anyone else can. He has "long felt that the only value of stock forecasters is to make fortune tellers look good."[2]

In 1992, Buffett admittedly stepped out of character and predicted that over the decade of the 1990s, it was unlikely that the S&P 500 Index would post returns similar to the above-average returns it accomplished in the 1980s. The prediction, however, had little to do with forecasting. During the 1980s, returns on equity did increase slightly above their historical trend. This increase was attributed more to lower corporate taxes and dramatic increases in leverage. Neither operating margins nor asset turnover ratios—truer indicators of underlying value—showed much change during this period. Of course, the stock market can endure long periods of over- and undervaluation, as happened in the 1980s, but stocks cannot continue to outperform their business fundamentals indefinitely.

Market levels do not stop Buffett from making purchases. Although high general market prices might diminish the number of attractive bargains outstanding, they will not prevent Buffett from buying a company that he finds attractive. However, when market prices are down and pessimism is up, the number of attractive bargains increases. In 1979, Buffett wrote an article entitled "You Pay a Very High Price in the Stock Market for a Cheery Consensus."[3] At the time, the Dow Jones Industrial Average was selling slightly below book value and stocks were earning, on average, 13 percent on equity. Interest rates on bonds fluctuated between 9 percent and 10 percent. Yet most pension managers purchased bonds over stocks. Compare this situation to investor attitudes in 1972, when stocks earned 11 percent on equity and the Dow Jones Industrial Average traded at 168 percent of book value. During this period, Buffett noted, pension managers moved heavily into stocks, selling bonds in order to buy equities.

What was the difference between 1972 and 1979? One possible explanation Buffett offered is that in 1979, portfolio managers felt that as long as the immediate future was unclear, it was best to avoid equity commitments. Such a mentality, Buffett said, must acknowledge the following: First, "The future is never clear," and second, "You pay a very high price for a cheery consensus."[4]

Buffett did not anticipate the periods in which the market was likely to go up or down. Rather, his goals were modest. "We simply attempt," he explained, "to be fearful when others are greedy and to be greedy only when others are fearful."[5] Of course, as Buffett pointed out, polling does not replace thinking. To earn superior profits, individuals are required to carefully evaluate a company's economic fundamentals. Embracing the latest investment style or fad cannot guarantee success.

Portfolio Insurance

During the 1980s, institutional portfolio managers were seduced by an investment strategy called "portfolio insurance," in which a portfolio is constantly rebalanced between risky and riskless assets so that its value does not fall below a prescribed minimum level. As a portfolio decreases in value, funds are shifted away from risky assets (stocks) to riskless assets (bonds or cash). As a portfolio's value rises, conversely, funds are shifted away from riskless assets to riskier assets. Because of the difficulty of shifting millions of dollars in individual securities, portfolio managers instead turned to stock index futures as a means to insure their portfolios.

Buffett worried that naive investors would be seduced into purchasing futures contracts in hopes of reaping large gains. The low margin requirements associated with futures contracts, he said, would also invite gamblers seeking quick profits. Such short-term mentality, he said, is the reason why promoters of penny stocks, casino gambling, and lottery tickets never face a shortage of takers. For the general health of the capital markets, what is needed, Buffett said, is long-term investors who seek out long-term prospects and invest accordingly.

To appreciate the absurdity of portfolio insurance, Buffett asks his readers to consider the rationale of a landowner who, after buying a farm, instructs his real estate agent to begin selling off plots the minute a neighboring farm is sold at a lower price. Or whether a large pension fund, owning shares in General Electric or Ford Motor, is logical in selling portions of its investments just because the last quoted share price was a downtick or in buying shares because of an uptick.

Recent commentaries have suggested that individuals are at a disadvantage when forced to compete against large institutional accounts. Such a conclusion, Buffett says, is wrong. Because of the erratic and illogical behavior of institutional investors, individuals can easily profit, as long as they stick to simple business fundamentals. According to Buffett, individuals are at a disadvantage only if they are forced to sell at unfavorable times. Buffett believes that investors must be financially and psychologically prepared to deal with the market's volatility. Investors should expect their common stocks to fluctuate. Buffett believes that unless you can watch your stock holdings decline by 50 percent without becoming panic-stricken, you should not be in the stock market.

Against the Grain

Buffett has gained the reputation as a savvy investor because of his ability to buy a good business when most of Wall Street either hates or is indifferent to that business. When Buffett bought stock in General Foods and Coca-Cola in the 1980s, most of Wall Street could find nothing exciting about these purchases. General Foods was thought to be a stodgy food company, and Coca-Cola had the reputation of being a safe, conservative, but unappealing institutional holding. After Buffett purchased shares in General Foods, earnings exploded as commodity deflation reduced costs and consumers increased spending. By the time Philip Morris bought General Foods in 1985, Buffett's investment had tripled. Since Berkshire's 1988–1989 purchase of Coca-Cola, the stock price has quadrupled.

In other cases, Buffett has shown that he was unafraid to make substantial purchases even during periods of financial panic. Buffett purchased The Washington Post Company at the height of the 1973–1974 bear market. He purchased GEICO Corporation as it stood on the verge of bankruptcy. He took a huge position in Washington Public Power Supply Systems bonds after the company defaulted. He also took a substantial position in RJR Nabisco high-yield bonds late in 1989, as the junk bond market began a free fall. "The most common cause of low prices," he said, "is pessimism—sometimes pervasive, sometimes specific to a company or industry. We want to do business in such an environment, not because we like pessimism but because we like the prices it produces. It's optimism that is the enemy of the rational buyer."[6]

The True Value of the Market

Buffett finds it odd that investors habitually dislike markets that are in their best interests and favor those markets that continually put them at a disadvantage. Unwittingly, investors dislike owning stocks when prices are going down and warm to those stocks whose prices are ever increasing. Of course, selling at lower prices and buying at higher prices is not profitable. When Buffett purchased Wells Fargo, the stock price had declined 50 percent from its high. Even though Buffett had purchased some shares of Wells Fargo at higher prices, Buffett welcomed the decline in price as a means of purchasing the shares at cheaper prices. According to Buffett, if you expect to continue to purchase stocks throughout your life, you should welcome price declines as a way to add stocks more cheaply to your portfolio. Logically, an investor would be better off if there were one big bear market during the purchasing period of their lives and one glorious bull market shortly before they planned to sell. Buffett points out that investors show no confusion about food prices. Knowing that they are going to purchase food forever, they enjoy lower prices and despise price increases. According to Buffett, as long as you feel good about the businesses you own, you should welcome lower prices as a way to profitably increase your holdings.

Buffett is convinced that, even though the market may temporarily ignore a company's economic fundamentals, eventually the market will acknowledge a company's good fortune. Such a notion is uncomfortable for those investors who have not done their financial homework and who depend on the stock market as the final arbiter. But that is precisely why people have difficulty making money in the stock market. Buffett is able to eliminate the difficulty of share price and value because he dismisses the notion that the stock market is the final arbiter. "As far as I am concerned," he says, "the stock market doesn't exist. It is there only as a reference to see if anybody is offering to do anything foolish."[7] Buffett recognizes that he is neither richer nor poorer because of the market's short-term fluctuations in price, since his holding period is longer term. Whereas most individuals cannot endure the discomfort associated with declining stock prices, Buffett is not unnerved because he believes that he can do a better job than the market in valuing a company. Buffett figures that if you can't, you don't belong in the game. It's like poker, he explains—if you have been in the game for a while and don't know who the patsy is, you're the patsy.

Buffett has long realized that Graham's precepts about the stock market were correct. The stock market is not a guide, but merely there to serve you in buying or selling your interests. For years, Buffett has owned Borsheims, See's Candy Shops, and the Buffalo News without relying on daily price quotes. The businesses have operated quite well, independent of the stock market. Why should it be any different for The Coca-Cola Company, The Washington Post Company, GEICO, and Capital Cities/ABC? Make no mistake, Buffett is acutely aware of the operations of his stock holdings, just as he is aware of the operations of his privately held companies. Buffett focuses on the sales, earnings, profit margins, and capital reinvestment requirements of these companies. Published stock quotes are inconsequential. As Buffett puts it, he would not care if the stock market closed for ten years—it closes every Saturday and Sunday and that has not bothered him yet.

ECONOMICS

Just as Buffett puts no confidence in the prospects of market timing, neither does he commit any resources to judging economic cycles. "If Fed Chairman Alan Greenspan were to whisper to me what his monetary policy was going to be over the next two years," says Buffett, "it wouldn't change one thing I do."[8] Both Buffett and Charlie Munger confess that they spend no time contemplating unemployment figures, interest rates, or currency exchanges. Neither do they let politics interfere with their investment decision-making process. According to Buffett, if the results of a political election were known beforehand, such knowledge would not change his investment approach one bit. Buffett figures that the economy, like a horse on a racetrack, will run quickly some days and slowly on others. Both Buffett and Munger are more interested in focusing on business fundamentals, management, and prices. However, Buffett does give a great deal of thought to inflation, particularly to how inflation affects business returns.

Inflation

Buffett maintains that inflation is a political not an economic phenomenon. Because there is, as yet, no permanent restraint on government spending, the constant printing of money will push inflation higher. Buffett admits that he is unsure when high inflation will return, but feels that deficit spending makes inflation inevitable. Surprisingly, Buffett is less fearful of the budget deficit than he is of the trade deficit. Because the United States has a very strong economic system, Buffett believes that the country can manage its budget deficit. The trade deficit, on the other hand, worries Buffett and forms an integral part of his bias toward high inflation.

During the 1980s, Americans consumed more than one hundred percent of our production, Buffett says. In other words, we not only consumed goods produced in the United States, but our appetite led us to devour foreign goods as well. In exchange for these foreign goods, we issued various claim checks, including

U.S. government and corporate bonds and U.S. bank deposits. These claim checks, given to foreigners, have been growing at an incredible rate. Because we are a wealthy country, this trade deficit can go unnoticed for some time, but eventually these claim checks will be exchanged for our assets (golf courses and hotels) and our manufacturing facilities.

Buffett recognizes that the easiest way for a country to manage its deficits is to debase these claims through higher inflation. Accordingly, Buffett says, the faith that foreign investors have placed in the ability of the United States to pay future claims may be misguided. When claim checks held by foreigners rise to an unmanageable level, the temptation to inflate may be irresistible. For a debtor country, Buffett says, inflation is the economic equivalent of the hydrogen bomb. For this reason, few debtor countries are allowed to export debt denominated in their home currency. Because of the economic integrity of the United States, foreigners have been willing to purchase our debts. Of course, Buffett concludes, if we use inflation to evade our debt, it won't be only foreign holders who will suffer.

Buffett is quick to point out that these external factors—the budget deficit and the trade deficit—because of their effect on inflation, "will be the most important factors in determining whether there are any real rewards from your investment in Berkshire Hathaway."[9] High rates of inflation place a burden on companies to produce a real return for their owners. In order for investors to achieve a real return, companies must earn, on equity, rates that are higher than the investors' misery index: the sum of taxes (ordinary income taxes on dividends and capital gains taxes on retained earnings) and inflation.

Income taxes, Buffett says, can never turn a positive business return into a negative return for owners. Even if tax rates were 90 percent, he says, there would be some real return for owners if the inflation rate were zero. But, as Buffett witnessed during the late 1970s when inflation rose sharply, businesses needed to clear a higher rate of return for owners. For companies earning 20 percent on equity, which, as Buffett points out, few accomplish, operating in an environment of 12 percent inflation leaves little for the owners. During a period of 50 percent tax brackets, a company earning 20 percent on equity and distributing all of these earnings to owners would net a 10 percent return. At 12 percent inflation, owners would have realized just 98 percent of their beginning year's purchasing power. At a 32 percent tax bracket, with inflation at 8 percent, companies earning 12 percent on equity return zero to their owners.

Traditional wisdom for years assumed that stocks were the perfect hedge against inflation. Investors believed that as owners, their companies could naturally pass on the cost of inflation to customers, hence preserving the owner's investment value. Buffett disagrees, pointing out that inflation does not guarantee companies higher returns on equity. Buffett explains that there are only five ways for companies to increase their return on equity:[10]

1. Increase asset turnover (ratio between sales and assets).
2. Widen operating margins.
3. Pay lower taxes.
4. Increase leverage.
5. Use cheaper leverage.

In the first approach, three kinds of assets are analyzed: accounts receivable, inventories, and fixed assets (plant and machinery). As Buffett notes, accounts receivable will rise proportionally as sales rise, whether the rise is a result of unit volume or inflation. So, says Buffett, we cannot improve return on equity from this angle. Inventories, Buffett admits, are not as simple. He notes that an increase in sales can expect to increase inventory turnover ratios. Over shorter periods, inventories can be volatile due to many factors, including supply disruptions and cost changes. Companies that use FIFO (first-in, first-out) inventory methods can improve returns on equity during inflationary times. But, as Buffett explains, even during the ten-year period ending with 1975 when inflation was generally rising, turnover ratios of the Fortune 500 increased only from 1.18/1 to 1.29/1. Inflation will have a tendency, initially, to increase turnover ratios when compared to fixed assets. Because sales will rise sooner than the fixed assets are depleted, higher turnover ratios are to be expected. However, as these fixed assets are replaced, turnover ratios will slow until the rise in inflation matches the rise in sales and fixed assets.

Most managers figure there is always a possibility of increasing operating margins. Wide margins will increase returns on equity. Buffett recognizes that inflation does little to help managers control costs. Major noninterest, nontax costs that companies confront are raw materials, energy, and labor costs. During inflationary periods, these costs are usually escalating. Statistically, Buffett points to the Federal Trade Commission reports identifying a universe of manufacturing companies that achieved 8.6 percent pretax margins on sales in the 1960s. By 1975, during a period of rising inflation, this same universe of companies achieved pretax margins of 8 percent. Despite rising inflation, margins declined.

With regard to lower income taxes, Buffett asks his readers to imagine that investors in U.S. corporations own Class D stock. Class A, B, and C stock is owned by federal, state, and local governments and represents their separate tax claims. While Class A, B, and C owners do not have a claim on the corporations assets, they do get a major share of the corporation's earnings. As Buffett explains, Class A, B, and C owners can vote to increase their interest in a corporation's earnings. Obviously, when Class A, B, and C owners do so, the Class D owners' share of earnings declines. Hence, return on equity declines. Buffett then asks if, during periods of rising inflation, can you assume that Class A, B, and C owners will vote to reduce their share of the company's earnings?

A company can increase returns on equity by increasing leverage or by using cheaper leverage (lower interest rates). However, inflation, Buffett says, will not cause borrowing rates to decline. On the contrary, as inflation increases, capital needs increase, forcing loan demand higher. Additionally, as inflation rises, lenders, distrustful of the future, require a premium for their loanable funds. Even if interest rates do not increase substantially, Buffett explains, the cost of replacing lower interest rate debt that has matured with slightly higher rates will become an expense for corporations.

An irony in business is that those companies who can best afford debt usually require little, and those companies that struggle to remain profitable are always standing in front of the banker's window. Even so, corporations anticipating higher capital needs due to inflation tend to load up on debt. In cases where business slows and capital needs increase, companies can continue to operate without going to the equity market for additional money or, in more dramatic cases, cutting their dividend. Increasing leverage, if managed properly, can increase returns on equity. However, as Buffett explains, during periods of rising inflation, the benefits of greater leverage are offset by the costs of higher interest rates.

Buffett examined the postwar historical returns on equity and concluded that, over time, these returns fluctuated very little. In looking at ten-year intervals following World War II, Buffett noted that returns on equity for the Dow Jones Industrials averaged 12.8 percent ending with 1955, 10.1 percent ending with 1965, and 10.9 percent ending with 1975. In analyzing the Fortune 500, Buffett pointed out that the ten-year returns ending with 1965 were 11.2 percent and in 1975, 11.8 percent. Over the thirty-year period, the return on equity for most U.S. businesses averaged 10–12 percent. Importantly, the returns show no correlation to the rise or decline in inflation. Hence, Buffett is correct in stating that high inflation rates do not help companies earn higher returns on equity.

Knowing that he will not benefit from inflation, Buffett instead seeks to avoid those businesses that will be hurt by inflation. Companies that require large amounts of fixed assets to operate are hurt by inflation. Companies requiring little in fixed assets are, Buffett says, still hurt by inflation but hurt a little less. And the ones that are hurt the least are those with a significant amount of economic goodwill.

Economic Goodwill

Economic goodwill is not the same as the more familiar accounting goodwill. Accounting goodwill is a balance sheet item; it is part of the calculation of book value. Economic goodwill is a larger but less precisely defined item that contributes to a company's intrinsic value.[11]

The first lesson of economic goodwill, Buffett points out, is that companies that generate above-average returns on capital are worth considerably more than the sum of their identifiable assets. For example, in 1972, Blue Chip Stamps purchased See's Candy Shops for $25 million. At that time, See's had $8 million in identifiable assets. With $8 million in assets and no debt, See's was able to earn annually $2 million after taxes, or 25 percent on capital. It was not the fair market value of See's plant, machinery, and inventory that produced this extraordinary return. Rather, Buffett explains, it was the reputation of See's as a purveyor of fine candies and service. Because of this reputation, See's could price its candies far above its production costs. That is the essence of economic goodwill. As long as that reputation remains intact, premium prices will continue to produce high returns, and economic goodwill will remain steady or, perhaps, even increase.

Accounting goodwill, in contrast, will not remain steady; because of accounting practices, it must diminish. According to generally accepted accounting principles (GAAP), when companies are purchased for an amount larger than the net assets (assets minus liabilities), the extra value is assigned to the asset side of the balance sheet and is entitled goodwill. Like other assets, this goodwill is then amortized over a forty-year period. Each year, one-fortieth of the value of goodwill is reduced and charged against earnings. Since Blue Chip Stamps purchased See's for $17 million over its tangible assets, a goodwill account was established on the asset side of Blue Chip's balance sheet. Each year, one-fortieth of this goodwill, or $425,000, is reduced on the balance sheet and charged against earnings. Over the years, then, See's accounting goodwill has been reduced, but the economic value, as long as See's reputation prospers, continues to grow.

Economic goodwill not only produces above-average returns on capital but its value tends to increase with inflation. This appreciation is fundamental in understanding Buffett's equity-investment strategy. To illustrate how this works, Buffett compares See's financial operations with a hypothetical company I will call Bee's. See's, you recall, earned $2 million on $8 million of assets. Buffett asks us to assume that Bee's earns the same $2 million but needed $18 million in assets for its operations. Bee's is earning 11 percent on capital and likely possesses little or no goodwill. Bee's probably would sell for $18 million, the value of its assets, since it is only able to generate an average return on those assets. Remember, companies that are able to generate above-average returns on capital often receive a purchase price greater than their net assets. Buffett paid $25 million for See's, $7 million dollars more than the value of Bee's, even though the earnings of these two companies are identical and See's has half as much in identifiable assets. Buffett asks us to consider if See's, with fewer assets, really is worth more than Bee's. The answer is "yes," Buffett says, as long as you believe that we live in a world of continuous inflation.

To appreciate the effect that inflation has on these two businesses, imagine what would happen if inflation doubled costs. In order to maintain the same level of profits, both companies would need to increase earnings to $4 million. That is not difficult, even if volume is flat and margins are unchanged. You can double profits if you double your prices. The crucial difference between See's and Bee's is the effect that inflation has on assets. Inflation allows both companies to raise their prices, but it also requires additional capital expenditures. Buffett figures that if sales double, more dollars will have to be invested in inventory to support these sales. Fixed assets may respond more slowly than inventory when confronted by inflation, but, eventually, plant and machinery will be replaced with higher-cost equipment.

Since See's had only $8 million in assets producing $2 million in earnings, to reach $4 million in earnings would require it to commit another $8 million in capital. Bee's, on the other hand, would require $18 million in capital to generate an additional $2 million in earnings. Bee's now generates $4 million in earnings on $36 million in assets. Still earning 11 percent on capital, Bee's would sell for approximately $36 million. Hence, Bee's owners have created one dollar of market value for every one dollar of invested capital. See's, now generating $4 million on $16 million of capital, logically would be worth $50 million. See's, Buffett points out, gained $25 million in market value by investing only $8 million in capital, or over three dollars for every one dollar invested.

Companies with a high ratio of fixed assets to sales generally earn low rates of return. These businesses, by design, require extensive capital reinvestment just to maintain operations. During periods of high inflation, these asset-heavy businesses can barely generate enough cash to keep up with their capital demands. Rarely can these companies afford to repurchase their own stock or meaningfully raise their dividend payments to owners. Essentially, companies that require large capital expenditures are cash users, not cash generators.

Buffett maintains that during inflationary periods, a disproportionate number of businesses were able to amass great fortunes because these businesses were able to combine their intangibles—economic goodwill—with minor needs for additional capital investment. As unrestricted earnings increased, management of these businesses was able to increase dividends and repurchase shares. "During inflation," Buffett claims, "goodwill is the gift that keeps giving."[12] Because Buffett has suffered through the economics of bad businesses, he is sensitive about purchasing or reinvesting in businesses that show poor returns. It was the ownership of See's that taught Buffett the value of economic goodwill. "We've made significant money in certain common stocks", says Buffett, "because of the lessons we learned at See's."[13]

PORTFOLIO MANAGEMENT

Buffett does not practice portfolio management, at least not in the traditional sense. Contemporary portfolio managers are cognizant of their stock weighting, industry diversification, and performance relative to a major index. Most managers attempt to balance the dollar amount of their individual stocks. They are also aware of how much money they have invested in various industries, including basic materials, capital goods, consumer cyclicals, consumer staples, finance, technology, energy, utilities, and transportation. Few, if any, portfolio managers are unaware of their equity performance compared to the S&P 500 Index and/or the Dow Jones Industrial Average. Buffett knows all these statistics, too, but he does not waste much energy worrying about them.

In Berkshire's 1991 annual report, Buffett explained how he approaches portfolio management. If he were limited to selecting companies that were based in Omaha, admittedly he would first ascertain the long-term characteristics of the various businesses. Second, he would judge the quality of the management. And finally, he would attempt to purchase a few of the very best businesses at reasonable prices. He would not be interested, he said, in purchasing shares in each business in town. Now, since the universe of companies that he can select from extends much further than Omaha, why should he behave any differently?

In 1971, pension fund managers were selling bonds to purchase stocks. Buffett admitted that there were many attractive companies for sale but few were available at what he considered to be reasonable prices. Berkshire's common stock portfolio in 1971 was worth $11.7 million. Three years later, during the bear market of 1974, these same pension fund managers were investing only 21 percent of their funds in stocks at prices that were dramatically cheaper. Buffett, on the other hand, was increasing Berkshire's commitment to common stocks. By 1975, Berkshire's common stocks were worth

$39 million. At the end of 1978, Berkshire's common stock portfolio had a market value of $220 million, with an unrealized gain of $87 million. In these three years, while the Dow Jones Industrial Average declined from 852 to 805, Berkshire had both realized and unrealized gains in common stocks of $112 million.

The Washington Post Company was Berkshire's first major common stock purchase. In 1973, Buffett invested $10 million in the company; by 1977, his investment had tripled. The Washington Post Company was the first of many publishing companies that Berkshire would purchase. Buffett also invested in advertising agencies and broadcasting companies. For years, Berkshire owned shares of both Interpublic Group and Ogilvy & Mather International. In the late 1970s, Buffett owned both Capital Cities and American Broadcasting Companies. In 1986, Berkshire would become instrumental in providing the financing for Capital Cities' acquisition of American Broadcasting Companies.

In 1978, Buffett made his largest dollar investment to date, $23.8 million in a company called SAFECO Corporation. According to Buffett, it was the best-run property and casualty company in the country, better even than Berkshire's own property and casualty companies. SAFECO, combined with Berkshire's investment in GEICO (Government Employees Insurance Company), accounted for 29 percent of Berkshire's common stock portfolio. Advertising, broadcasting, and publishing accounted for 37 percent of Berkshire's portfolio. Almost two-thirds of Berkshire's portfolio was invested in only two industry groups: finance and consumer cyclicals.

In 1980, Berkshire owned eighteen companies that had a market value of over $5 million. In addition to advertising, broadcasting, insurance, and publishing companies, Buffett also owned a bank (National Detroit), a food company (General Foods), mining companies (Aluminum Company of America, Kaiser Aluminum & Chemical, Cleveland-Cliffs Iron Company), a retailer (F. W. Woolworth), a service company (Pinkerton's) and a tobacco company (R. J. Reynolds). This would be Buffett's most diversified portfolio. He had representation in all major industry groups except capital goods, energy, technology, and utilities.

To date, Buffett has not owned a technology company; he admits he would be unable to understand the company well enough to make an informed judgement. In addition, he has not owned utility companies; he was never attracted to an industry where the profits were regulated. Buffett did invest temporarily in oil: Amerada Hess in 1979 and Exxon in 1984. Over the years, Buffett purchased some stocks for arbitrage (see Chapter 6); Arcata Corporation (1981), Beatrice Companies (1985), and Lear Siegler (1986) were arbitrage positions. Although the potential for profits was small, Buffett used arbitrage as a way to increase the returns he could otherwise achieve by holding cash equivalents.

By 1986, Berkshire had invested in five common stock positions: Capital Cities/ABC, GEICO Corporation, The Washington Post Company, Handy & Harman, and Lear Siegler. As mentioned, Lear Siegler was an arbitrage position and Handy & Harman, a producer of gold and silver products, was only 2.4 percent of Berkshire's $1.9 billion portfolio. Buffett's three major positions—Capital Cities/ABC, GEICO, and The Washington Post Company—were worth $1.7 billion and represented 93 percent of Berkshire's common stock portfolio. That year, Buffett could not find any other common stocks that met his test for being a good business, run by capable management and available at a reasonable price.

During the October 1987 market crash, prices fell momentarily to attractive levels, but Buffett was unable to add any significant positions to Berkshire's common stock portfolio before prices rose again. By year end, Berkshire's common stock portfolio reached, for the first time, more than $2 billion. Amazingly, Buffett now owned only three companies. Capital Cities/ABC was worth $1 billion, GEICO, $750 million; and The Washington Post Company, $323 million. Undoubtedly, no other professional portfolio manager with more than $2 billion in capital limited himself to three companies.

In 1988, Buffett quietly purchased more than 14 million shares of Coca-Cola. It was his first major purchase since the Capital Cities/ABC acquisition in 1986. By year end, Berkshire had invested $592 million in Coca-Cola. The following year, Buffett added another 9,177,500 shares, bringing Berkshire's investment in Coca-Cola to more than $1 billion. It was a very bold and profitable move. By the end of 1989, Berkshire's unrealized gain in Coca-Cola was $780 million.

During 1989–1993, the number of companies in Berkshire's common stock portfolio increased, including nine companies by the end of 1993. Coca-Cola, by far, was the largest holding at $4.1 billion; it represented 37 percent of Berkshire's portfolio. The second largest position was occupied by GEICO, valued at $1.7 billion, followed by The Gillette Company at $1.4 billion, Capital Cities/ABC at $1.2 billion, Wells Fargo & Company at $878 million, Federal Home Loan Mortgage at $681 million, The Washington Post Company at $440 million, General Dynamics at $401 million, and Guinness plc at $270 million. The top four positions represented 76 percent of Berkshire's portfolio. The Washington Post Company, once Berkshire's largest position, represented 3.9 percent of Berkshire's common stock portfolio. By industry group, 52 percent of Berkshire's portfolio was invested in consumer staples, 29 percent in finance, 15 percent in consumer cyclical, and 4 percent in capital goods. For a year-by-year view of Berkshire's portfolio, see Tables A.1 through A.18 in the Appendix.

From his experience, Buffett has learned that good businesses enable the investor to make an easy decision, but tough businesses require difficult decisions. If the decision to purchase a business is not easy, he will not pursue the company. Buffett's willingness to say "no" comes from his direct experience with Ben Graham. Buffett can remember how difficult it was recommending stocks to Graham, only to be turned down most of the time. Graham, Buffett recalls, was never willing to purchase a stock unless all the facts were in his favor. This ability to say "no" is a tremendous advantage for an investor.

Much of Buffett's success in managing Berkshire's investment portfolio can be attributed to his inactivity. Most investors cannot resist the temptation to constantly buy or sell stocks. While Buffett worked in New York, he remembers "people coming up to (him) all the time, whispering into (his) ear about some wonderful business. I was a wonderful customer for the brokerages," Buffett says. "Trouble was, everyone else was, too."[14] According to Buffett, investors feel the need to purchase far too many stocks, rather than wait for that one exceptional company. Tinkering with a portfolio each day is unwise, he says. In his mind, it is easier to buy and hold outstanding businesses than to constantly switch from "far-from-great" businesses. Buffett does not believe he has the talent to frequently buy and sell mediocre businesses that depend more on future market prices than the progress of the company's economic fundamentals. He is content not purchasing or selling a single share of his major holdings throughout the year. "Lethargy bordering on sloth," he says, "remains the cornerstone of our investment style."[15]

In Buffett's opinion, investors are better served if they concentrate on locating a few spectacular investments rather than jumping from one mediocre idea to another. He believes that his success can be traced to a few investments. If, over his career, you eliminate one dozen of Buffett's best decisions, his investment performance would be no better than average. According to him, "An investor should act as though he had a lifetime decision card with just twenty punches on it. With every investment decision his card is punched, and he has one fewer available for the rest of his life."[16] If investors were restrained in this way, Buffett figures that they would wait patiently until a great investment opportunity surfaced.

Because of the tax on capital gains, Buffett figures that his buy-and-hold strategy has a financial advantage over investment approaches that emphasize short-term trading. To explain, he asks us to imagine what happens if we buy a $1 investment that doubles in price each year. If we sell the investment at the end of the first year, we would have a net gain of $.66 (assuming we're in a 34 percent tax bracket). If the investment continues to double each year, and we continue to sell, pay the tax, and reinvest the proceeds, at the end of twenty years we would gain $25,200 after paying taxes of $13,000. If, on the other hand, we purchased a $1 investment that doubled each year and was not sold until the end of twenty years, we would gain $692,000 after paying taxes of approximately $356,000.

Buffett has learned from experience that good, well-managed businesses often are not available at reasonable prices. When he comes across a wonderful business for sale at an attractive price, he buys a significant position. His purchase is not deterred by pessimistic economic forecasts or gloomy stock market predictions. If he is convinced that an investment is attractive, he buys boldly. Buffett's rationale for concentrating his investments is further explained in Berkshire's 1991 annual report. Here, Buffett shared portions of a letter John Maynard Keynes wrote to a business associate, F. C. Scott. "As time goes on, I get more and more convinced that the right method in investments is to put fairly large sums into enterprises which one thinks one knows something about and in management of which one thoroughly believes. It is a mistake to think that one limit's one's risk by spreading too much between enterprises about which one knows little and has no special reason for special confidence . . . . One's knowledge and experience is definitely limited and there are seldom more than two or three enterprises at any given time which I personally feel myself entitled to put full confidence."[17]

In addition to Keynes, Buffett's legitimacy for limiting the number of stocks in Berkshire's portfolio is found in Philip Fisher's teachings. Fisher, like Keynes, felt that too many stocks increased the riskiness of the portfolio. A portfolio manager forced to analyze and follow a large number of stocks runs the risk of putting too much money in bad investments and not enough money in the spectacular investments. Berkshire's heavy concentration in just a few companies would be inappropriate for most insurance companies. Buffett's policy of concentration has the probability of producing above-average, long-term results. Of course, in any one given year, he has the potential to look either incredibly intelligent or foolish, depending on the vagaries of the stock market.

Buffett is remarkably unconcerned about the price performance of his common stocks compared to a stock market index. He judges the success of his common stocks by their operating performance, not by their short-term (daily, weekly, monthly, yearly) temperamental price quotes. In the long run (years), he knows that if the operating performance of his business is superior, the market will, at some point, price the stock higher.

LOOK-THROUGH EARNINGS

Just as Buffett pays little attention to stock market prices, he is not terribly concerned with GAAP reported earnings. He loses no sleep over the fact that accounting rules about how earnings must be reported create, in effect, a false reading for Berkshire Hathaway.

The percentage of voting stock owned determines which one of three accounting methods an investor can use to report earnings. If you, the investor, own more than 50 percent of a company's voting stock, accounting rules say that you can fully consolidate all revenues and expenses and deduct for minority interest the percentage of earnings you do not own. In the second category, ownership of 20–50 percent of a company's voting stock leads to certain presumptions that an investor can influence the operations of the company. Because of this ability, ownership is accounted for under the equity method. All of the earnings are not consolidated; only your percentage share of the earnings are included. In the third category, less than 20 percent of the voting stock, you include only the proportional share of dividends (if any) in your own reported earnings. The undistributed or retained earnings of the company are not included in your income statement. All of Berkshire Hathaway's common stocks fall into this third category.[18]

Because of the accounting rules, Berkshire's large dollar investment in common stocks has a material effect on its corporate earnings. Presently, Berkshire's share of undistributed earnings from its common stock investments is almost as large as the combined earnings of its consolidated subsidiaries. For example, in 1990, Berkshire owned 18 percent of Capital Cities/ABC. In that year, Capital Cities/ABC earned $465 million. Although Berkshire was the owner of $83 million in earnings (18 percent of $465 million), it could only report $530,000 in dividend income: 18 percent of the Capital Cities/ABC dividends less $70,000 in taxes paid. Berkshire could not report the $82 million that stayed with Capital Cities/ABC as retained earnings.

This accounting restriction would be unacceptable to most business managers, who feel compelled to report all of their earnings. Buffett's strategy, on the other hand, has nothing to do with maximizing reported earnings. The underlying economics of Berkshire's uncontrolled businesses are excellent, and Buffett was able to obtain a partial ownership of these businesses at prices far more reasonable than if he had tried to buy the entire company. He would rather own 10 percent of a well-managed company at $1X per share than own 100 percent of the same company at $2X per share. If you consider an equal dollar investment, Buffett prefers to own $2 earnings that are not reportable to Berkshire than purchase $1 of earnings that is reportable. The value to Berkshire Hathaway is not determined by whether it can report a company's retained earnings. The ultimate value to Berkshire depends on how the retained earnings are reinvested and what that reinvestment produces in future earnings. How earnings are reported is less important than how they are used. "We care not whether the auditors hear a tree fall; we do care who owns the tree and what's next done with it."[19]

To help owners appreciate the value of Berkshire Hathaway's common stock "nonreported" earnings, Buffett coined the term "look-through" earnings. Berkshire Hathaway's look-through earnings are made up of the operating earnings of its consolidated businesses (including dividends from common stock investments), the retained earnings of its common stock investments, and an allowance for the tax that Berkshire would have had to pay if the retained earnings had actually been paid. Each year, Buffett includes a table to help shareholders understand the contribution that look-through earnings have for Berkshire Hathaway.

In 1991 (Table 3.1), Berkshire's share of retained earnings from "investees" (companies in which Berkshire owned common stock) was $230 million. Subtracting taxes owed if those earnings were paid out, the remaining unreported earnings were $200 million. If you add the $200 million in unreported earnings to Berkshire's $316 million in operating earnings, the total 1991 look-through earnings were $516 million. Buffett points out that 44 percent of Berkshire's earnings that year were "iceberg" earnings—only a portion appears above the surface. In 1993 (Table 3.1), Berkshire's share of retained earnings from investees reached $439 million. After tax, unreported earnings were $378 million. Berkshire's total look-through earnings in 1993 were $856 million. In that year, 44 percent of Berkshire's earnings were iceberg earnings.

Buffett's long-term goal for Berkshire Hathaway is to have its intrinsic value increase, on average, 15 percent annually. He believes that if look-through earnings increase 15 percent annually, Berkshire's business will grow at the same rate. Indeed, Buffett has calculated that, since 1965, Berkshire's look-through earnings have grown at almost the same 23 percent annual rate as its gain in book value.

LEMMINGS

Lemmings are small rodents indigenous to the tundra region and are noted for their mass exodus to the sea. In normal periods, lemmings move about during their spring migration in search of food and new shelter. Every three to four years, however, something odd begins to happen. Because of high breeding and low

Table 3.1 Berkshire Hathaway "Look-Through Earnings"

Berkshire's Major Investees	Berkshire's Approximate Ownership at Year-End			Berkshire's Share of Undistributed Operating Earnings (in millions)		
	1993	1992	1991	1993	1992	1991
Capital Cities/ABC, Inc.	13.0%	18.2%	18.1%	$83[b]	$70	$61
The Coca-Cola Company	7.2%	7.1%	7.0%	94	82	69
Federal Home Loan Mortg. Corp.	6.8%[a]	8.2%[a]	3.4%[a]	41[b]	29[c]	15
GEICO Corp.	48.4%	48.1%	48.2%	76[c]	34[c]	69[c]
General Dynamics	13.9%	14.1%	—	25	11[b]	—
The Gillette Company	10.9%	10.9%	11.0%	44	38	23[b]
Guinness plc	1.9%	2.0%	1.6%	8	7	—
The Washington Post Company	14.8%	14.6%	14.6%	15	11	10
Wells Fargo & Company	12.2%	11.5%	9.6%	53[b]	16[b]	(17)[b]
Berkshire's share of undistributed earnings of major investees				$439	$298	$230
Hypothetical tax on these undistributed investee earnings[d]				(61)	(42)	(30)
Reported operating earnings of Berkshire				478	348	316
Total look-through earnings				$856	$604	$516

Source: Berkshire Hathaway 1992 and 1993 annual reports.

[a]Net of minority interest in Wesco.

[b]Calculated on average ownership for the year.

[c]Excludes realized capital gains, which have been recurring and significant.

[d]The tax rate used is 14%, which is the rate Berkshire pays on the dividends it receives.

mortality, the population of lemmings begins to rise. As soon as their ranks swell, lemmings begin an erratic movement under darkness. Soon, this bold group begins to move in daylight. When confronted by barriers, the number of lemmings in the pack increases until a panic-like reaction drives them through or over the obstacle. As this behavior intensifies, lemmings begin to challenge other animals they normally would avoid. Although many lemmings die from starvation, predators, and accidents, most reach the sea. There they plunge in and swim until they die from exhaustion. The behavior of lemmings is not fully understood. Zoologists theorize that the mass migration of lemmings occurs because of changes in their food supply and/or stressful conditions. The crowding and competition among lemmings possibly evokes a hormonal change that induces an alteration in behavior.

Because financial markets are moved, dramatically, by moblike action, investment professionals have long been interested in the psychological theories of human behavior. Ben Graham offered a story to help illustrate the irrational behavior of certain investors. Buffett shared Graham's analogy with his readers in Berkshire's 1985 annual report. An oil prospector, moving to his heavenly reward, was met by St. Peter with bad news. "You're qualified for residence," said St. Peter, "but, as you can see, the compound reserved for oil men is packed. There's no way to squeeze you in." After thinking for a moment, the prospector asked if he might say just four words to the present occupants. That seemed harmless to St. Peter, so the prospector cupped his hand and yelled, "Oil discovered in hell." Immediately the gates to the compound opened and all the oil men marched out to head for the nether regions. Impressed, St. Peter invited the prospector to move in and make himself comfortable. The prospector paused. "No", he said, "I think I'll go along with the rest of the boys. There might be some truth to that rumor after all."

It is perplexing to Buffett that, with so many well-educated, experienced professionals working on Wall Street, there is not a more logical and rational force in the market. In fact, stocks with the highest percent of institutional ownership are often the most volatile in price. Business managers cannot determine their share prices. They can only hope to encourage investors, by releasing corporate information, to act rationally. The wild swings in share prices, Buffett notes, have more to do with the "lemming-like" behavior of institutional investors than with the aggregate returns of the company they own.

Buffett confides that his long-term buy-and-hold strategy is out of step with the present-day thinking of institutional money managers. Most money managers are quick to restructure (buy or sell) their portfolios whenever Wall Street dictates a new preference. Their portfolios are diversified among the major industry groups, more to protect themselves from being out of step with the market than from any deeply felt sense that the companies within the industries represent good value. In Buffett's opinion, the term "institutional investor" is becoming an oxymoron. Referring to money managers as investors is, he says, like calling a person who engages in one-night stands romantic.

Critics argue that, because of the standard practices of diversification, money managers behave more conservatively than Buffett. Buffett disagrees. He does admit that money managers invest their money in a more conventional manner. However, he argues that conventionality is not synonymous with conservatism. Rather, conservative actions rise from facts and reasoning. Buffett gains no confidence because "important" people agree with him. Neither does he lose confidence because they disagree with his investment approach. Whether he acts conventionally or unconventionally, whether people agree or disagree, Buffett maintains that he manages money conservatively.

The failure of most portfolio managers to exceed the major indices is not a reflection of intelligence, Buffett says, but a symptom of the institutional decision-making process. According to Buffett, most institutional decisions are made by groups or committees who possess a strong desire to conform to generally accepted portfolio safeguards. The institution that compensates the money manager equates safe with average. Adherence to standard diversification practices, rational or irrational, is rewarded over independent thinking. "Most managers," Buffett has said, "have very little incentive to make the intelligent-but-with-some-chance-of-looking-like-an-idiot decision. Their personal gain/loss ratio is all too obvious; if an unconventional decision works out well, they get a pat on the back, and if it works out poorly, they get a pink slip. Failing conventionally is the route to go; as a group, lemmings may have a rotten image, but no individual lemming has ever received bad press."[20]

FOUR

Buying a Business

THERE IS NO FUNDAMENTAL difference, according to Warren Buffett, between buying a business outright and buying shares in a business. It has always been his preference to directly own a company, for it permits him to influence the most critical issue in a business: capital allocation. Otherwise, his choice is to own a portion of a company by purchasing its common stock. The disadvantage of not controlling a business, Buffett explains, is offset by two distinct advantages: first, the arena for selecting noncontrolled businesses, the stock market, is significantly larger, and, second, the stock market provides more opportunities for finding bargains. In either case—whether purchasing a controlled or noncontrolled business—Buffett continually follows the same equity-investing strategy: He looks for companies he understands, with favorable long-term prospects that are operated by honest and competent people and, importantly, are available at attractive prices.

"When investing," he says, "we view ourselves as business analysts not as market analysts, not as macroeconomic analysts, and not even as security analysts."[1] This means that when he evaluates a potential acquisition or stock purchase, Buffett works first and foremost from the perspective of a businessperson. He looks at the business holistically, examining all quantitative and qualitative aspects of its management, its financial position, and its purchase price.

75

If we go back through time and review all of Buffett's purchases, looking for the commonalities, it is possible to discern a set of basic principles, or tenets, that guide his decisions. If we extract these tenets and spread them out for a closer look, we see that they naturally group themselves into four categories:

1. Business tenets—three basic characteristics of the business itself.
2. Management tenets—three important qualities that senior managers must display.
3. Financial tenets—four critical financial decisions that the company must maintain.
4. Market tenets—two interrelated cost guidelines.

Of course, not all of Buffett's acquisitions will display all the tenets, but, taken as a group, these tenets constitute the core of his equity investment approach.

These twelve tenets also serve as the principles by which Buffett runs his own company, Berkshire Hathaway. Buffett walks his talk. The same qualities he looks for in the businesses he buys, he expects to see when he walks through the front door of his office each day.

BUSINESS TENETS

For Buffett, stocks are an abstraction.[2] He does not think in terms of market theories, macroeconomic concepts, or sector trends. Rather, his investment actions are related only to how a business operates. He believes that if people are drawn to an investment because of superficial notions, rather than business fundamentals, they are more likely to be scared away at the first sign of trouble and, in all likelihood, lose money in the process. Instead, Buffett concentrates on learning all he can about the business under consideration, focusing on three main areas:

1. Is the business simple and understandable?
2. Does the business have a consistent operating history?
3. Does the business have favorable long-term prospects?

Simple and Understandable

In Buffett's view, an investor's financial success is in direct proportion to the degree to which he or she understands the investment. This understanding is a distinguishing trait that separates investors with a business orientation from most hit-and-run investors, people who merely buy shares of stock.

Over the years, Buffett has owned a vast array of businesses: a gas station; a farm implement business; textile companies; a major retailer; banks; insurance companies; advertising agencies; aluminum and cement companies; newspapers; oil, mineral, and mining companies; food, beverage, and tobacco companies; and television and cable companies. Some of these have been controlled by Buffett, and in other cases, he was or is a minority shareholder. In either case, Buffett is acutely aware of how these businesses operate. He understands the revenues, expenses, cash flow, labor relations, pricing flexibility, and capital-allocation needs of each of Berkshire's holdings.

Buffett is able to maintain a high level of knowledge about Berkshire's businesses because he purposely limits his selections to companies that are within his area of financial and intellectual understanding. "Invest within your circle of competence," he counsels. "It's not how big the circle is that counts, it's how well you define the parameters."[3]

Critics argue that Buffett's self-imposed restrictions exclude him from industries that offer the greatest investment potential, such as technology. In response, Buffett observes that investment success is not a matter of how much you know but how realistically you define what you do not know. "An investor needs to do very few things right as long as he or she avoids big mistakes."[4] Above-average results, Buffett has learned, are often produced by doing ordinary things. The key is to do those ordinary things exceptionally well.

Consistent Operating History

Buffett not only avoids the complex, he avoids purchasing companies that are either solving difficult business problems or fundamentally changing the direction of the company because their previous plans were unsuccessful. It has been Buffett's experience that the best returns are achieved by companies that have been producing the same product or service for several years. Undergoing major business changes increases the likelihood of committing major business errors.

Buffett's belief is that "severe change and exceptional returns usually don't mix."[5] Most individuals, unfortunately, invest as if the opposite were true. Lately, investors have scrambled to purchase stocks from companies that are in the midst of a corporate reorganization. For some unexplained reason, Buffett says, these investors are so infatuated with the notion of what tomorrow may bring that they ignore today's business reality.

Buffett's experience in business operations and investment has taught him that "turn-arounds" seldom turn. Energy can be more profitably expended by purchasing good businesses at reasonable prices than difficult businesses at cheaper prices. "Charlie [Munger] and I have not learned how to solve difficult business problems," Buffett explains. "What we have learned is to avoid them. To the extent that we have been successful, it is because we concentrated on identifying one-foot hurdles that we could step over rather than because we acquired any ability to clear seven-footers."[6]

Favorable Long-Term Prospects

According to Buffett, the economic world is divided into a small group of franchises and a much larger group of commodity businesses, of which most are not worth purchasing. He defines a franchise as a company providing a product or service that is (1) needed or desired, (2) has no close substitute, and (3) is not regulated. These traits allow a franchise to regularly increase the prices of its product or service without fear of losing market share or unit volume. Often a franchise can raise its prices even when demand is flat and capacity is not fully utilized. This pricing flexibility is one of the defining characteristics of a franchise; it allows franchises to earn above-average returns on invested capital. Another defining characteristic is that franchises possess a greater amount of economic goodwill, which enables them to better withstand the effects of inflation.

Conversely, a commodity business offers a product that is virtually indistinguishable from the products of its competitors. Years ago, basic commodities included oil, gas, chemicals, wheat, copper, lumber, and orange juice. Today, computers, automobiles, airline service, banking, and insurance have become commodity-type products. Despite mammoth advertising budgets, they are unable to achieve meaningful product differentiation.

Commodity businesses, generally, are low-returning businesses and "prime candidates for profit trouble."[7] Since their product is basically no different from anyone else's, they can only compete on the basis of price, cutting into profit margins severely. The only other way to turn a profit is during periods of tight supply. In fact, a key to determining the long-term profitability of a commodity business, Buffett notes, is the ratio of "supply-tight to supply-ample years." However, this ratio is often fractional. The most recent supply-tight period in Berkshire's textile division, Buffett quips, lasted the "better part of a morning."

After analyzing a company's economic characteristics, Buffett next judges its competitive strengths and weaknesses. "What I like," he confides, "is economic strength in an area where I understand it and where I think it will last."[8]

Economic strength is most often found in franchises. One strength is the potential to freely raise prices and earn high rates on invested capital. Another is the ability to survive economic mishaps and still endure. It is comforting, Buffett says, to be in a business where mistakes can be made and still above-average returns can be achieved. "Franchises," he tells us, "can tolerate mismanagement. Inept managers may diminish a franchise's profitability, but they cannot inflict mortal damage."[9]

A major weakness with franchises is that their value is perishable. Success will inevitably attract other entrepreneurs. Competition will ensue. Substitute products will be introduced, and the differentiation between products will narrow. During this competitive period, a franchise slowly deteriorates into what Buffett calls a "weak franchise" and then further into a "strong business." Eventually, the once-promising franchise may be reduced to a commodity business.

When that happens, the value and importance of good management increase exponentially. A franchise can survive inept management; a commodity business cannot.

MANAGEMENT TENETS

The highest compliment Buffett can pay a manager is that the manager unfailingly behaves and thinks like an owner of the company. Managers who behave like owners tend not to lose sight of the company's prime objective—increasing shareholder value—and they tend to make rational decisions that further that goal. Buffett also greatly admires managers who take seriously their responsibility to report fully and genuinely to shareholders, and who have the courage to resist what he has termed the "institutional imperative"—blindly following industry peers.

In considering a business acquisition, Buffett looks hard at the quality of management. He tells us that the companies Berkshire purchases must be operated by honest and competent people, managers for whom he can feel admiration and trust. Specifically, he considers these main areas:

1. Is management rational?
2. Is management candid with the shareholders?
3. Does management resist the institutional imperative?

Rationality

The most important management act is allocation of the company's capital. It is the most important because allocation of capital, over time, determines shareholder value. Deciding what to do with the company's earnings—reinvest in the business or return money to shareholders—is, in Buffett's mind, an exercise in logic and rationality. "Rationality is the quality that Buffett thinks distinguishes his style with which he runs Berkshire—and the quality he often finds lacking in other corporations," writes Carol Loomis of *Fortune*.[10]

The question of where to allocate earnings is linked to where that company is in its life cycle. As a company moves through its economic life cycle, its growth rates, sales, earnings, and cash flows change dramatically. In the development stage, a company loses money as it develops products and establishes markets. During the next stage, rapid growth, the company is profitable but growing so fast that the company cannot support the growth; often it has to not only retain all of its earnings but also borrow money or issue equity to finance this growth.

In the third stage, maturity, a company's growth rate slows and the company begins to generate more cash than it needs for development and operating costs. In the last stage, decline, the company suffers declining sales and earnings but continues to generate excess cash. It is in phases three and four, but particularly three, that the question arises: How should those earnings be allocated?

If the extra cash, reinvested internally, can produce an above-average return on equity, a return that is higher than the cost of capital, then the company should retain all of its earnings and reinvest them. That is the only logical course. Retaining earnings in order to reinvest in the company at *less* than the average cost of capital is completely irrational. It is also quite common.

A company that provides average or below-average investment returns but generates cash in excess of its needs has three options: (1) It can ignore the problem and continue to reinvest at below average rates, (2) it can buy growth, or (3) it can return the money to shareholders. It is at this crossroad that Buffett keenly focuses on management's behavior. It is here that management will behave rationally or irrationally.

Generally, managers who continue to reinvest despite below-average returns do so in the belief that the situation is temporary. They are convinced that with managerial prowess, they can improve their company's profitability. Shareholders become mesmerized with management's forecast of improvements. If a company continually ignores this problem, cash will become an increasingly idle resource and stock price will decline. A company with poor economic returns, excess cash, and a low stock price will attract corporate raiders, which often is the beginning of the end of current management tenure. To protect themselves, executives frequently choose the second option instead: purchasing growth by acquiring another company.

Announcing acquisition plans has the effect of exciting shareholders and dissuading corporate raiders. However, Buffett is skeptical of companies that need to buy growth. For one thing, growth often comes at an overvalued price. For another, a company that must integrate and manage a new business is apt to make mistakes that could be costly to shareholders.

In Buffett's mind, the only reasonable and responsible course for companies that have a growing pile of cash that cannot be reinvested at above-average rates is to return that money to the shareholders. For that, there are two methods available: raising the dividend or buying back shares.

With cash in hand from their dividends, shareholders have the opportunity to look elsewhere for higher returns. On the surface, this seems a good deal, and therefore many people view increased dividends as a sign of companies that are doing well. Buffett believes this is so only if investors can get more for their cash than the company could generate if it retained the earnings and reinvested in the company.

Over the years, Berkshire Hathaway has earned very high returns from its capital and has retained all of its earnings. With such high returns, shareholders would have been ill served if they were paid a dividend. Not surprisingly, Berkshire does not pay a dividend. And that's just fine with the shareholders. In 1985, Buffett asked shareholders which of three dividend options they preferred: (1) continuing to reinvest all earnings and pay no cash dividend, (2) pay out modest dividends, 5 percent to 15 percent of operating earnings, (3) pay out dividends at a rate typical of American industry, 40 percent to 50 percent of earnings. A very large majority of those who responded—88 percent—preferred to continue the existing policy. The ultimate test of owners' faith is allowing management to reinvest 100 percent of earnings; Berkshire owners have a lot of faith in Buffett.

If the real value of dividends is sometimes misunderstood, the second mechanism for returning earnings to the shareholders—stock repurchase—is even more so. The benefit to the owners is, in many respects, less direct, less tangible, and less immediate.

When management repurchases stock, Buffett feels that the reward is twofold. If the stock is selling below its intrinsic value, then purchasing shares makes good business sense. If a company's stock price is $50 and its intrinsic value is $100, then each time management buys its stock, they are acquiring $2 of intrinsic value for every $1 spent. Transactions of this nature can be very profitable for the remaining shareholders.

Furthermore, Buffett says, when executives actively buy the company's stock in the market, they are demonstrating that they have the best interests of their owners at hand, rather than a careless need to expand the corporate structure. That kind of stance sends good signals to the market, attracting other investors looking for a well-managed company that increases shareholders' wealth. Frequently, shareholders are rewarded twice—once from the initial open market purchase and then subsequently as investor interest has a positive effect on price.

Candor

Buffett holds in high regard managers who report their companies' financial performance fully and genuinely, who admit mistakes as well as share successes, and are in all ways candid with shareholders. In particular, he respects managers who are able to communicate the performance of their company without hiding behind generally accepted accounting principles (GAAP).

Financial accounting standards only require disclosure of business information classified by industry segment. Some managers exploit this minimum requirement and lump together all of the company's businesses into one industry segment, making it difficult for owners to understand the dynamics of their separate business interests. "What needs to be reported," argues Buffett, "is data—whether GAAP, non-GAAP, or extra-GAAP—that helps the financially literate readers answer three key questions: (1) Approximately how much is this company worth? (2) What is the likelihood that it can meet its future obligations? and (3) How good a job are its managers doing, given the hand they have been dealt?"[11]

Berkshire Hathaway's annual reports meet GAAP obligations but go much further. Buffett includes the separate earnings of each of Berkshire's businesses and any other additional information he feels owners would deem valuable when judging a company's economic performance. Buffett admires the CEO who is able to report to his shareholders in the same candid fashion.

He also admires those with the courage to discuss failure openly. According to Buffett, most annual reports are a sham. Over time, every company makes mistakes, both large and inconsequential. Too many managers, he believes, report with excess optimism rather than honest explanation, serving perhaps their own interests in the short term but no one's interests in the long run.

In his annual reports to Berkshire Hathaway shareholders,

Buffett is very open about Berkshire's economic and management performance, both good and bad. Throughout the years, he has admitted the difficulties that Berkshire encountered in both the textile and insurance businesses, and his own management failures in regards to these businesses. In the 1989 Berkshire Hathaway Annual Report, he started a formal practice of listing his mistakes, called "Mistakes of the First Twenty-Five Years (A Condensed Version)." Two years later, the title was changed to "Mistake Du Jour." Here, Buffett confessed not only mistakes made but opportunities lost because he failed to act appropriately.

Critics have argued that Buffett's practice of publicly admitting his mistakes is made easier because by owning 42 percent of Berkshire's common stock, he never has to worry about being fired. This is true. But beyond this criticism, something more is being created in management reporting. It is Buffett's belief that candor benefits the manager at least as much as the shareholder. "The CEO who misleads others in public," he says, "may eventually mislead himself in private."[12] Buffett credits Charlie Munger with helping him understand the value of studying one's mistakes, rather than concentrating only on success.

The Institutional Imperative

If management stands to gain wisdom and credibility by facing mistakes, why do so many annual reports trumpet only successes? If allocation of capital is so simple and logical, why is capital so poorly allocated? The answer, Buffett has learned, is an unseen force he calls "the institutional imperative"—the lemminglike tendency of corporate management to imitate the behavior of other managers, no matter how silly or irrational it may be.

It was, Buffett confesses, the most surprising discovery of his business career. At school he was taught that experienced managers of companies were honest, intelligent, and automatically made rational business decisions. Once out in the business world, he learned instead that "rationality frequently wilts when the institutional imperative comes into play."[13]

According to Buffett, the institutional imperative exists when "(1) an institution resists any change in its current direction; (2) just as work expands to fill available time, corporate projects or acquisitions will materialize to soak up available funds; (3) any business craving of the leader, however foolish, will quickly be supported by detailed rate-of-return and strategic studies prepared by his troops; and (4) the behavior of peer companies, whether they are expanding, acquiring, setting executive compensation or whatever, will be mindlessly imitated."[14]

Jack Ringwalt, head of National Indemnity, helped Buffett discover the destructive power of the imperative. While the majority of insurance companies were writing insurance policies on terms guaranteed to produce inadequate returns or worse, a loss, Ringwalt stepped away from the market and refused to write policies. Likewise, both Munger and Buffett abruptly altered the direction of Mutual Savings when it was clear the strategy of the savings and loan industry was leading to disaster.

Most managers are unwilling to look foolish and expose their company to an embarrassing quarterly loss when other "lemming" companies are still able to produce quarterly gains, even though they assuredly are "heading into the sea." Shifting direction is never easy. It is often easier to follow other companies down the same path leading to failure than alter the direction of the company. Admittedly Buffett and Munger don't have to worry about getting fired, and this frees them to make unconventional decisions. Still, a manager with strong communication skills should be able to convince owners to accept a short-term loss in earnings if it means superior results over time. The inability to resist the institutional imperative, Buffett has learned, often has less to do with the owners of the company than the willingness of its managers to accept fundamental change.

Even when managers accept the notion that their company must change or face the possibility of shutting down, carrying out this plan is too difficult for most managers to accomplish. Instead, many succumb to the temptation to buy a new company rather than face the financial facts of the current problem.

Why would they do this? Buffett isolates three factors he feels most influence management's behavior. First, most managers cannot control their lust for activity. Such hyperactivity often finds its outlet in business takeovers. Second, most managers are constantly comparing their business's sales, earnings, and executive compensation to other companies within and beyond their industry. These comparisons, Buffett notes, invite corporate hyperactivity. Lastly,

Buffett believes that most managers have an exaggerated sense of their own management capabilities.

Another common problem is poor allocation skills. As Buffett points out, CEOs often rise to their position by excelling in other areas of the company, including administration, engineering, marketing, or production. Because they have little experience in allocating capital, most CEOs, instead, turn to their staff members, consultants, or investment bankers for advice. Here the institutional imperative begins to enter the decision-making process. If the CEO craves a potential acquisition that requires a 15 percent return on investment to justify the purchase, it is amazing, Buffett points out, how smoothly his troops report back to him that the business can actually achieve 15.1 percent.

The final justification for the institutional imperative is mindless imitation. If companies A, B, and C are behaving in a similar manner, then, reasons the CEO of company D, it must be all right for our company to behave the same way. It is not venality or stupidity, Buffett claims, that positions these companies to fail. Rather, it is the institutional dynamics of the imperative that make it difficult to resist doomed behavior. Speaking before a group of Notre Dame students, Buffett displayed a list of thirty-seven failed investment banking firms. All of these firms, he explained, failed even though the volume of the New York Stock Exchange multiplied fifteenfold. These firms were headed by hard-working individuals with very high IQs, all of whom had an intense desire to succeed. Buffett paused; his eyes scanned the room. "You think about that," he said sternly. "How could they get a result like that? I'll tell you how," he said, "mindless imitation of their peers."[15]

Buffett has been fortunate to work with some of the brightest managers in corporate America, including Tom Murphy and Dan Burke at Capital Cities/ABC, Roberto Goizueta and Donald Keough at Coca-Cola, and Carl Reichardt at Wells Fargo. However, there is a point where even the brightest and most capable manager cannot rescue a difficult business. "If you put those same guys to work in a buggy whip company," Buffett says, "it wouldn't have made much difference."[16] What Buffett is saying is that no matter how impressive management is, he will not invest in people alone. "When a management with a reputation for brilliance tackles a business with a reputation for poor fundamental economics," he writes, "it is the reputation of the business that stays intact."[17]

For the most part, valuing the ability of managers is a subjective effort that defies quantification. Nonetheless, there are some quantifiable measurements available. And they are the same measures by which economic performance is gauged: return on equity, cash flow, and operating margins.

FINANCIAL TENETS

The financial tenets by which Buffett values both managerial excellence and economic performance are all grounded in some typically Buffettlike principles. For one thing, he does not take yearly results too seriously. Instead, he focuses on four- or five-year averages. Oftentimes, he notes, profitable business returns might not coincide with the time it takes for the planet to circle the sun. He also has little patience with accounting sleight-of-hand that produces impressive year-end numbers but little real value. Instead, he is guided by these principles:

1. Focus on return on equity, not earnings per share.
2. Calculate "owner earnings" to get a true reflection of value.
3. Look for companies with high profit margins.
4. For every dollar retained, make sure the company has created at least one dollar of market value.

Return on Equity

Customarily, analysts measure annual company performance by looking at earnings per share. Did they increase over last year? Are they high enough to brag about? Buffett considers earnings per share a smokescreen. Since most companies retain a portion of their previous year's earnings as a way of increasing their equity base, he sees no reason to get excited about record earnings per share. There is nothing spectacular about a company that increases earnings per share by 10 percent if, at the same time, it is growing its equity base by 10 percent. That's no different, he explains, from putting money in a savings account and letting the interest accumulate and compound.

"The primary test of managerial economic performance," he

asserts, "is the achievement of a high earnings rate on equity capital employed (without undue leverage, accounting gimmickry, etc.) and not the achievement of consistent gains in earnings per share."[18] To measure a company's annual performance, Buffett prefers return on equity—the ratio of operating earnings to shareholder's equity.

To use this ratio, we need to make several adjustments. First, all marketable securities should be valued at cost and not at market value because values in the stock market as a whole can greatly influence the returns on shareholder's equity in a particular company. For example, if the stock market rose dramatically in one year, thereby increasing the net worth of a company, a truly outstanding operating performance would be diminished when compared to a larger denominator. Conversely, falling prices reduce shareholders' equity, which means that mediocre operating results appear much better than they really are.

Second, investors must also control the effects that unusual items may have on the numerator of this ratio. Buffett excludes all capital gains and losses as well as any extraordinary items that may increase or decrease operating earnings. He is seeking to isolate the specific annual performance of a business. He wants to know how well management accomplishes its task of generating a return on the operations of the business, given the capital it employs. That, he says, is the single best judge of management's economic performance.

Furthermore, Buffett believes that a business should achieve good returns on equity while employing little or no debt. We know that companies can increase their return on equity by increasing their debt-to-equity ratio. Buffett is aware of this, but the idea of adding a couple of points to Berkshire Hathaway's return on equity simply by taking on more debt does not impress him. "Good business or investment decisions," he says, "will produce quite satisfactory economic results with no aid from leverage."[19] Furthermore, highly leveraged companies are vulnerable during economic slowdowns. He would rather err on the side of financial quality than risk the welfare of Berkshire's owners by increasing the risk that is associated with debt.

Despite his conservative stance, Buffett is not phobic when it comes to borrowing money. In fact, he prefers to borrow money in anticipation of using it farther down the road, rather than borrowing the money after a need is announced. It would be ideal, Buffett notes, if the timing of business acquisitions profitably coincided with the availability of funds. However, experience has shown that just the opposite occurs. Cheap money has a tendency to force prices of assets higher. Tight money and higher interest rates raise liability costs and often force the price of assets downward. Just when the best prices are available for purchasing businesses, the cost of money (higher interest rates) is likely to diminish the attractiveness of the opportunity. For this reason, Buffett says, companies should manage their assets and liabilities independently of each other.

This philosophy of borrowing now in the hope of finding a good business opportunity later will penalize near-term earnings. However, Buffett acts only when he is reasonably confident the return of a future business will more than offset the expense of the debt. In addition, because the availability of attractive business opportunities is limited, Buffett wants Berkshire to be prepared. "If you want to shoot rare, fast moving elephants," he advises, "you should always carry a gun."[20]

Buffett does not give any suggestions as to what debt levels are appropriate or inappropriate for a business. Understandably, different companies, depending on their cash flows, can manage different levels of debt. What Buffett does say is that a good business should be able to earn a good return on equity without the aid of leverage. Companies that are only able to earn good returns on equity by employing significant debt should be viewed suspiciously.

"Owner Earnings"

Investors, warns Buffett, should be aware that accounting earnings per share are the starting point for determining the economic value of a business, not the ending point. "The first point to understand," he says, "is that not all earnings are created equal."[21] Companies with high assets to profits, he points out, tend to report ersatz earnings. Because inflation extracts a toll on asset-heavy businesses, the earnings of these businesses take on a "mirage-like" quality. Hence, accounting earnings are only useful to the analyst if they approximate the expected cash flow of the company.

But even cash flow, Buffett warns, is not a perfect tool for measuring value; often, it misleads investors. Cash flow is an appropriate way to measure businesses that have large investments in the beginning and smaller outlays later on, companies such as real estate, gas fields, and cable companies. Manufacturing companies, on the other hand, which require ongoing capital expenditures, are not accurately valued using only cash flow.

A company's cash flow is customarily defined as net income after taxes plus depreciation, depletion, amortization, and other noncash charges. The problem with this definition, explains Buffett, is that it leaves out a critical economic fact: capital expenditures. How much of the year's earnings must the company use for new equipment, plant upgrades, and other improvements needed to maintain its economic position and unit volume? According to Buffett, approximately 95 percent of America's businesses require capital expenditures that are roughly equal to their depreciation rates. You can defer capital expenditures for a year or so, he says, but if over a long period you don't make the necessary expenditures, your business will surely decline. These capital expenditures are as much an expense to a company as are labor and utility costs.

Popularity of cash-flow numbers heightened during the leverage buyout period of the 1980s because the exorbitant prices paid for businesses were justified by a company's cash flow. Buffett believes that cash flow numbers "are frequently used by marketers of business and securities in attempts to justify the unjustifiable and thereby sell what should be unsalable. When earnings look inadequate to service debt of a junk bond or justify a foolish stock price, how convenient it becomes to focus on cash flow."[22] But you cannot focus on cash flow, Buffett warns, unless you are willing to subtract the necessary capital expenditures.

Instead of cash flow, Buffett prefers to use what he calls "owner earnings"—a company's net income plus depreciation, depletion, and amortization, less the amount of capital expenditures and any additional working capital that might be needed. Owner earnings, Buffett admits, do not provide the precise calculations that many analysts demand. Calculating future capital expenditures often requires rough estimates. Still, quoting Keynes, he says, "I would rather be vaguely right than precisely wrong."

Profit Margins

Like Philip Fisher, Buffett is aware that great businesses make lousy investments if management cannot convert sales into profits. In his experience, managers of high-cost operations tend to find ways to continually add to overhead, whereas managers of low-cost operations are always finding ways to cut expenses.

Buffett has little patience for managers who allow costs to escalate. Frequently, these same managers have to initiate a restructuring program to bring costs in line with sales. Each time a company announces a cost-cutting program, he knows this company has not figured out what expenses can do to a company's owners. "The really good manager," Buffett says, "does not wake up in the morning and say, 'This is the day I'm going to cut costs,' any more than he wakes up and decides to practice breathing."[23]

Buffett singles out the accomplishments of Carl Reichardt and Paul Hazen at Wells Fargo, and Tom Murphy and Dan Burke at Capital Cities/ABC for their relentless attack on unnecessary expenses. These managers, he says, "abhor having a bigger head count than is needed" and both managerial teams "attack costs as vigorously when profits are at record levels as when they are under pressure."[24] Buffett himself can be tough when it comes to costs and unnecessary expenses. He is very sensitive about Berkshire's profit margins. He understands the right size staff for any business operation and believes that for every dollar of sales, there is an appropriate level of expenses.

Berkshire Hathaway is a unique corporation. The corporate staff at Kiewit Plaza would have difficulty fielding a softball team. Berkshire Hathaway does not have a legal department, or a public or investor relations department. There are no strategic planning departments staffed with MBA-trained workers plotting mergers and acquisitions. Berkshire does not employ security guards, limo drivers, or messengers. Berkshire's after-tax overhead corporate expense runs less than 1 percent of operating earnings. Compare this, says Buffett, to other companies with similar earnings but 10 percent corporate expenses; shareholders lose 9 percent in the value of their holdings simply because of corporate overhead.

The One-Dollar Premise

There is a quick test that can be used to judge not only the economic attractiveness of a business but how well management has accomplished its goal of creating shareholder value: If Buffett has selected a company with favorable long-term economic prospects, run by able and shareholder-oriented managers, the proof will be reflected in the increased market value of the company.

We know that the stock market will track business value reasonably well over long periods, although, in any one year, prices can gyrate widely for reasons other than value. The same, Buffett explains, holds true for retained earnings. If a company employs retained earnings nonproductively over an extended period, eventually the market (justifiably) will price the shares of the company disappointingly. Conversely, if a company has been able to achieve above-average returns on augmented capital, that success will be reflected in increased stock price.

In Buffett's quick test, the increase should, at the very least, match the amount of retained earnings, dollar for dollar. If the value goes up greater than the retained earnings, so much the better. All in all, Buffett explains, "Within this gigantic auction arena, it is our job to select a business with economic characteristics allowing each dollar of retained earnings to be translated eventually into at least a dollar of market value."[25]

MARKET TENETS

All the principles embodied in the tenets described so far lead to one decision point: buying or not buying shares in a company. Anyone at that point must weigh two factors: Is this company a good value, and is this a good time to buy it—that is, is the price favorable?

Price is established by the stock market. Value is determined by the analyst, after weighing all the known information about a company's business, management, and financial traits. Price and value are not necessarily equal. If the stock market were efficient, prices would instantaneously adjust to all available information. Of course we know this does not occur. The prices of securities move above and below company values for numerous reasons, not all of them logical.

Theoretically, the actions of an investor are determined by the differences between price and value. If the price of a business is below its per-share value, a rational investor will purchase shares of the business. Conversely, if the price of a business is higher than its determined value, that investor will pass. As the company moves through its economic life cycle, the analyst will periodically reassess the company's value in relation to market price, and buy, sell, or hold shares accordingly. In sum, then, rational investing has two components:

1. What is the value of the business?
2. Can the business be purchased at a significant discount to its value?

Determine the Value

The traditional ways of valuing a business make use of three general approaches: liquidation, going-concern, or market. Liquidation value is the cash value generated by selling the assets of the business net of all liabilities. Liquidation value requires no consideration of the future earnings of the business since the presumption is the business will no longer be viable. Going-concern value, on the other hand, determines the future cash flows an owner of the business can expect to receive. These future cash flows are discounted back to a present value using an appropriate rate. When future cash flows are too difficult to compute, analysts often use the market approach: comparing the company to other similar publicly traded companies, and applying an appropriate multiple.

Which approach does Buffett use? The best system, he says, was determined more than fifty years ago by John Burr Williams in *The Theory of Investment Value* (North-Holland, 1938). Paraphrasing Williams's theory, Buffett tells us the value of a business is determined by the net cash flows expected to occur over the life of the business discounted at an appropriate interest rate. "So valued," Buffett says, "all businesses, from manufacturers of buggy whips to operators of cellular telephones, become economic equals."[26]

The mathematical exercise, Buffett tells us, is very similar to valuing a bond. A bond has both a coupon and a maturity date that determines its future cash flow. If you add all the bond's coupons and divide the sum by the appropriate discount rate, the price of the bond will be revealed. To determine the value of a business, the analyst estimates the "coupons" that the business will generate for a period into the future, and then discounts all of these coupons back to the present.

For Buffett, determining a company's value is easy as long as you plug in the right variables: the stream of cash and the proper discount rate. If he is unable to project with confidence what the future cash flows of a business will be, he will not attempt to value the company. This is the distinction of his approach. Although he admits that Microsoft is a dynamic company and he highly regards Bill Gates as a manager, Buffett confesses to not having a clue how to estimate the future cash flows of this company. If the business is simple and understandable, if it has operated with consistent earnings power, Buffett is able to determine the future cash flows with a high degree of certainty. The circle of competence that he refers to is reflected in his ability to project into the future. In Buffett's mind, the predictability of a company's future cash flow should take on a "coupon-like" certainty that is found in bonds.

After he has determined the future cash flows of a business, Buffett applies the discount rate. Many people will be surprised to learn that the discount rate that Buffett uses is simply the rate of the long-term U.S. government bond, nothing else. That is as close as anyone can come to a risk-free rate.

Academics argue that a more appropriate discount rate would be the risk-free rate of return (the long-term bond rate) plus an equity risk premium, added to reflect the uncertainty of the company's future cash flows. Although Buffett does admit that as interest rates decline he is apt to be more cautious in applying the long-term rate, he does not add a risk premium to his formula for the simple reason that he avoids risk. First, Buffett eliminates the financial risk associated with debt financing by excluding from purchase those companies with high debt levels. Second, business risk is reduced, if not eliminated, by focusing on companies with consistent and predictable earnings. "I put a heavy weight on certainty," he says. "If you do that, the whole idea of a risk factor doesn't make any sense to me. Risk comes from not knowing what you're doing."[27]

Despite Buffett's claims, critics argue that estimating future cash flow is tricky, and selecting the proper discount rate can leave room for substantial errors in valuation. Instead, these critics have employed various shorthand methods to identify value: low price-to-earnings ratios, low price-to-book values, and high dividend yields. Practitioners have vigorously back tested these ratios and concluded that success can be had by isolating and purchasing companies that possess exactly these financial ratios.

People who consistently purchase companies that exhibit low price-to-earnings, low price-to-book, and high dividend yields are customarily called "value investors." People who claim to have identified value by selecting companies with above-average growth in earnings are called "growth investors." Typically, growth companies possess high price-to-earnings ratios and low dividend yields. These financial traits are the exact opposite of what value investors look for in a company.

Investors who seek to purchase value often must choose between the "value" and "growth" approach to selecting stocks. Buffett admits that years ago he participated in this intellectual tug-of-war. Today he thinks the debate between these two schools of thought is nonsense. Growth and value investing are joined at the hip, says Buffett. Value is the discounted present value of an investment's future cash flow; growth is simply a calculation used to determine value.

Growth in sales, earnings, and assets can either add or detract from an investment's value. Growth can add to the value when the return on invested capital is above average, thereby assuring that when a dollar is being invested in the company, at least a dollar of market value is being created. However, growth for a business earning low returns on capital can be detrimental to shareholders. For example, the airline business has been a story of incredible growth, but its inability to earn decent returns on capital have left most owners of these companies in a poor position.

All the shorthand methods—high or low price-earnings ratios, price-to-book ratios, and dividend yields, in any number of combinations—fall short, Buffett says, in determining whether "an investor is indeed buying something for what it is worth and is therefore truly operating on the principle of obtaining value for his investments . . . . Irrespective of whether a business grows or doesn't, displays volatility or smoothness in earnings, or carries a high price or low in relation to its current earnings and book value, the investment shown by the discounted-flows-of-cash calculation to be the cheapest is the one that the investor should purchase."[28]

Buy at Attractive Prices

Focusing on businesses that are understandable, with enduring economics, run by shareholder-oriented managers does not guarantee success, Buffett notes. First, he has to buy at sensible prices and then the company has to perform to his business expectations. If we make mistakes, Buffett confesses, it is either because of (1) the price we paid, (2) the management we joined, or (3) the future economics of the business. Miscalculations in the third instance are, he notes, the most common.

It is Buffett's intention not only to identify businesses that earn above-average returns, but to purchase these businesses at prices far below their indicated value. Graham taught Buffett the importance of buying a stock only when the difference between its price and its value represented a margin of safety.

The margin-of-safety principle assists Buffett in two ways. First, it protects him from downside price risk. If Buffett calculates the value of a business to be only slightly higher than its per share price, he will not buy the stock; he reasons that if the company's intrinsic value were to dip even slightly because he misappraised the company's future cash flow, eventually the stock price would drop, too, perhaps below what he paid for it. But if the margin between the purchase price and the intrinsic value of the company is large enough, the risk of declining intrinsic value is less. If Buffett purchases a company at a 25 percent discount to intrinsic value and the value subsequently declines by 10 percent, his original purchase price will still yield an adequate return.

The margin of safety also provides opportunities for extraordinary stock returns. If Buffett correctly identifies a company possessing above-average economic returns, the value of the shares of stock over the long term will steadily march upwards as the share price mimics the returns of the business. If a company consistently earns 15 percent on equity, its share appreciation will advance more each year than the share price of a company that earns 10 percent on equity. Additionally, if Buffett, by using the margin of safety, is able to buy this outstanding business at a significant discount to its intrinsic value, Berkshire will earn an extra bonus when the market corrects the price of the business. "The market, like the Lord, helps those who help themselves," Buffett says. "But unlike the Lord, the market does not forgive those who know not what they do."[29]

THE INTELLIGENT INVESTOR

The most distinguishing trait of Buffett's investment philosophy is the clear understanding that, by owning shares of stock, he owns businesses, not pieces of paper. The idea of buying stock without understanding the company's operating functions—including a company's products and services, labor relations, raw material expenses, plant and equipment, capital reinvestment requirements, inventories, receivables, and working capital needs—is unconscionable, says Buffett. This mentality is reflected in the attitude of a business owner as opposed to a stock owner. In the summation of *The Intelligent Investor* Benjamin Graham wrote, "Investing is most intelligent when it is most businesslike." These words are, Buffett says, "the nine most important words ever written about investing."

A person who holds stocks has the choice to become the owner of a business or the bearer of tradable securities. Owners of common stocks who perceive that they merely own a piece of paper are far removed from the company's financial statements. These owners behave as if the market's ever-changing price is a more accurate reflection of their stock's value than the businesses' balance sheet and income statement. They draw or discard stocks like playing cards. For Buffett, the activities of a common-stock holder and a businessperson are intimately connected. Both should look at ownership of a business in the same way. "I am a better investor because I am a businessman," confesses Buffett, "and a better businessman because I am an investor."[30]

Buffett is often asked what types of companies he will purchase in the future. First, he says, he will avoid commodity businesses and managers in which he has little confidence. What he will purchase is the type of company that he understands, one that possesses good economics and is run by trustworthy managers. "A good business is not always a good purchase," Buffett says, "although it is a good place to look for one."[31]

FIVE

Permanent Holdings

I T IS WARREN BUFFETT'S practice to let companies inform
him by their operating results, not by their short-term stock
quotes, whether Berkshire's investments are successful. He is convinced that although the stock market, in the short run, may ignore a business's financial results, it will, over time, confirm a
company's success or failure at providing increased shareholder
value. Buffett remembers Ben Graham telling him that "in the
short run, the market is a voting machine but in the long run it is
a weighing machine."[1] He is willing to be patient. In fact, as long
as Berkshire's businesses are increasing shareholder value at a satisfactory rate, he would prefer that the stock market delay its rec-
ognition, thereby allowing him the opportunity to purchase more
shares at bargain prices.

Sometimes the market will quickly confirm Buffett's judgment
that a company is a good investment. When that happens, he is
not compelled to sell just because of short-term appreciation. He
considers the Wall Street maxim "you never go broke taking a
profit" to be foolish advice. Fisher taught him that either the investment you hold is a better investment than cash or it is not.
Buffett says that he is "quite content to hold any security indefi-

nitely, so long as the prospective return on equity capital of the underlying business is satisfactory, management is competent and honest, and the market does not overvalue the business."[2] If the stock market does significantly overvalue a business, he will sell. In addition, Buffett will sell a fairly valued or undervalued security if he needs the proceeds to purchase something else—either a business that is even more undervalued or one of equal value that he understands better.

Beyond this investment strategy, however, Buffett confessed in 1987 that there are three common-stock positions that he will not sell, regardless of how seriously the stock market may overvalue their shares: The Washington Post Company, GEICO Corporation, and Capital Cities/ABC. In 1990, he added The Coca-Cola Company to this list of permanent common-stock holdings.

This 'till-death-do-us-part attitude places these four investments on the same commitment level as Berkshire's controlled businesses. Permanent status is not something Buffett hands out indiscriminately. And it should be noted that a company is not automatically "permanent" on the day Buffett buys it. Berkshire Hathaway has owned shares of The Washington Post Company for twenty years and GEICO for eighteen years. Buffett first purchased Capital Cities in 1977. Even Coca-Cola, first purchased in 1988, was not elevated to permanent status until 1990.

At the time of acquisition, each of these four companies possessed attributes that qualified them for purchase. It is these attributes that are worth studying.

THE WASHINGTON POST COMPANY

The principal business activities of The Washington Post Company include newspaper publishing, television broadcasting, cable television systems, and magazine publishing. The newspaper division publishes *The Washington Post, The Everett Herald*, and the Gazette Newspapers, a group of fourteen weekly newspapers. The television broadcasting division owns six television stations located in Detroit; Miami; Houston and San Antonio, Texas; Hartford, Connecticut; and Jacksonville, Florida. The cable television systems division provides cable service to 463,000 subscribers located in fifteen midwestern, southern, and western States. The magazine publishing division publishes *Newsweek*, with domestic circulation of more than 3 million and more than 700,000 sales internationally.

In addition to the four major divisions, The Washington Post Company owns the Stanley H. Kaplan Educational Centers, a chain of schools where students are tutored for college admission tests. It also owns Legi-Slate, a company that provides computerized information on the legislative and regulatory activities of the United States government. The company owns 50 percent of the *International Herald Tribune* and 28 percent of Cowles Media, the publisher of the *Minneapolis Star* and *Tribune*, and it has also formed a limited partnership with American Personal Communications, which has developed a personal communications system in the Washington, D.C., area.

By the end of 1993, The Washington Post Company was a $3-billion-dollar company generating $1.5 billion in annual sales. Its accomplishments are especially impressive when you consider that sixty years ago the company had one business—publishing a newspaper.

In 1931, the *Washington Post* was one of five dailies competing for readers. Two years later, the *Post*, unable to pay for its newsprint, was placed in receivership. That summer, the company was sold at auction to satisfy creditors. Eugene Meyer, a millionaire financier, bought the *Washington Post* for $825,000. For the next two decades, he supported the paper until it turned a profit. Management of the paper passed to Philip Graham, a brilliant Harvard-educated lawyer, who had married Meyer's daughter, Katherine. In 1954, Phil Graham convinced Eugene Meyer to purchase a rival newspaper, the *Times-Herald*. Later, Graham purchased *Newsweek* magazine and two television stations before his tragic death in 1963. It is Phil Graham who is credited with transforming the *Washington Post* from a single newspaper into a media and communications company.

After Graham's death, control of the *Washington Post* passed to Katherine Graham. Although she had no experience in managing a major corporation, she quickly distinguished herself by confronting difficult business issues. Much of Mrs. Graham's success can be attributed to her genuine affection for the *Post*. She had observed how her father and husband had both struggled to keep the company viable. Katherine Graham realized that to be successful, the company would need a decision maker, not a caretaker. "I quickly learned that things don't stand still," she said. "You have to make decisions."[3] Two decisions that had a pronounced impact on the *Washington Post* were hiring Ben Bradlee as managing editor of the newspaper and then inviting Warren Buffett to become a director of the company. Bradlee encouraged Katherine Graham to publish the Pentagon Papers and to pursue the Watergate investigation, which earned the *Washington Post* a reputation for prize-winning journalism. Buffett taught Katherine Graham how to run a successful business.

Buffett first met Katherine Graham in 1971. At that time, Buffett owned stock in the *New Yorker*. Hearing that the magazine might be for sale, he asked Katherine Graham whether the *Washington Post* would be interested in purchasing it. Although the sale never materialized, Buffett came away very much impressed with the publisher of the *Post*.

At about that time, the *Post*'s financial structure was headed for profound changes. Under the terms of a trust established by Eugene and Agnes Meyer, Katherine and Phil Graham owned all of the voting stock of the *Washington Post*. After Graham's death, Katherine Graham inherited control of the company. Over the years, Eugene Meyer had gifted thousands of shares of private *Post* stock to several hundred employees in gratitude for their loyalty and service. He also had funded the company's profit-sharing plan with private stock. As the company prospered, the value of the *Washington Post* stock skyrocketed from $50 per share in the 1950s to $1,154 by 1971. The profit-sharing plan and the personal holdings of employees required the company to maintain a market for the stock. This arrangement proved to be an unproductive use of the company's cash. In addition, the Graham and Meyer families were facing stiff inheritance taxes.

In 1971, Katherine Graham decided to take the *Washington Post* public, thus erasing the burden of maintaining a market in its own stock, and enabling the family heirs to more profitably plan for their estates. The Washington Post Company was divided in two classes of stock. Class A common stock elected a majority of the board of directors. Katherine Graham held 50 percent of the class A stock, thus effectively controlling the company. Class B stock elected a minority of the board of directors. In June of 1971, The

Washington Post Company issued 1,354,000 shares of class B stock. Remarkably, two days later, despite governmental threats, Katherine Graham gave Ben Bradlee permission to publish the Pentagon Papers.

In 1972, the share price of the *Post* climbed steadily, from $24.75 in January to $38 in December. Although business at the paper was improving, the mood on Wall Street was turning gloomy. In early 1973, the Dow Jones Industrial Average began to slide. By spring, it was down more than one hundred points to 921. The *Washington Post* share price was slipping as well; by May, it was down 14 points to $23. Wall Street brokers were buzzing about IBM—the stock had declined more than 69 points, breaking through its 200-day moving average—warning that the breakdown signaled a bad omen for the rest of the market. That same month, gold broke through $100 an ounce, the Federal Reserve boosted the discount rate to 6 percent and the Dow fell 18 points, its biggest loss in three years. By June, the discount rate was raised again, and the Dow Jones Industrial Average was headed down through the 900 level. And all the while, Buffett was quietly buying shares in the *Washington Post.* By June, he had purchased 467,150 shares of the company at an average price of $22.75, a purchase worth $10,628,000 (see Figure 5.1).

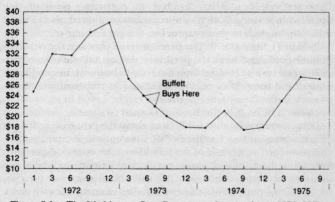

Figure 5.1. The Washington Post Company price per share, 1972–1975.

Today, Donald E. Graham, son of Phil and Katherine Graham, is publisher of the paper and president, chief executive officer, and chairman of the board of The Washington Post Company. Don Graham graduated magna cum laude from Harvard in 1966, having majored in English history and literature. While at Harvard, he was editor of the *Crimson*, the university's newspaper. After graduation, Graham served two years in the army. Knowing that he would eventually lead the *Washington Post*, Graham first decided to get better acquainted with the city. He took the unusual path of joining Washington's metropolitan police force. After spending four months at the police academy, he was a patrolman for the next fourteen months, walking the beat in the ninth precinct. In 1971, Graham joined the *Post* as a metro reporter. Later, he worked ten months as a reporter for *Newsweek* at the Los Angeles bureau. Graham returned to the *Post* in 1974 and became the assistant managing sports editor. That year, he was added to the company's board of directors.

When Buffett purchased *Post* stock in 1973, Katherine Graham was initially unnerved. The idea of a nonfamily member owning so much *Post* stock, even though the stock was noncontrolling, was unsettling to her. Buffett assured Katherine Graham that Berkshire's purchase was for investment purposes only. To reassure her, he suggested that Don Graham be given a proxy to vote Berkshire's shares. That clinched it. Katherine Graham responded by inviting Buffett to join the board of directors in 1974, and soon made him chairman of the finance committee.

Buffett's role at the *Washington Post* is widely documented. He helped Katherine Graham persevere during the strikes of the 1970s, and he also tutored Don Graham in business, helping him understand the role of management and its responsibility to its owners. Buffett's influence at the *Post* can be found in various actions taken by both Katherine and Donald Graham.

Don Graham is unmistakably clear about the prime objective of The Washington Post Company. "We will continue to manage the company for the benefit of shareholders," he writes, "especially long-term shareholders whose perspective extends well beyond quarterly or even yearly results. We will not measure our success by the size of our revenues or the number of companies we control."[4] Graham vows always to "manage costs rigorously" and "to be disciplined about the uses we make of our cash."

Tenet: Simple and Understandable

Buffett's grandfather once owned and edited the *Cuming County Democrat*, a weekly newspaper in West Point, Nebraska. His grandmother helped out at the paper and also set the type at the family's printing shop. His father, while attending the University of Nebraska, edited the *Daily Nebraskan*. Buffett himself was once the circulation manager for the *Lincoln Journal*. It has often been said that if Buffett had not embarked on a business career, he most surely would have pursued journalism.

In 1969, Buffett bought his first major newspaper, the *Omaha Sun*, along with a group of weekly papers. Although he respected high-quality journalism, Buffett thought of newspapers first and always as businesses. He expected profits, not influence, to be the rewards for a paper's owners. Owning the *Omaha Sun* taught Buffett the business dynamics of a newspaper. He had four years of hands-on experience running a newspaper before he bought his first share of the *Washington Post*.

Tenet: Consistent Operating History

Buffett tells Berkshire's shareholders that his first financial connection with The Washington Post Company was at age thirteen. He delivered both the *Washington Post* and the *Times-Herald* on his paper route while his father served in Congress. Buffett likes to remind others that with this dual delivery route, he merged the two papers long before Phil Graham bought the *Times-Herald*.

Obviously Buffett was aware of the newspaper's rich history. And he considered *Newsweek* magazine a predictable business. He quickly learned the value of the company's television stations. The Washington Post Company had been reporting for years the stellar performance of its broadcast division. Buffett's personal experience with the company and its own successful history led him to believe that the company was a consistent and dependable business performer.

Tenet: Favorable Long-Term Prospects

"The economics of a dominant newspaper," Buffett wrote in 1984, "are excellent, among the very best in the world."[5] Of the roughly

1,700 newspapers in the United States, approximately 1,600 operate without any direct competition. The owners of newspapers, he noted, like to believe that the exceptional profits they earn each year are a result of their paper's journalistic quality. The truth, said Buffett, is that even a third-rate newspaper can generate adequate profits if it is the only paper in town. Now it's true that a high-quality paper will achieve a greater penetration rate, but even a mediocre paper, he explains, is essential to a community for its bulletin-board appeal. Every business in town, every home seller, every individual who wants to get a message out to the community, needs the circulation of a newspaper to do so. Like Lord Thomson, Buffett believed that owning a newspaper was like receiving a royalty on every business in town that wanted to advertise.

In addition to their franchise quality, newspapers possess valuable economic goodwill. As Buffett points out, newspapers have low capital needs, so they can easily translate sales into profits. Even when a newspaper installs expensive computer-assisted printing presses and newsroom electronic systems, they are quickly paid for by lower fixed-wage costs. Newspapers also are able to increase prices relatively easily, thereby generating above-average returns on invested capital and reducing the harmful effects of inflation. Buffett figures that a typical newspaper could double its price, as did *USA Today*, and still retain 90 percent of its readership.

Tenet: Determine the Value

In 1973, the total market value for The Washington Post Company was $80 million. Yet, Buffett claims that "most security analysts, media brokers, and media executives would have estimated WPC's intrinsic value at $400 to $500 million."[6] How did Buffett arrive at that estimate? Let us walk through the numbers, using Buffett's reasoning.

We'll start by calculating owner earnings (see Chapter 4) for that year: net income ($13.3 million) plus depreciation and amortization ($3.7 million) minus capital expenditures ($6.6 million) yields 1973 owner earnings of $10.4 million. If we divide these earnings by the long-term U.S. government bond yield (6.81 percent), the value of The Washington Post Company reaches $150 million, almost twice the market value of the company but well short of Buffett's estimate.

Buffett tells us that, over time, the capital expenditures of a newspaper will equal depreciation and amortization charges, and therefore net income should approximate owner earnings. Knowing this, we can simply divide net income by the risk-free rate and now reach a valuation of $196 million.

If we stop here, the assumption is that the increase in owner-earnings will equal the rise in inflation. But we know that newspapers have unusual pricing power; because most are monopolies in their community, they can raise their prices at rates higher than inflation. If we make one last assumption—that the *Washington Post* has the ability to raise real prices by 3 percent—the value of the company is closer to $350 million. Buffett also knew that the company's 10 percent pretax margins were below its 15 percent historical average margins, and he knew that Katherine Graham was determined that the *Post* would once again achieve these margins. If pretax margins improved to 15 percent, the present value of the company would increase by $135 million, bringing the total intrinsic value to $485 million.

Tenet: Buy at Attractive Prices

Even the most conservative calculation of the company's value indicates that Buffett bought The Washington Post Company for at least half of its intrinsic value. He maintains that he bought the company at less than one-quarter of its value. Either way, he clearly bought the company at a significant discount to its present value. Buffett satisfied Ben Graham's premise that buying at a discount creates a margin of safety.

Tenet: Return on Equity

When Buffett purchased stock in the *Washington Post*, its return on equity was 15.7 percent. This was an average return for most newspapers and only slightly better than the average return on equity for the Standard & Poor's Industrial Index. But within five years, the *Post's* return on equity doubled. By then it was twice as high as the S&P Industrials and 50 percent higher than the average newspaper. Over the next ten years, the *Post* maintained its supremacy reaching a high of 36.3 percent return on equity in 1988.

These above-average returns are more impressive when you observe that the company has, over time, purposely reduced its debt. In 1973, long-term debt to shareholder's equity stood at 37.2 percent, the second highest ratio in the newspaper group. Astonishingly, by 1978, Katherine Graham had reduced the company's debt by 70 percent. In 1983, long-term debt to equity was a low 2.7 percent—one-tenth the newspaper group average—yet the *Post* generated a return on equity 10 percent higher than these same companies. In 1986, after investing in cellular telephone systems and purchasing Capital Cities' fifty-three cable systems, debt in the company was at an uncharacteristic high of $336 million. Within a year, it was reduced to $155 million. By 1992, long-term debt was $51 million and the company's long-term debt to equity was 5.5 percent, compared to the industry average of 42.7 percent.

Tenet: Profit Margins

Six months after WPC went public, Katherine Graham met with Wall Street security analysts. The first order of business, she told them, was to maximize profits from the company's existing operations. Profits continued to rise at the television stations and *Newsweek*, but profitability at the newspaper was leveling off. Much of the reason, said Mrs. Graham, was high production costs, namely wages. After the *Post* purchased the *Times-Herald*, profits at the company had surged. Each time the unions struck the paper (1949, 1958, 1966, 1968, 1969) management had opted to pay their demands rather than risk a shutdown of the paper. During this time, Washington, D.C., was still a three-newspaper town. Throughout the 1950s and 1960s, increasing wage costs dampened profits. This problem, Mrs. Graham told the analysts, was going to be solved.

As union contracts began to expire in the 1970s, Mrs. Graham enlisted labor negotiators who took a hard line with the unions. In 1974, the company defeated a strike by the Newspaper Guild and after lengthy negotiations, the printers settled on a new contract.

Mrs. Graham's firm stance on labor contracts came to a head during the pressmen's strike in 1975. The strike was violent and bitter. Because the pressmen had vandalized the pressroom before striking, sympathy for their cause was lost. Management worked the presses. Members of the guild and the printers union crossed the picket lines. After four months, Mrs. Graham announced that the company was hiring nonunion pressmen. The company had won.

In the early 1970s, the financial press wrote, "The best that could be said about The Washington Post Company's performance was it rated a gentleman's C in profitability."[7] Pretax margins in 1973 were 10.8 percent—well below the company's historical 15 percent margins earned in the 1960s. After successfully renegotiating the union contracts, the *Post's* fortunes improved. By 1978, profit margins had leaped to 19.3 percent—an 80 percent improvement within five years. Buffett's bet had paid off. By 1988, the *Post's* pretax margin reached a high of 31.8 percent, which compared favorably to its newspaper group average of 16.9 percent and the Standard & Poor's Industrial average of 8.6 percent. Although the company's margins have declined somewhat in the early 1990s, they remain substantially higher than the industry average.

Tenet: Rationality

The Washington Post Company generates substantial cash flow for its owners. Because it generates more cash than can be reinvested in its primary businesses, management is confronted with two rational choices: return the money to shareholders and/or profitably invest the cash in new investment opportunities. It is Buffett's preference to have companies return excess earnings to shareholders. The Washington Post Company, while Katherine Graham was president, was the first newspaper company in its industry to repurchase shares in large quantities. Between 1975 and 1991, the company bought an unbelievable 43 percent of its shares at an average price of $60 per share (see Figure 5.2)

A company can also choose to return money to shareholders by increasing the dividend. In 1990, confronted with a substantial cash reserves, The Washington Post Company voted to increase

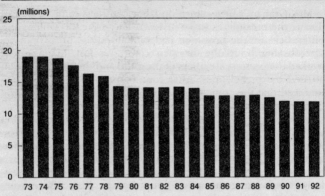

Figure 5.2. The Washington Post Company common shares outstanding.

the annual dividend to its shareholders from $1.84 to $4.00, a 117 percent increase (see Figure 5.3).

In addition to returning excess cash to its owners, The Washington Post Company has made several profitable business purchases. In 1986, the company purchased cable properties from Capital Cities, thus enabling Cap Cities to purchase the ABC Tele-

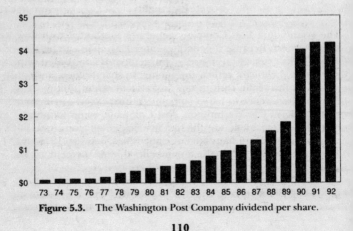

Figure 5.3. The Washington Post Company dividend per share.

vision Network. The *Post* also was an early investor in the cellular telephone industry. In 1993 the company purchased two television stations in Texas.

Don Graham's goal is to develop substantial cash flows at favorable investment costs. Knowing that countless businesses are available for purchase, Graham has developed specific guidelines that assist him in saying "no" to a business opportunity, which he admits is more important than saying "yes." He looks for a business that "has competitive barriers, does not require extensive capital expenditures, and has reasonable pricing power." Furthermore, he notes, "We have a strong preference for businesses we know" and given the choice, "we're more likely to invest in a handful of big bets rather than spread our investment dollars around thinly."[8] Graham's acquisition approach mimics Buffett's strategy at Berkshire Hathaway.

In the early 1990s, the dynamics of the newspaper business changed. In 1990, the recession that gripped the nation was particularly brutal in the Mid-Atlantic region. Sales and earnings at the *Washington Post* declined measurably that year. Buffett admittedly was surprised by the detrimental effects this early recession had on both the *Buffalo News* and the *Washington Post*. The question he asked himself was whether this downturn was part of a predictable economic cycle or represented a more threatening secular change in the newspaper business.

Newspapers, Buffett concluded, would remain above-average businesses when compared to American industry in general, but they were destined to become less valuable than he or any other media analyst had predicted years earlier, because newspapers had lost their pricing flexibility. In previous years, when the economy slowed and advertisers cut spending, newspapers could maintain profitability by raising lineage rates. Today, newspapers are no longer monopolies. Advertisers have found cheaper ways to reach their customers: cable television, direct mail, and newspaper inserts. Advertising dollars are more widely dispersed and the dominance of newspapers as advertising vendors has diminished.

By 1991, Buffett was convinced that the change in profitability of newspapers represented a long-term secular change as well as a temporary cyclical change. "The fact is," he confessed, "newspaper, television, and magazine properties have begun to resemble businesses more than franchises in their economic behavior."[9] Cyclical changes hurt short-term earnings but do not reduce a company's intrinsic value. Secular changes reduce earnings and also reduce intrinsic value. However, the change in intrinsic value of The Washington Post Company , Buffett said, was moderate compared to other media companies. The reasons were twofold. First, the *Post's* $50 million long-term debt was more than offset by its $400 million in cash holdings. The *Washington Post* is the only public newspaper that is essentially free of debt. "As a result," Buffett said, "the shrinkage in the value of their assets has not been accentuated by the effects of leverage."[10] Second, he noted, The Washington Post Company has been exceptionally well-managed.

Tenet: The One-Dollar Premise

Buffett's goal is to select companies in which each dollar of retained earnings is translated into at least one dollar of market value. This test can quickly identify companies whose managers, over time, have been able to optimally invest their company's capital. If retained earnings are invested in the company and produce above-average return, the proof will be a proportionally greater rise in the company's market value.

From 1973 to 1992, The Washington Post Company earned $1.755 billion for its owners. From these earnings, the company paid shareholders $299 million and retained $1.456 billion to reinvest in the company. In 1973, the total market value of WPC was $80 million. Since that time, the market value has grown to $2.71 billion (see Table 5.1). The change in market value from 1973 to 1992 was $2.630 billion. Over those twenty years, for every $1.00 WPC has retained, it has created $1.81 in market value for its shareholders.

Summary

Buffett has told us that even third-rate newspapers can earn substantial profits. Since the market does not require high standards of a paper, it is up to management to impose its own. And it is management's high standards and abilities that can differentiate their business returns when compared to its peer group. In 1973, if Buffett had invested in Gannett, Knight-Ridder, New York

Table 5.1   The Washington Post Company—Change in Market Value
(figures in $ millions)

	Net Income	Dividend Payment	Retained Earnings	Market Value
1973	13.3	1.9	11.4	80.8
1974	14.4	2.4	12.0	81.3
1975	12.0	2.4	9.6	100.3
1976	24.5	2.2	22.3	219.8
1977	35.5	3.0	32.5	291.9
1978	49.7	4.8	44.9	369.9
1979	43.0	5.6	37.4	299.3
1980	34.3	6.2	28.1	316.3
1981	32.7	7.0	25.7	441.3
1982	52.4	7.9	44.5	780.8
1983	68.4	9.4	59.0	1038.0
1984	85.9	11.2	74.7	1122.6
1985	114.3	12.9	101.4	1522.6
1986	100.2	14.4	85.8	2000.9
1987	186.7	16.4	170.3	2402.0
1988	269.1	20.1	249.0	2710.9
1989	197.9	23.5	174.4	3515.1
1990	174.6	48.5	126.1	2348.5
1991	118.7	49.9	68.8	2301.3
1992	127.8	49.7	78.1	2710.6

Notes: Total retained earnings 1973–1993 equal $1,456. Change in market value 1973–1992 equals $2,629.80. *For every one dollar in retained earnings,* **$1.81** *was created in market value.*

Times, or Times Mirror the same $10 million he did in The Washington Post Company, his investment returns would have been above average (see Figure 5.4), reflecting the exceptional economics of the newspaper business during this period. But the extra $200 million to $300 million in market value that WPC gained over its peer group, Buffett notes, "came, in very large part, from the superior nature of the managerial decisions made by Kay (Katherine Graham) as compared to those made by managers of most other media companies."[11] Katherine Graham had the brains to purchase large quantities of WPC stock at bargain prices. She also had the courage, he says, to confront the labor unions, reduce expenses, and increase the business value of the paper.

Figure 5.4. Common stock price of The Washington Post Company compared to the S&P 500 and publishing (newspapers) indexes.

Over the years, investors have shown commonsense by purchasing shares in The Washington Post Company pushing its stock price closer to its intrinsic value. Berkshire, Buffett says, received a "triple-dip" from its investment in WPC. First, the media business has soared over the last twenty years. Second, the discount to the underlying intrinsic value of the company has narrowed. Third, the per-share business value of the company increased faster because of stock repurchases. In all, the rise in the stock price outpaced the rise in the company's intrinsic value.

In 1985, when WPC's market value was $1.5 billion, Buffett was aware that the increase in the company's per-share value could not match its earlier growth rates. Today, at close to $3 billion in market value, this is especially true. Now that media companies are losing their franchiselike qualities, management decisions should distinguish companies going forward. Washington Post shareholders are fortunate that Katherine Graham positioned the company so favorably. It has practically no debt and a history of vigorously controlling costs. Furthermore, the company is shareholder-conscious. These attributes will distinguish WPC as it participates in a more combative business environment.

When Capital Cities purchased ABC, Buffett was forced to resign from the board of The Washington Post Company. Still, eight years later, his influence is firmly imbedded in the company's management-owner philosophy.

GEICO CORPORATION

GEICO Corporation is an insurance organization whose affiliates are personal line property and casualty insurers. The largest subsidiary, Government Employees Insurance Company (GEICO), writes preferred-risk private passenger automobile insurance for government employees and military personnel. The company also writes homeowners and other lines of insurance for qualified applicants. Another subsidiary, GEICO General Insurance Company, writes private passenger automobile insurance for other applicants. Today, GEICO is the country's eighth largest private passenger carrier.

GEICO was founded in 1936 by Leo Goodwin, an insurance accountant.[12] Goodwin's idea was to form a company that only insured preferred-risk drivers and to sell this insurance directly by mail. Goodwin had discovered that government employees, as a group, had fewer accidents than the general public. He also knew that by selling insurance policies directly to the driver, the company could eliminate the overhead expenses associated with insurance agents, which typically cost 10–25 percent of every premium dollar. Goodwin figured that if he isolated careful drivers and passed along the savings of issuing insurance policies directly, he would have a recipe for success.

Goodwin invited a Fort Worth, Texas, banker named Cleaves Rhea to be his partner. Goodwin invested $25,000 and owned 25 percent of the stock. Rhea owned 75 percent of GEICO by investing $75,000. In 1948, the company was moved from Texas to Washington, D.C. That year, the Rhea family decided to sell its interest in the company. Rhea employed Lorimer Davidson, a Baltimore bond salesperson, to assist him in disposing of his stock. Davidson enlisted David Kreeger, a Washington, D.C., lawyer, to help him find buyers. It was Kreeger who approached the Graham–Newman Corporation. Ben Graham decided to buy half of Rhea's stock for $720,000; the other half of Rhea's holdings was purchased by Kreeger and Davidson's Baltimore associates. The

Securities and Exchange Commission forced Graham–Newman, because it was an investment fund, to limit its holdings of GEICO to 10 percent of the insurance company. Hence, Graham had to distribute GEICO's stock to the fund's partners. Years later, when GEICO became a billion-dollar company, Graham's personal shares were worth millions.

Lorimer Davidson, at Goodwin's invitation, joined GEICO's management team. In 1958, he became chairman and led the company until 1970. During this period, the board extended the eligibility for GEICO's car insurance to include professional, managerial, technical, and administrative workers. GEICO's insurance market now included 50 percent of all car owners, up from 15 percent. The new strategy was a success. Underwriting profits soared because the new insured group turned out to be composed of careful drivers, just like government employees.

These were the company's golden years. Between 1960 and 1970, insurance regulators were mesmerized by GEICO's success, and shareholders saw their share price soar. The company's premium-to-surplus ratio rose above 5:1. This ratio measures the risk that a company takes (premiums written) compared to its policyholder's surplus (capital that is used to pay claims). Traditionally, this ratio does not exceed 3:1. Because insurance regulators were so impressed with GEICO, the company was allowed to exceed the industry average ratio.

By the late 1960s, GEICO's fortunes were beginning to dim. In 1969, the company reported that it had underestimated its reserves for that year by $10 million. Instead of earning $2.5 million, the company actually posted a loss. The adjustment to income was made the next year, but again the company understated reserves—this time by $25 million—so 1970s underwriting profit instead showed a disastrous loss.

The revenues an insurance company receives from policyholders are called earned premiums. From these premiums, the company promises to provide coverage to the automobile driver during the year. Costs to an insurance company include insured losses, which are claims brought by the driver, and loss expenses, the administrative cost of settling the claim. These total costs must reflect not only payments made during the year, but estimates of claims yet to be paid. Estimates, in turn, are divided into two categories, "claim costs and expenses," which the company expects to pay during the year, and "adjustment reserves," set aside to cover underestimated reserves from earlier years. Because of litigation, some insurance claims are not settled for several years and often involve substantial payments for legal and medical expenses. The problem confronting GEICO was not only had it written insurance policies that were poised to create an underwriting loss, but its estimates for earlier reserves were inadequate as well.

In 1970, Davidson retired and was replaced by David Kreeger, the Washington lawyer. Running the company fell to Norman Gidden, who served as president and chief executive officer. What happened next suggests that GEICO was attempting to grow out of its reserve mess created in 1969 and 1970. Between 1970 and 1974, the number of new auto policies grew at a 11 percent annual rate compared to the 1965–1970 period, which averaged 7 percent. In addition, in 1972, the company embarked on an expensive and ambitious decentralization program that required it to make significant investments in real estate, computer equipment, and personnel.

By 1973, the company, facing fierce competition, lowered its eligibility standards and expanded its market share. Now GEICO's automobile drivers, for the first time, included blue-collar workers and drivers under age twenty-one, two groups with checkered driving histories. Both of these strategic changes, the corporate expansion plan and the plan to insure a greater number of motorists, occurred simultaneously with the lifting of the country's 1973 price controls. Soon, auto repair and medical care costs exploded.

Underwriting losses at GEICO began to appear in the fourth quarter of 1974. For the year, the company reported a $6 million underwriting loss, its first underwriting loss in twenty-eight years. Amazingly, the premium to surplus ratio that year was 5:1. Nonetheless, the company continued to pursue growth, and by the second quarter of 1975, GEICO reported more losses and announced it was eliminating the company's $.80 dividend. Gidden employed the consulting firm of Milliman & Robertson to make recommendations on how GEICO could reverse its slide. The results of the study were not encouraging. The company, they said, was under-reserved by $35 million to $70 million and would need a capital infusion to stay viable. The board accepted Milliman & Robertson's study and made the announcement to its shareholders. In addition, the board projected that 1975's underwriting loss

117

would approach a staggering $140 million (the actual result was $126 million). Shareholders and insurance regulators were dumbfounded.

In 1972, GEICO's share price reached an all-time high of $61 (see Figure 5.5). By 1973, the share price was cut in half, and in 1974 it fell further to $10. In 1975, when the board announced the project losses, the stock dropped to $7. Several stockholders, charging fraud, filed class-action suits against the company. Executives at GEICO blamed inflation and outrageous legal and medical costs for the company's woes. But these problems confronted all insurers. GEICO's problem was that it had moved away from its successful tradition of insuring only careful drivers. Furthermore, it was no longer checking corporate expenses. As the company expanded the list of insured drivers, its earlier loss assumptions were woefully inadequate to cover the new and more frequent claims. At a time when the company was underestimating its insured losses, it simultaneously was increasing fixed expenses.

At the March 1976 GEICO annual meeting, Gidden confessed that another president might have handled the company's problems better. He announced that the company's board of directors had appointed a committee to seek new management. Still,

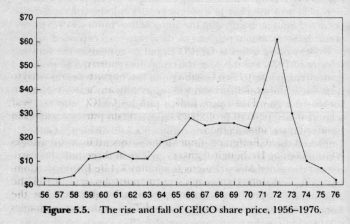

Figure 5.5. The rise and fall of GEICO share price, 1956–1976.

GEICO's share price was weakening. It was now $5 and heading lower.[13]

After the 1976 annual meeting, GEICO announced that John J. Byrne, a forty-three-year-old marketing executive of Traveler's Corporation, would become GEICO's new president. Soon after Byrne's appointment, the company announced a $76 million preferred stock offering to shore up its capital. Shareholders had lost hope and the stock price drifted down to $2 per share. During this period, Buffett quietly and doggedly purchased stock in GEICO. As the company teetered on the edge of bankruptcy, he invested $4.1 million in the company, gathering 1,294,308 shares at an average price per share of $3.18.

Tenet: Simple and Understandable

When Buffett attended Columbia University in 1950, he noticed that his teacher, Ben Graham, was a director of GEICO. His curiosity stimulated, Buffett went to Washington, D.C., one weekend to visit the company. On a Saturday, he knocked on the company's door and was let in by a janitor, who led him to the only executive in the office that day, Lorimer Davidson. Buffett had many questions and Davidson spent the next five hours schooling Buffett on GEICO's distinctions. Philip Fisher would have been impressed.

Later, when Buffett returned to Omaha and his father's brokerage firm, he recommended the purchase of GEICO to the firm's clients. He himself invested $10,000, approximately two-thirds of his net worth, in GEICO stock. Many investors resisted Buffett's recommendation. Even Omaha's insurance agents complained to Howard Buffett that his son was promoting an "agentless" insurance company. Frustrated, Buffett sold his GEICO shares a year later, at a 50 percent profit, and did not again purchase shares in the company until 1976.

Undaunted, Buffett continued to recommend insurance stocks to his clients. He bought Kansas City Life at three times its earnings. He owned Massachusetts Indemnity & Life Insurance Company in Berkshire Hathaway's security portfolio, and in 1967 he purchased controlling interest in National Indemnity. For the next ten years, Jack Ringwalt educated Buffett on the mechanics of running an insurance company. This experience, more than any other, helped Buffett understand how an insurance company makes money. It also, despite GEICO's shaky financial situation, gave Buffett confidence to purchase the company.

In addition to Berkshire's $4.1 million dollar common stock investment, Buffett also invested $19.4 million in GEICO's convertible preferred stock issue, which raised additional capital for the company. Two years later, Berkshire converted these preferred shares into common, and in 1980, he invested another $19 million of Berkshire's money in the company. Between 1976 and 1980, Berkshire invested a total of $47 million, purchasing 7.2 million shares of GEICO at an average price of $6.67 per share. Berkshire now owned 33 percent of the company. By 1980, Berkshire's investment had appreciated 123 percent. It was then worth $105 million and became Buffett's largest holding.

Tenet: Consistent Operating History

On first reaction, we might assume that Buffett violated his consistency tenet. Clearly, GEICO's operations in 1975 and 1976 were anything but consistent. When Byrne became president of GEICO, his job was to turn around the company, and "turnarounds," Buffett has said, seldom turn. So how do we explain Berkshire's purchase of GEICO?

For one thing, it appears to be a turnaround exception. Byrne successfully turned the company and positioned it to compete again for insurance. But more importantly, Buffett said, GEICO was not terminal, only wounded. Its franchise of providing low cost agentless insurance was still intact. Furthermore, in the marketplace, there still existed safe drivers who could be insured at rates that would provide a profit for the company. On a price basis, GEICO would always beat its competitors. For decades, GEICO generated substantial profits for its owners by capitalizing on its competitive strengths. These strengths, said Buffett, still in place. GEICO's troubles in the 1970s had nothing to do with a diminution of its franchise. Rather the company, because of operating and financial troubles, became sidetracked. Even with no net worth, GEICO was still worth a lot of money because its franchises were intact.

Tenet: Favorable Long-Term Prospects

Although automobile insurance is a commodity product, Buffett says a commodity business can make money if it has a cost advantage that is both sustainable and wide. This description aptly fits GEICO. We also know that management in a commodity business is a crucial variable. GEICO's leadership, since Berkshire's purchase, has demonstrated that it, too, has a competitive advantage.

Tenet: Candor

When John (Jack) Byrne took over GEICO in 1976, he convinced both insurance regulators and competitors that if GEICO went bankrupt, it would be bad for the entire industry. His plan for rescuing the company included raising capital, obtaining a reinsurance treaty with other companies to reinsure a portion of GEICO's business, and cutting costs aggressively. "Operation Bootstrap," as Byrne called it, was the battle plan aimed at returning the company to profitability.

In his first year, Byrne closed 100 offices, reduced employment from 7,000 to 4,000, and turned in its license to sell insurance in both New Jersey and Massachusetts. Byrne told New Jersey regulators that he would not renew 250,000 policies in the state, which were costing the company $30 million a year. Next, he did away with the computerized systems that allowed policyholders to renew their insurance without providing updated information. When Byrne required this new information, he found the company was underpricing 9 percent of its renewal policies. When GEICO repriced these policies, 400,000 policyholders decided to discontinue their insurance. Altogether, Byrne's actions reduced the number of policyholders from 2.7 million to 1.5 million, and the company went from being the nation's eighteenth largest insurer in 1975 to thirty-first a year later. Despite this reduction, GEICO, after losing $126 million in 1976, earned an impressive $58.6 million on $463 million in revenues in 1977, Byrne's first full year of responsibility.

Clearly, GEICO's dramatic recovery was Byrne's doing, and his steadfast discipline on corporate expenses sustained GEICO's recovery for years. Byrne told shareholders that the company must return to its first principle of being the low-cost provider of insurance. His reports detailed how the company continually reduced costs. Even in 1981, when GEICO was the country's seventh largest writer of automobile insurance, Byrne shared his secretary with two other executives. He boasted how the company serviced 378 policies per GEICO employee, up from 250 policies per employee years earlier. During the turnaround years, he was always a great motivator. "Byrne," said Buffett, "is like the chicken farmer who rolls an ostrich egg into the hen house and says, 'Ladies, this is what the competition is doing.'"[14]

Over the years, Byrne happily reported the successful progress of GEICO; he was equally candid with his shareholders when the news turned bad. In 1985, the company temporarily stumbled when it had underwriting losses. Writing in the company's first quarter report to shareholders, Byrne "likened the company's plight to that of the pilot who told his passengers, 'the bad news is that we are lost, but the good news is that we are making great time.'"[15] The company quickly regained its footing and the following year posted profitable underwriting results. But, just as important, the company gained the reputation of being candid with its shareholders.

Although Jack Byrne resigned from GEICO in 1986 to head Fireman's Fund, the company's reputation for candid reporting still exists today. In 1991, the company earned the *Washington Post's* "The Tell It Like It Is Award." "Once again," wrote the *Post*, "Chairman Bill Snyder and Vice Chairman Lou Simpson have given shareholders an unvarnished view of the company's highs and lows."[16]

Tenet: The Institutional Imperative

Insurance companies can profit in two ways: (1) by earning an underwriting profit on the insurance policies they issue, and (2) by investing smartly the premium dollars that policyholders pay. As a general rule, profits from underwriting are small compared to the profits generated by investments—so much so that when the financial markets offer high returns, insurance companies will even sell policies at a loss to gather more premium dollars to invest. The chief investment officer is responsible for a significant portion of the company's earnings.

Louis Simpson, GEICO's co-chief executive officer, is responsible for the company's capital operations, including its investment pool. Simpson graduated with a master's degree in economics from Princeton. After a brief stint as a teacher at his alma mater, he accepted a position with the investment firm of Stein Roe & Farnham. In 1969, he joined Western Asset Management, where he became president and chief executive officer before joining GEICO in 1979. When Buffett, along with Jack Byrne, interviewed Simpson, he remembers his independent attitude. "He has the ideal temperament for investing," Buffett says. "He derives no particular pleasure from operating with or against the crowd. He is comfortable following his own reason."[17] Buffett instinctively knew that Simpson had the characteristics necessary to resist the institutional imperative and avoid mindless imitation.

The willingness to act and think independently is found in the investment guidelines that Simpson developed for GEICO.[18] The first guideline is "Think independently." Simpson is skeptical of Wall Street's conventional wisdom. Instead, he searches for his own. Like Buffett, he is a voracious reader of daily newspapers, magazines, journals, and annual reports. He believes that after receiving the basic financial training, the most important job of a investment manager is to keep reading and reading until an idea materializes. Simpson is constantly on the prowl for good ideas but resists the overt suggestions of most brokerage analysts. "Lou is a quiet guy. In this modern world, everybody would rather talk on the phone than do the basic work. Lou does the basic work," said one former GEICO director.[19]

GEICO's second guideline is "Invest in high-return businesses run for shareholders." Simpson seeks companies with sustainable above-average profitability. Then he interviews the company management to ascertain whether their priorities are maximizing shareholder value or expanding corporate empires. Simpson looks for managers who have a significant investment stake in their own company and are straightforward in their dealings with the company's owners, treating them like partners. Lastly, he quizzes management on their willingness to divest unprofitable businesses and use excess cash to repurchase shares for the owners.

GEICO's third guideline is "Pay only a reasonable price, even for an excellent business." Simpson is a very patient investor. He is willing to wait until the price of business becomes attractive. The greatest business in the world, Simpson confesses, is a bad investment if the price is too high. The fourth guideline is "Invest for the long-term." Simpson pays no attention to the stock market and never tries to predict short-term market movements. "In many ways," he writes, "the stock market is like the weather in that if you don't like the current conditions all you have to do is wait awhile."[20]

GEICO's last guideline is "Do not diversify excessively." Simpson figures that a widely diversified portfolio will only provide mediocre results. He admits that his talks with Buffett helped crystallize his thinking on this subject. Simpson's tendency is to concentrate his equity holdings. In 1991, GEICO's $800 million equity portfolio contained eight stocks.

From 1979, when Simpson assumed control, to 1989, the equity portfolio generated an average annual compounded rate of return of 26.1 percent—compared to 17.4 percent for the Standard & Poor's 500 Index. Since 1990, GEICO's equity portfolio has appreciated at a 16.5 percent annualized rate, while the S&P 500 increased at 10.8 percent. Over the years, Simpson has steered GEICO's investment portfolio away from junk bonds and risky real estate holdings. While other insurance investment officers surrendered to the institutional imperative and risked the net worth of their company, Simpson, investing conservatively, produced above-average returns for GEICO's shareholders. "Louis Simpson," trumpets Buffett, "is the best investment manager in the property-casualty business."[21]

Tenet: Rationality

Over the years, Jack Byrne, his successor Bill Snyder, and Lou Simpson have demonstrated rational behavior managing GEICO's corporate assets. After Byrne took charge of GEICO's underwriting debacle, he positioned the company for controlled growth. It was more profitable, Byrne figured, to grow at a slower rate that allowed the company to carefully monitor its losses and expenses than to grow twice as fast if it meant losing financial control. Since then, GEICO has continually earned underwriting profits for its owners.

In fact, Simpson's investment achievements have provided more capital surplus than has been needed to cover estimated losses. In a nutshell, the company's capital has been accumulating at a faster

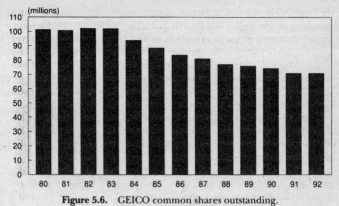

Figure 5.6. GEICO common shares outstanding.

rate than could be used in its business. A good indication of management's ability to make rational decisions, as well as its loyalty to shareholders, is the willingness to use cash to increase the dividend or buy back shares rather than needlessly expand the corporate empire.

In 1983, the company was unable to invest its cash profitably and decided to return the money to its shareholders by offering to repurchase shares. "Either our standards are too high or the price we're willing to pay (for acquisitions) is too low," said Louis Simpson.[22] Since 1983, GEICO has repurchased, on a postsplit basis, 30 million shares, reducing the company's total common shares outstanding by 30 percent (see Figure 5.6).[23]

In addition to buying back stock, GEICO has also generously increased the dividend it pays to its shareholders. In 1980, the company's split-adjusted dividend was $.09 per share (see Figure 5.7). By 1992, the dividend paid was $.60 per share. Since 1980, GEICO has increased its dividend to shareholders at a 21 percent annual rate.

Tenet: Return on Equity

Since 1982, GEICO's return on equity has averaged 21.2 percent, twice as good as that of the industry average. In the early 1990s,

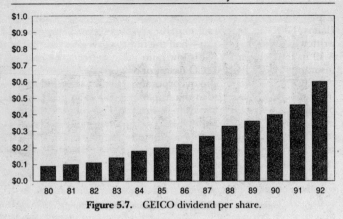

Figure 5.7. GEICO dividend per share.

return on equity declined because its equity grew faster than its earnings. Hence, part of the financial logic of paying out increasing dividends and buying back stock is to reduce capital and maintain an acceptable return on equity.

Despite the recent decline, GEICO's return on equity has been consistently superior to other insurance companies in the property-casualty index. In 1980, it was 30.8 percent—almost twice as high as the peer group average. Although return on equity declined in 1984 and 1988, GEICO continued to outperform the industry average. In 1992, GEICO's return on equity dropped to 14.0 percent, much of that attributable to the natural disasters that struck the country in that year, including Hurricane Andrew.

Tenet: Profit Margins

Investors can compare profitability of insurance companies in several ways. Pretax margins are one of the best measures. Over a ten-year period, GEICO's average pretax margins have been the most consistent (with the lowest standard deviation) of any peer group company.

GEICO pays meticulous attention to all its expenses, and it

closely tracks the expenses associated with settling insurance claims. GEICO's corporate expenses as a percent of premiums written averages 15 percent—half the industry average (see Table A.19 in the Appendix). This low ratio partly reflects the cost of insurance agents that GEICO does not have to pay.

GEICO's combined ratio of corporate expenses and underwriting losses (see Table A.20 in the Appendix) has been demonstrably superior to the industry average. From 1977 through 1992, the industry average has beaten GEICO's combined ratio only once, in 1977. Since then, GEICO's combined ratio has averaged 97.1 percent, more than ten percentage points better than the industry average. GEICO has shown an underwriting loss only twice— once in 1985 and again in 1992. The underwriting loss in 1992 was accentuated by the unusual number of natural disasters that struck the country that year. Without Hurricane Andrew and other major storms, GEICO's combined ratio would have been low, 93.8 percent.

Tenet: Determine the Value

When Buffett started buying GEICO, the company was close to bankruptcy. But he says GEICO was worth a substantial sum, even with a negative net worth, because of the company's insurance franchise. Still, in 1976, the company, since it had no earnings, defied a mathematical determination of value as put forth by John Burr Williams. Williams postulated that the value of a business is determined by the net cash flows expected to occur over the life of a business discounted at an appropriate rate. Despite the uncertainty over GEICO's future cash flows, Buffett was sure that the company would survive and earn money in the future. How much and when was open to speculation.

In 1980, Berkshire Hathaway owned one-third of GEICO, invested at a cost of $47 million. That year, GEICO's total market value was $296 million. Even then, Buffett estimated that the company possessed a significant margin of safety. In 1980, the company earned $60 million on $705 million in revenues. Berkshire's share of GEICO's earnings was $20 million. According to Buffett, "to buy a similar $20 million of earnings in a business with first-class economic characteristics and bright prospects would cost a minimum of $200 million"—more if the purchase was for a controlling interest in a company.[24]

Even so, Buffett's $200 million assumption is realistic, given the theory by Williams. Assuming that GEICO could sustain this $60 million in earnings without the aid of any additional capital, the present value of GEICO, discounted at the then-current 12 percent rate for a thirty-year U.S. government bond, would have been $500 million—almost twice GEICO's 1980 market value. If the company could grow this earnings power at 2 percent real, or at 15 percent before current inflation, the present value of GEICO would increase to $600 million, and Berkshire's share would equal $200 million. In other words, in 1980, the market value of GEICO's stock was less than half the discounted present value of its earnings power.

Tenet: The One-Dollar Premise

Since 1980, the market value of GEICO has grown from $296 million to $4.6 billion in 1992 (see Table 5.2)—an increase of $4.3 billion. During these thirteen years, GEICO earned $1.7 billion. It paid shareholders, in common stock dividends, $280 million and retained $1.4 billion for reinvestment. Thus, for every dollar retained, GEICO created $3.12 in market value for its shareholders. This financial accomplishment demonstrates not only GEICO's superior management and niche marketing, but its ability to reinvest shareholder's money at optimal rates.

Further proof of GEICO's superiority: A $1 investment in GEICO in 1980, excluding dividends, increased to $27.89 by 1992. This is an astonishing 29.2 percent compounded annual rate of return, far greater than the 8.9 percent industry average and the Standard & Poor's 500 Index during the same period (see Figure 5.8).

Summary

Recently, Bill Snyder, who replaced Jack Byrne as chairman and chief executive officer of GEICO in 1986, announced that he was retiring a year early. Both he and Byrne, together, have decided

Table 5.2 GEICO Corporation—Change in Market Value
(figures in $ millions)

	Net Income	Dividend Payment	Retained Earnings	Market Value
1980	59.6	9.7	49.9	296.3
1981	64.4	10.3	54.1	559.0
1982	77.5	11.3	66.2	879.7
1983	94.8	15.0	79.8	1185.3
1984	100.4	17.1	83.3	1088.4
1985	77.6	18.2	59.4	1539.6
1986	119.3	18.5	100.8	1646.5
1987	150.2	22.4	127.8	1790.0
1988	134.4	25.7	108.7	1914.6
1989	213.1	27.5	185.6	2314.3
1990	208.4	30.1	178.3	2407.7
1991	196.4	32.6	163.8	2827.6
1992	172.7	42.4	130.3	4627.0

Notes: Total retained earnings 1980–1992 equal $1,388. Change in market value 1980–1992 equals $4,331. *For every one dollar in retained earnings, **$3.12** was created in market value.*

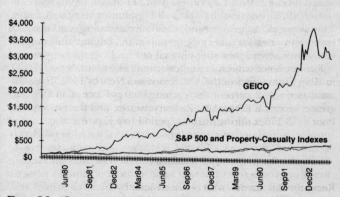

Figure 5.8. Common stock price of GEICO compared to the S&P 500 and Property-Casualty indexes.

to form a new insurance company. They are purchasing from GEICO two insurance businesses: Merastar Insurance Company of Chattanooga, Tennessee, and Southern Heritage Insurance Company in Atlanta, Georgia. Combined premium revenue for these companies amounts to $38 million. GEICO announced that Tony Nicely and Louis Simpson will become co-chief executives of the company. Nicely will manage the insurance operations and Simpson will remain head of capital operations.

GEICO's franchise of profitably selling low-cost, agentless insurance is firmly in place. The company's dedication to controlling expenses is embedded in the corporate culture. Simpson's outstanding track record implies that GEICO's investment portfolio is well positioned, and the company has earned the reputation of treating shareholders well. These combined strengths led *Forbes* to announce, in its "Annual Report on American Industry," that GEICO is *the* insurance company of the 1990s.[25]

Buffett's vote is in as well. Over the years, Berkshire's position in GEICO has steadily increased. Today, Berkshire owns 48 percent of the company.

CAPITAL CITIES/ABC

Capital Cities/ABC (Cap Cities) is an $11 billion media and communications business that owns and operates a television and radio network, television and radio broadcasting stations, and produces video for cable programming. In addition, the company publishes newspapers, shopping guides, and various business and specialized magazines, periodicals, and books.

Cap Cities operates the ABC Television Network, which has 228 affiliated television stations reaching 99.9 percent of all U.S. television homes, and the ABC Radio Networks, which serve approximately 3,175 radio affiliates. Cap Cities pays for the cost of producing or purchasing the broadcast rights for its network programs and also pays affiliated television and radio stations to broadcast the programs, including commercial announcements. Revenues come from the sale to advertisers of time in network programs for commercial announcements.

Cap Cities owns eight television stations, nine AM radio stations, and eight FM radio stations. All of the company's television stations are affiliated with the ABC Television Network, and fourteen of the company's seventeen radio stations are affiliated with the ABC Radio Network.

The company's video enterprise is actively involved in the production and supply of cable programming. Cap Cities owns 80 percent of ESPN, the premier cable sports network and the largest cable network in the country. ESPN reaches 61 million homes in the United States and 34 million homes in 75 countries worldwide. Cap Cities owns 37.5 percent of The Arts and Entertainment Network, which provides cable programming of cultural and entertainment events, and one-third of Lifetime, a cable service devoted to women's lifestyle and health programs. The company also owns equity positions in television and theatrical production companies in Germany, France, and Spain.

Cap Cities publishes eight daily newspapers, seventy-five weekly newspapers, and fifty-six shopping guides and real estate magazines in twelve states. Specialized publications include the Agriculture Publishing Group, Chilton Publications, Fairchild Publications Group, and the Financial Services and Medical Group, which publish several magazines, including *Institutional Investor* and *Internal Medicine News*.

The company reports sales and income divided by broadcasting and publishing. In 1992, broadcasting income—including network programming, television and radio broadcasting, and video programming—was $619 million on $4.2 billion in revenue. The publishing group earned $136 million on $1.1 billion in revenue. Cap Cities' 1992 total operating income was $755 million on $5.3 billion in revenue.

Cap Cities had its beginnings in the news business. In 1954, Lowell Thomas, the famous journalist, his business manager Frank Smith, and a group of associates bought Hudson Valley Broadcasting Company, which included an Albany, New York, television and AM radio station. At that time, Thomas Murphy, now chairman of Cap Cities, was a product manager at Lever Brothers. Frank Smith, who was a golfing partner of Murphy's father, hired his friend's son to manage the company's television station. In 1957, Hudson Valley purchased a Raleigh-Durham television station and the company's name was changed to Capital Cities Broadcasting, reflecting that both Albany and Raleigh were capitals of their respective states.

In 1960, Murphy hired Dan Burke to manage the Albany station. Burke, who recently retired as chief executive officer of Cap Cities, is the brother of Murphy's Harvard classmate, Jim Burke, who later became chairman of Johnson & Johnson. Dan Burke, an Albany native, was left in charge of the television station, while Murphy returned to New York, where he was named president of Capital Cities in 1964. Thus began one of the most successful corporate partnerships in American business. During the next three decades, Murphy and Burke ran Capital Cities. Together they made more than thirty broadcasting and publishing acquisitions, the most notable being the purchase of the ABC Network in 1985.

Buffett first met Tom Murphy in the late 1960s at a New York luncheon arranged by one of Murphy's classmates. Supposedly, Murphy was so impressed with Buffett that he invited him to join the board of Capital Cities.[26] Buffett declined, but he and Murphy became close friends, keeping in touch over the years. Buffett first invested in Capital Cities in 1977; unexplainably, but profitably, he sold the position the following year.

In December 1984, Murphy approached Leonard Goldenson, who was chairman of American Broadcasting Companies, with the idea of merging the two companies. Although initially rebuffed, Murphy contacted Goldenson again in January 1985. The FCC had increased the number of television and radio stations that a single company could own from seven to twelve, effective in April that year. This time Goldenson agreed. Goldenson, who was seventy-nine years old, was concerned about who would eventually manage American Broadcasting Companies. Although ABC had several potential candidates, none was, in Goldenson's opinion, ready for leadership. Murphy and Burke were considered the best managers in the media and communications industry. By agreeing to merge with Cap Cities, Goldenson was assuring that ABC would remain in strong management hands. American Broadcasting Companies entered the negotiating room with high-priced investment bankers. Murphy, who always negotiated his own deals, brought his trusted friend Warren Buffett. Together they worked out the first-ever sale of a television network and the largest media merger in history.

Capital Cities offered American Broadcasting Companies a total package worth $121 per ABC share ($118 in cash per share and one-tenth warrant to purchase Capital Cities worth $3 per share).

This offer was twice the value at which ABC's stock traded the day before the announcement. To finance the $3.5 billion deal, Capital Cities would borrow $2.1 billion from a banking consortium, sell overlapping television and radio stations worth approximately $900 million dollars, and also sell restricted properties that a network was not allowed to own, including cable properties subsequently sold to The Washington Post Company. The last $500 million came from Buffett. He agreed that Berkshire Hathaway would purchase three million newly issued shares of Cap Cities at a price of $172.50 per share. Murphy again asked his friend to join the board of Capital Cities and this time Buffett agreed.

Tenet: Simple and Understandable

After serving on the board of The Washington Post Company for more than ten years, Buffett understood the business of television broadcasting and magazine publishing. His long experience with newspaper publishing has been noted as well. Buffett's understanding of television networks grew with Berkshire's own purchase of ABC once in 1978 and again in 1984.

Tenet: Consistent Operating History

Both Capital Cities and American Broadcasting Companies had profitable operating histories dating back more than thirty years. American Broadcasting Companies averaged 17 percent return on equity and 21 percent debt to capital from 1975 through 1984. Capital Cities, during the ten years before its offer to purchase ABC, averaged 19 percent return on equity and 20 percent debt to capital.

Tenet: Favorable Long-Term Prospects

Broadcasting companies and networks are blessed with above-average economics. Like newspapers, and for much the same reasons, they generate a great deal of economic goodwill. Once a broadcasting tower is built, capital reinvestment and working capital needs are minor, and inventory investment is nonexistent. Movies and programs can be bought on credit and settled later when advertising dollars roll in. As a general rule, broadcasting companies produce above-average returns on invested capital and generate substantial cash in excess of their operating needs.

The risks to networks and broadcasters include government regulation, changing technology, and shifting advertising dollars. Governments can deny the renewal of a company's broadcasting license, but this is rare. Cable programs, in 1985, were a minor threat to the networks. Although some viewers tuned in cable shows, the overwhelming majority of television viewers still preferred network programming. Also during the 1980s, advertising dollars for free-spending consumers were growing substantially faster than the country's gross domestic product. To reach a mass audience, advertisers still counted on network broadcasting. The basic economics of networks, broadcasting companies, and publishers were, in Buffett's mind, above average and in 1985, the long-term prospects for these businesses were highly favorable.

Tenet: Determine the Value

Berkshire's $517 million investment in Cap Cities at that time was the single largest investment Buffett ever made. How Buffett determined the combined value of Capital Cities and American Broadcasting is open to speculation. Murphy agreed to sell Buffett three million shares of Capital Cities/ABC for $172.50 per share. But we know that price and value are often two different figures. Buffett's practice, we have learned, is to acquire a company only when there is a significant margin of safety between the company's intrinsic value and its purchase price. However, with the purchase of Capital Cities/ABC, he admittedly compromised this principle.

If we discount Buffett's offer of $172.50 per share by 10 percent (the approximate yield of the thirty-year U.S. government bond in 1985) and multiply this value by 16 million shares (Cap Cities had 13 million shares outstanding plus 3 million issued to Buffett), the present value of this business would need to have earnings power of $276 million. Capital Cities' 1984 earnings net after depreciation and capital expenditures was $122 million.

American Broadcasting Companies' net income after depreciation and capital expenditures was $320 million. The combined earnings power of these two companies was $442 million. But the combined company would have substantial debt: the approximately $2.1 billion that Murphy was to borrow would cost the company $220 million a year in interest. So the net earnings power of the combined company was approximately $200 million.

There were additional considerations. Murphy's reputation for improving the cash flow of purchased businesses simply by reducing expenses was legendary. Capital Cities' operating margins were 28 percent, whereas ABC's were 11 percent. If Murphy could improve the operating margins of the ABC properties by one-third, to 15 percent, the company would throw off an additional $125 million each year, and the combined earnings power would equal $325 million annually. The per-share present value of a company earning $325 million with 16 million shares outstanding discounted at 10 percent was $203 per share—a 15 percent margin of safety over Buffett's $172.50 purchase price. "I doubt if Ben's (Ben Graham) up there applauding me on this one," Buffett quipped.[27]

The margin of safety that Buffett accepted could be expanded if we make certain assumptions. Buffett says that conventional wisdom during this period argued that newspapers, magazines, or television stations would be able to forever increase earnings at 6 percent annually—without the need for any additional capital.[28] The reasoning, explains Buffett, was that capital expenditures would equal depreciation rates and the need for working capital would be minimal. Hence, income could be thought of as freely distributed earnings. This means that an owner of a media company possessed an investment, a perpetual annuity, that would grow at 6 percent for the foreseeable future without the need of any additional capital. Compare that, Buffett suggests, to a company that is only able to grow if capital is reinvested. If you owned a media company that earned $1 million and expected to grow at 6 percent, it would be appropriate, says Buffett, to pay $25 million dollars for this business ($1 million divided by a risk-free rate of 10 percent less the 6 percent growth rate). Another business that earned $1 million but could not grow earnings without reinvested capital might be worth $10 million ($1 million dividend by 10 percent).

If we take this finance lesson and apply it to Cap Cities, the value of Cap Cities increases from $203 per share to $507, or a 66 percent margin of safety over the $172.50 price that Buffett agreed to pay. But there are a lot of "ifs" in these assumptions. Would Murphy be able to sell a portion of Capital Cities/ABC combined properties for $900 million (he actually got $1.2 billion)? Would he be able to improve operating margins at American Broadcasting Companies? Would he be able to continually count on the growth of advertising dollars?

Buffett's ability to obtain a significant margin of safety in Capital Cities was complicated by several factors. First, the stock price of Cap Cities had been rising over the years (see Figure 5.9). Murphy and Burke were doing an excellent job of managing the company, and the company's share price reflected this. So, unlike GEICO, Buffett did not have the opportunity to purchase Cap Cities cheaply because of a temporary business decline. The stock market didn't help, either. And, because this was a secondary stock offering, Buffett had to take a price for Cap Cities' shares that was close to its then-trading value.

If there was any disappointment over the issue price, Buffett was comforted by the quick appreciation of those same shares. On Friday, March 15, 1985, Capital Cities' share price was $176. On Monday afternoon, March 18, the announcement was made that Capital Cities would purchase American Broadcasting Companies. The next day, by the market close, Capital Cities' share price

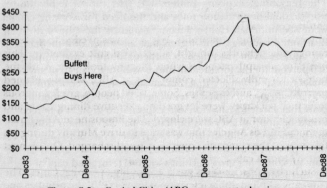

Figure 5.9. Capital Cities/ABC common stock price.

was $202.75. In four days the price had risen 26 points, a 15 percent appreciation. Buffett's profit was $90 million and the deal was not due to close until January 1986.

The margin of safety that Buffett received buying Capital Cities was significantly less compared with other companies he had purchased. So why did he proceed? The answer was Tom Murphy. Had it not been for Murphy, Buffett admittedly would not have invested in the company. Murphy was Buffett's margin of safety. Capital Cities/ABC is an exceptional business, the kind of business that attracts Buffett. But there was also something special about Murphy. "Warren adores Tom Murphy," said John Byrne. "Just to be partners with him is attractive to (Buffett)."[29]

Cap Cities' management philosophy is decentralization. Murphy and Burke hire the best people possible and then leave them alone to do their job. All decisions are made at the local level. Burke found this out early in his relationship with Murphy. Burke, while managing the Albany TV station, mailed updated reports weekly to Murphy, who never responded. Burke finally got the message. Murphy promised Burke, "I won't come to Albany unless you invite me—or I have to fire you."[30] Murphy and Burke help set yearly budgets for their companies, and operating performance is reviewed quarterly. With these two exceptions, managers are expected to operate their businesses as if they owned them. "We expect a great deal from our managers," writes Murphy.[31]

And one thing Capital Cities' managers are expected to do is control costs. When they fail, Murphy is not shy about getting involved. When Capital Cities purchased ABC, Murphy's talent for cutting costs was badly needed. Networks had a tendency to think in terms of ratings, not profits. Whatever was needed to increase ratings, the networks thought, superseded cost evaluation. This mentality abruptly stopped when Murphy took over. With the help of carefully selected committees at ABC, Murphy pruned payrolls, perks, and expenses. Some 1,500 people, given generous severance packages, were let go. The executive dining room and private elevator at ABC were closed. The limousine at ABC Entertainment in Los Angeles that was used to drive Murphy during his first tour of the company's operation was discharged. On his next visit, he took a cab.

Such cost-consciousness was a way of life at Capital Cities. The company's Philadelphia television station, WPVI, the number one station in the city, had a news staff of 100 compared with 150 at the CBS affiliate across town. Before Murphy arrived at ABC, the company employed 60 people to manage ABC's five television stations. Today, 6 people manage eight stations. WABC TV in New York used to employ 600 people and generate 30 percent pretax margins. It now employs 400 people and margins are more than 50 percent. Once a cost crisis was resolved, Murphy depended on Burke to manage operating decisions. He concentrated on acquisitions and shareholder assets.

Tenet: The Institutional Imperative

The basic economics of the broadcasting and network business assured Cap Cities it would generate ample cash flow. However, the industry's basic economics, coupled with Murphy's penchant for controlling costs, meant that Cap Cities would have overwhelming cash flow. From 1988 through 1992, Cap Cities generated $2.3 billion in unencumbered cash. Given these resources, some managers might be unable to resist the temptation to spend the money, buying businesses and expanding the corporate domain. Murphy, too, bought a few businesses. In 1990, he spent $61 million acquiring small properties. At that time, the general market for most media properties was priced too high, he said.

Acquisitions have been very important to Cap Cities in the development of its growth. Murphy is always on the lookout for media properties, but he remains steadfast in his discipline not to overpay for a company. Cap Cities, with its enormous cash flow, could easily gobble up other media properties, but "Murphy would sometimes wait for years until he found the right property. He never made a deal just because he had the resources available to do it."[32] Murphy and Burke also realized that the media business was cyclical, and if it was built on too much leverage, the risk to shareholders would be unacceptable. "Murphy never did a deal that either of us thought was capable of mortally wounding us," Burke said.[33]

A company that generates more cash than can be profitably reinvested in its business can buy growth, reduce leverage, or return the money to shareholders. Since Murphy was unwilling to pay the high asking prices for media companies, he chose, instead, to

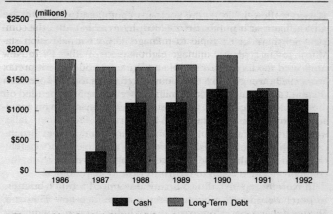

Figure 5.10. Capital Cities/ABC cash equivalents and long-term debt.

reduce leverage and buy back stock. In 1986, after the acquisition of ABC, total long-term debt at Cap Cities was $1.8 billion, and debt to capital was 48.6 percent. Cash and cash equivalents at 1986 year end amounted to $16 million. By 1992, long-term debt at the company was $964 million, and debt to capital dropped to 20 percent. Furthermore, cash and cash equivalents increased to $1.2 billion, making the company essentially debt-free (see Figure 5.10). Murphy's strengthening of Cap Cities' balance sheet substantially reduced the risk of the company. What he did next substantially increased the value.

Tenet: Rationality

In 1988, Cap Cities announced that it had authorized the repurchase of up to 2 million shares, 11 percent of the company's outstanding stock. In 1989, the company spent $233 million purchasing 523,000 shares of stock at an average price of $445. This price was 7.3 times the company's operating cash flow, compared to the asking prices of most other media companies that were selling at 10–12 times cash flow. The following year, the company purchased 926,000 shares at an average price of $477, or 7.6 times operating cash flow. In 1992, the company continued to buy back its stock. That year it purchased 270,000 shares at an average cost of $434 per share, or 8.2 times cash flow. The price it paid for itself, Murphy reiterated, was still less than the price of other advertiser-supported media companies he and Burke considered attractive. From 1988 through 1992, Cap Cities purchased a total of 1,953,000 shares of stock, investing $886 million (see Figure 5.11).

Since 1992 Cap Cities has been interested in making a large acquisition in the $5 billion to $8 billion range. Preliminary talks were held with Paramount Communications and Turner Broadcasting, but major acquisitions were not available at prices that would provide shareholders a reasonable return. Instead, the company decided again to return its cash to shareholders.

In November 1993, the company announced a Dutch auction to purchase up to 2 million shares at prices between $590 and $630 per share. Berkshire participated in the auction, submitting 1 million of its 3 million shares. This act alone caused widespread speculation. Was the company, unable to find an appropriate acquisition, putting itself up for sale? Was Buffett, by selling a third of his position, giving up on the company? Cap Cities denied the rumors. Opinions surfaced that Buffett would not have tendered stock that surely would have fetched a higher price if indeed the company were for sale. The company eventually purchased

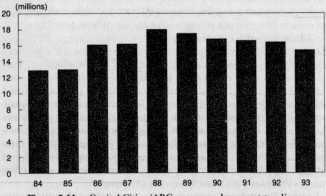

Figure 5.11. Capital Cities/ABC common shares outstanding.

1.1 million shares of stock—1 million of them from Berkshire—at an average price of $630 per share. Buffett has been able to redeploy $630 million dollars without disrupting the market place for Cap Cities shares. And he is still the largest shareholder of the company, owning 13 percent of the shares outstanding.

Buffett's admiration for Murphy is more easily appreciated when you realize how much money Cap Cities generated over the years and how responsibly it was allocated. Since 1977, Murphy has reduced shares outstanding by 17 percent, cut long-term debt in half, and raised cash equivalents to more than $1 billion. Also, Cap Cities is managed in the same decentralized fashion as Berkshire Hathaway. Buffett only involves himself in Berkshire's noninsurance businesses as they relate to compensation and capital reinvestment. Buffett is very willing, like Murphy, to allow his subsidiaries to operate independently. He is also willing, as is Murphy, to become intensely involved when costs get out of line. Both men share the same aversion to shareholder waste.

Buffett has observed the operations and management of countless businesses over the years. But according to him, Cap Cities is the best managed publicly owned company in the country. To prove his point, when Buffett invested in Cap Cities, he assigned all voting rights for the next eleven years to Murphy and Burke, as long as either one continued to manage the company. And if that is not enough to convince you of the high regard Buffett holds for these men, consider this: "Tom Murphy and Dan Burke are not only great managers," Buffett claims, "they are precisely the sort of fellows that you would want your daughter to marry."[34]

The value of Tom Murphy to Cap Cities and to Berkshire Hathaway has increased measurably as the outlook for the television network business has declined. Like The Washington Post Company, Cap Cities, in 1990, was confronted with an economic cyclical downturn that affected the company's profits, coupled with a secular downturn in the business that affected its intrinsic value. Increased competition has made it difficult to raise prices on advertising. This was one of the economic marvels of the network broadcasting business—the ability to aggressively raise prices. A franchise that loses its pricing power quickly becomes an ordinary business, and the value of management to the company's shareholders becomes more meaningful.

Today, the network business is facing increased competition

from cable and videos at a time when advertising dollars are stretched thin. Networks, Buffett explains, are in the business of selling information and entertainment for what he refers to as "eyeballs." Today, cable programs, pay-for-view shows, and videos all compete for the same eyeballs. Now, with approximately 500 eyeballs in the country and still only twenty-four hours in the day, the competition for television viewers is intense. When Cap Cities purchased ABC, the networks' share of the television audience was above 80 percent. Today, it is 60 percent. Buffett remembers a few years ago watching a sporting event with Murphy on a large-screen TV and commenting on how wonderful the picture was. "I liked it better," replied Murphy, "when it was on an eight-inch screen in black and white and there were only three channels."[35]

Tenets: The One-Dollar Premise; Return on Equity; Profit Margins

From 1985 through 1992, the market value of Capital Cities/ABC grew from $2.9 billion to $8.3 billion (see Table 5.3). During this same period, the company retained $2.7 billion in earnings, thereby creating $2.01 in market value for every $1 reinvested.

Table 5.3 Capital Cities/ABC—Change in Market Value
(figures in $ millions)

	Net Income	Dividend Payment	Retained Earnings	Market Value
1985	142.2	2.6	139.6	2918.0
1986	181.9	3.2	178.7	4323.0
1987	279.1	3.2	275.9	5586.0
1988	387.1	3.4	383.7	6520.0
1989	485.7	3.5	482.2	9891.0
1990	477.8	3.4	474.4	7694.0
1991	374.7	3.3	371.4	7213.0
1992	389.3	3.3	386.0	8349.4

Notes: Total retained earnings 1985–1992 equal $2,692. Change in market value 1985–1992 equals $5,431. *For every one dollar in retained earnings,* **$2.01** *was created in market value.*

This accomplishment is especially noteworthy considering that the company endured both a cyclical downturn in earnings, in 1990–1991, and a decline in its intrinsic value from secular changes in the network-broadcasting business. During this period, Berkshire's investment in Capital Cities/ABC grew from $517 million to $1.5 billion, a 14.5 percent compounded annual rate of return—better than both CBS and the Standard & Poor's 500 Index.

If the intrinsic value of Capital Cities/ABC has declined, why then has Buffett refused to sell his entire position? Undoubtedly, part of the reason is his personal relationship with Murphy. Murphy has rightly earned Buffett's respect as a manager who will not waste shareholder value. Another important reason why Buffett has not sold his Capital Cities position is that the company still provides economic returns that are better than the average American industry. "Television networks are a business that's tougher but still very good with very good management. It generates a lot of cash," Buffett says.[36]

During the 1970s and 1980s, the return on equity of Capital Cities was consistently five to seven percentage points higher than the Standard & Poor's 500 Index (see Figure 5.12). The company's pretax margins were triple the average American business (see Figure 5.13). After Capital Cities bought ABC, both pretax margins

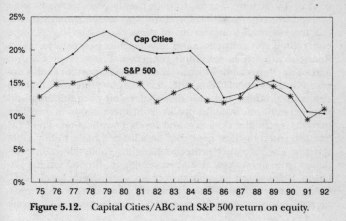

Figure 5.12. Capital Cities/ABC and S&P 500 return on equity.

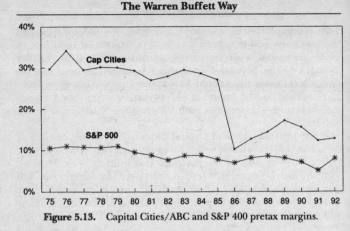

Figure 5.13. Capital Cities/ABC and S&P 400 pretax margins.

and return on equity declined from their higher levels but still remained better than the average company and were steadily improving until the 1990–1991 recession. Today, return on equity for Capital Cities has dropped to an average level but pretax margins remain demonstrably higher.

The FCC has recognized the changing economics of network broadcasting and admits that the three major networks no longer control TV viewing. For more than twenty years networks were banned from owning television shows and barred from the lucrative market syndicating reruns of these programs. In 1993, the court lifted this restriction and now permits networks to take a financial interest in television programs. Program production and ownership, claims Murphy, is the most important future opportunity for Capital Cities/ABC. It is Murphy's intention that the company produce and own more television programming and thus generate meaningful profits from these shows in ancillary markets, including domestic and foreign syndication. The FCC has also voted to allow networks, on a limited basis, to buy cable systems. The rule once protected fledgling cable television companies from networks and was responsible for forcing Capital Cities, in 1986, to sell its cable properties when it purchased ABC. Lastly, networks have been aggressively purchasing foreign commercial television broadcasters. Cap Cities, adding to its equity ownerships in German, French, and Spanish television and production companies, recently purchased a 21 percent stake in Luxembourg-based Scandinavian Broadcasting System, one of the region's first broadcasters. All of these changes have increased the intrinsic value of Capital Cities/ABC.

Summary

Berkshire Hathaway has more than $2 billion invested in media and communications companies, including Capital Cities/ABC, The Washington Post Company, and *Buffalo News*. Berkshire's look-through earnings and intrinsic value have both declined as a result of cyclical and secular changes in this industry. However, Cap Cities, Washington Post, and *Buffalo News* possess above-average economics. The reason, claims Buffett, is Stan Lipsey's leadership at the *Buffalo News* and the exceptional management at Washington Post and Cap Cities.

What sets these companies apart is that while other media companies, using leverage, were busy overpaying for properties, Cap Cities and The Washington Post did not allow the institutional imperative to sway their thinking. Instead, they reduced debt and bought back shares rather than pay irrational prices for other companies. Now that the secular changes have unfolded, Cap Cities and Washington Post are the only two publicly traded media companies that are essentially debt free. Other companies that paid outrageous prices for acquisitions now find themselves struggling to pay interest costs at a time when earnings are shrinking. Buffett is more comfortable owning Cap Cities and the Washington Post than he would be owning any other media company. Still, he expects both of these companies to generate returns higher than the average business. But, he admits, "gone are the days of bullet-proof franchises and cornucopian economics."[37]

THE COCA-COLA COMPANY

Coca-Cola is the world's largest manufacturer, marketer, and distributor of carbonated soft drink concentrates and syrups. The company's soft drink product, first sold in the United States in 1886, is now sold in more than 195 countries worldwide.

Buffett's relationship with Coca-Cola dates back to his childhood. He had his first Coca-Cola when he was five years old. Soon afterwards, he started buying six Cokes for twenty-five cents from his grandfather's grocery store and reselling them in his neighborhood for five cents each. For the next fifty years, Buffett admits, he observed the phenomenal growth of Coca-Cola but purchased textile mills, department stores, and windmill and farming equipment manufacturers. Even in 1986, when he formally announced that Cherry Coke would become the official soft drink of Berkshire Hathaway's annual meetings, Buffett still had not purchased a share of Coca-Cola. It was not until two years later, in the summer of 1988, that Buffett began to purchase his first shares of Coca-Cola.

Tenet: Simple and Understandable

The business of Coca-Cola is relatively simple. The company purchases commodity inputs and combines them to manufacture a concentrate that is sold to bottlers, who combine the concentrate with other ingredients. The bottlers then sell the finished product to retail outlets, including minimarts, supermarkets, and vending machines. The company also provides soft drink syrups to fountain retailers, who sell soft drinks to consumers in cups and glasses. The company's name brand products include Coca-Cola, Diet Coke, Sprite, Mr. PiBB, Mello Yello, Ramblin' Root Beer, Fanta soft drinks, Tab, and Fresca. The company's beverages also include Hi-C brand fruit drinks, Minute Maid orange juice, Powerade, Nestea, and Nordic Mist. The company owns 44 percent of Coca-Cola Enterprises, the largest bottler in the United States, and 53 percent of Coca-Cola Amatil, an Australian bottler that has interests not only in Australia but in New Zealand and Eastern Europe.

The strength of Coca-Cola is not only its name brand products but includes its unmatched worldwide distribution system. Today, international sales of Coca-Cola products account for 67 percent of the company's total sales and 81 percent of its profits. In addition to Coca-Cola Amatil, the company has equity interests in bottlers located in Mexico, South America, Southeast Asia, Taiwan, Hong Kong, and China. In 1992, the company sold more than 10 billion cases of beverage products.

Tenet: Favorable Long-Term Prospects

Shortly after Berkshire's 1989 public announcement that it owned 6.3 percent of The Coca-Cola Company, Buffett was interviewed by Mellisa Turner, a business writer for the Atlanta *Constitution.* She asked Buffett a question he has been asked often: Why hadn't he purchased shares in the company sooner? By way of an answer, Buffett related what he was thinking at the time he finally made the decision.

"Let's say you were going away for ten years," he said, "and you wanted to make one investment and you know everything that you know now, and you couldn't change it while you're gone. What would you think about?"[38] Of course the business would have to be simple and understandable. Of course the company would have to have demonstrated a great deal of business consistency over the years. And of course the long-term prospects would have to be favorable. "If I came up with anything in terms of certainty, where I knew the market was going to continue to grow, where I knew the leader was going to continue to be the leader—I mean worldwide—and where I knew there would be big unit growth, I just don't know anything like Coke," Buffett explained. "I'd be relatively sure that when I came back they would be doing a hell of a lot more business than they do now."[39]

But why purchase at that particular time? Coca-Cola's business attributes, as described by Buffett, have existed for several decades. What caught his eye, he said, were the changes occurring at Coca-Cola during the 1980s under the leadership of Roberto Goizueta and Donald Keough.

The 1970s were a dismal period for Coca-Cola. The decade was marred by disputes with bottlers, accusations of mistreatment of migrant workers at the company's Minute Maid groves, environmentalists' claim that Coke's "one way" containers contributed to the country's growing pollution problem, and the Federal Trade Commission charge that the company's exclusive franchise system violated the Sherman Anti-Trust Act. Coca-Cola's international business was reeling as well. The Arab boycott of Coke, caused by the company's issuing an Israeli franchise, dismantled years of investment. Japan, where the company's earnings were growing the fastest, was a battlefield of corporate mistakes. Coke's twenty-six ounce take-home bottles were exploding—literally—

on store shelves. In addition, Japanese consumers angrily objected to the company's use of artificial coal-tar coloring in Fanta Grape. When the company developed a new version using real grape skins, the bottles fermented and the grape soda was tossed in Tokyo Bay.

During the 1970s, Coca-Cola was a fragmented and reactive company rather than an innovator setting the pace within the beverage industry. Paul Austin was appointed chairman of the company in 1971, after serving as president since 1962. Despite its problems, the company continued to generate millions of dollars in earnings. But instead of reinvesting in its own beverage market, Austin diversified the company, investing in water projects and shrimp farms, despite their slim profit margins. Austin also purchased a winery. Shareholders bitterly opposed this investment, arguing that Coca-Cola should not be associated with alcohol. To deflect criticism, Austin directed unprecedented amounts of money to advertising campaigns.

Meanwhile, Coca-Cola earned 20 percent on equity. However, pretax margins were slipping (see Figure 5.14). The market value of the company at the end of the bear market of 1974 was $3.1 billion (see Figure 5.15). Six years later, the value of the company was $4.1 billion. From 1974–1980, the company's market value rose an average annual rate of 5.6 percent, vastly underperforming the Standard & Poor's 500 Index. For every dollar the company retained in those six years, it only created $1.02 of market value.

Coca-Cola's corporate woes were exacerbated by Austin's behavior.[40] He was intimidating and unapproachable. Furthermore, his wife, Jeane, was a disruptive influence within the company. She redecorated corporate headquarters with modern art, shunning the company's classic Norman Rockwell paintings. She even ordered a corporate jet to help her facilitate the search for works of art. But it was her last order that contributed to her husband's downfall.

In May 1980, Mrs. Austin ordered the company's park closed to employee luncheons. Their food droppings, she complained, attracted pigeons on the well-manicured lawns. Employee morale hit an all-time low. Robert Woodruff, the company's ninety-one-year-old patriarch, who led Coca-Cola from 1923 until 1955 and was still chairman of the board's finance committee, had heard enough. He demanded Austin's resignation and replaced him with Roberto Goizueta.

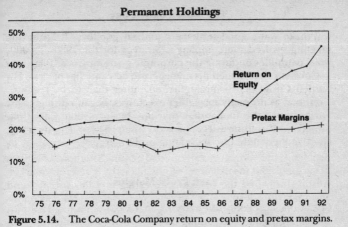

Figure 5.14. The Coca-Cola Company return on equity and pretax margins.

Goizueta, raised in Cuba, was Coca-Cola's first foreign chief executive officer. Goizueta was as outgoing as Austin was reticent. One of Goizueta's first acts was to bring together Coca-Cola's top fifty managers for a meeting in Palm Springs, California. "Tell me what we're doing wrong," he said. "I want to know it all and once it's settled, I want 100 percent loyalty. If anyone is not happy, we

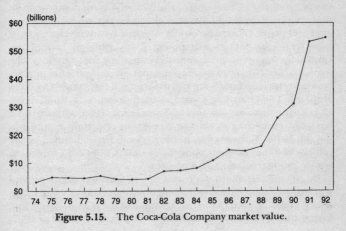

Figure 5.15. The Coca-Cola Company market value.

will make you a good settlement and say goodbye."[41] From this meeting evolved the company's "Strategy for the 1980s," a 900-word pamphlet outlining the corporate goals for Coca-Cola.

Goizueta encouraged his managers to take intelligent risks. He wanted Coca-Cola to initiate action rather than to be reactive. Goizueta, as do many new chief executives, began cutting costs. Furthermore, he demanded that any business that Coca-Cola owned must optimize its return on assets. These actions translated, immediately, into increasing profit margins.

Tenet: Profit Margins

Coca-Cola's pretax profit margins, in 1980, were a low 12.9 percent. Margins had been falling for five straight years and were substantially below the company's 1973 margins of 18 percent. In Goizueta's first year, pretax margins rose to 13.7 percent; by 1988, when Buffett bought his Coca-Cola shares, margins had climbed to a record 19 percent.

Tenet: Return on Equity

In the company's "Strategy for the 1980s," Goizueta pointed out that the company would divest any business that no longer generated acceptable returns on equity. Any new business venture must have sufficient real growth potential to justify an investment. Coca-Cola was no longer interested in battling for share in a stagnant market. "Increasing earnings per share and effecting increased return on equity are still the name of the game," Goizueta argued.[42] The chairman's words were followed by actions. Coca-Cola's wine business was sold to Seagrams in 1983. Although the company earned a respectable 20 percent return on equity during the 1970s, Goizueta was not impressed. He demanded better returns and the company obliged. By 1988, Coca-Cola's return on equity had increased to 31.8 percent.

By any measurement, Goizueta's Coca-Cola was doubling and tripling the financial accomplishments of Austin's Coca-Cola. The results could be seen in the market value of the company. In 1980, Coca-Cola had a market value of $4.1 billion. By the end of 1987, even after the stock market crash in October, the market value of Coca-Cola had risen to $14.1 billion (see Figure 5.15). In seven years, Coca-Cola's market value rose an average annual rate of 19.3 percent. For every dollar Coca-Cola retained during this period, it gained $4.66 in market value.

Tenet: Candor

Goizueta's strategy for the 1980s pointedly included shareholders. "We shall, during the next decade, remain totally committed to our shareholders and to the protection and enhancement of their investment," he wrote.[43] "In order to give our shareholders an above average total return on their investment, we must choose businesses that generate returns in excess of inflation." Goizueta not only had to grow the business, which required capital investment, he was also obliged to increase shareholder value. To do so, Coca-Cola, by increasing profit margins and return on equity, was able to pay increasing dividends while simultaneously reducing the dividend payout ratio. In the 1980s, dividends to shareholders were increasing 10 percent per year while the payout ratio was declining from 65 percent to 40 percent. This enabled Coca-Cola to reinvest a greater percentage of the company's earnings to help sustain its growth rate while not shortchanging shareholders.

Each year in its annual report Coca-Cola begins the financial review and management's discussion by stating its primary objective: "Management's primary objective is to maximize shareholder value over time." The company's business strategy emphasizes maximizing long-term cash flows. In order to do so, the company focuses on investing in the high-return soft drink business, increasing returns on existing businesses, and optimizing the cost of capital. If successful, the evidence will be growth in cash flow, increased return on equity, and an increased total return to shareholders.

Tenet: Rationality

The growth in net cash flow has allowed Coca-Cola to increase its dividend to shareholders and also repurchase its shares in the open market. In 1984, the company authorized its first ever buy back, announcing it would repurchase 6 million shares of stock. The company has continued to repurchase its shares every year since then, for a total repurchase of 414 million shares at a total cost of $5.3 billion. This represents more than 25 percent of the company's outstanding shares at the beginning of 1984. The value of the shares repurchased, based on the closing price on December 31, 1993, was $18.5 billion.

In July 1992, Coca-Cola announced that through the year 2000, it would buy back 100 million shares of its stock, representing 7.6 percent of the company's outstanding shares. Remarkably, the company will be able to accomplish this while it continues its aggressive investment in overseas markets. The buy back, claims Goizueta, can be accomplished because of the company's strong cash generating abilities. Between 1993 and 1996, the company, after capital expenditures, will have more than $3 billion to begin its share repurchase program.

Tenet: "Owner Earnings"

In 1973, "owner earnings" (net income plus depreciation minus capital expenditures) were $152 million (see Figure 5.16). By 1980, owner earnings were $262 million, an 8 percent annual compounded growth rate. From 1981 through 1988, owner earnings grew from $262 million to $828 million, a 17.8 percent average annual compounded growth rate. The growth in owner earnings is reflected in the share price of Coca-Cola. In analyzing ten-year periods, from 1973–1982, the total return of Coca-Cola grew at a 6.3 percent average annual rate. From 1983–1992 the total return of Coca-Cola grew at a 31.1 percent average annual rate.

Tenet: Determine the Value

When Buffett first purchased Coca-Cola in 1988, people asked, "Where is the value in Coke?" The company's price was fifteen times earnings and twelve times cash flow, a 30 percent and 50 percent premium to the market average. Buffett paid five times book value for a company with a 6.6 percent earning yield. He was

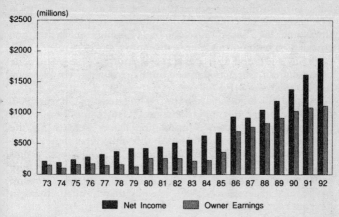

Figure 5.16. The Coca-Cola Company net income and "owner earnings."

willing to do that because of Coke's extraordinary level of economic goodwill. The company was earning a 31 percent return on
equity while employing relatively little in capital investment. Of
course, Buffett has explained that price tells nothing about value.
The value of Coca-Cola, like any other company, is determined by
the net cash flows expected to occur over the life of the business,
discounted at an appropriate interest rate.

In 1988, owner earnings (net cash flow) of Coca-Cola equalled
$828 million (see Table 5.4). The thirty-year U.S. Treasury bond
(the risk-free rate) at this time traded near a 9 percent yield. If
Coca-Cola's 1988 owner earnings were discounted by 9 percent
(remember, Buffett does not add an equity risk premium to the
discount rate), the value of Coca-Cola would have been $9.2 bil-
lion. When Buffett purchased Coca-Cola, the market value of the
company was $14.8 billion indicating that Buffett might have over-
paid for the company. But $9.2 billion represents the discounted
value of Coca-Cola's current owner earnings. Because the market
was willing to pay a price for Coca-Cola that was 60 percent higher
than $9.2 billion, it indicated that buyers perceived part of the
value of Coca-Cola to be its future growth opportunities.

Table 5.4 The Coca-Cola Company—"Owner Earnings" Analysis (figures in $ millions)

	Annual Sales	Annual Income	Depreciation	Capital Expenditures	Owner Earnings
73	2145	215	59.1	121.3	152.8
74	2522	196	59.5	150.1	105.4
75	2872	239	67.7	143.3	163.4
76	3032	285	71.7	182.2	174.5
77	3559	326	85.4	260.9	150.5
78	4337	374	95.0	306.0	163.0
79	4961	420	117.0	409.3	127.7
80	5912	422	138.0	298.0	262.0
81	5889	447	144.9	329.6	262.3
82	6249	512	150.7	400.3	262.4
83	6829	558	156.0	492.0	222.0
84	7364	629	170.0	565.0	234.0
85	7904	678	335.0	652.0	361.0
86	8669	934	430.0	665.0	699.0
87	7658	916	153.0	300.0	769.0
88	8338	1045	170.0	387.0	828.0
89	8966	1193	184.0	462.0	915.0
90	10236	1382	236.0	593.0	1025.0
91	11572	1618	254.0	792.0	1080.0
92	13074	1884	310.0	1083.0	1111.0
			Compounded Annual Growth Rates		
1973–1980	15.6%	10.1%	12.9%	13.7%	8.0%
1981–1988	5.1%	12.9%	2.3%	2.3%	17.8%
1988–1992	11.9%	15.9%	16.2%	29.3%	7.6%

When a company is able to grow owner earnings without the need for additional capital, it is appropriate to discount owner earnings by the difference between the risk-free rate of return and the expected growth of owner earnings. Analyzing Coca-Cola, we find that owner earnings from 1981 through 1988 grew at a 17.8 percent annual rate—faster than the risk-free rate of return. When this occurs, analysts use a two-stage discount model. This model is a way of calculating future earnings when a company has extraordinary growth for a limited number of years, and then a period of constant growth at a slower rate.

We can use this two-stage process to calculate the 1988 present value of the company's future cash flows. In 1988, Coca-Cola's owner earnings were $828 million. If we assume that Coca-Cola would be able to grow owner earnings at 15 percent per year for the next ten years (a reasonable assumption, since that rate is lower than the company's previous seven-year average), by year ten owner earnings will equal $3.349 billion. Let us further assume that starting in year eleven, growth rate will slow to 5 percent a year. Using a discount rate of 9 percent (the long-term bond rate at the time), we can calculate that the intrinsic value of Coca-Cola in 1988 was $48.377 billion (see Table A.21 in the Appendix).[44]

We can repeat this exercise using different growth-rate assumptions. If we assume that Coca-Cola can grow owner earnings at 12 percent for ten years followed by 5 percent growth, the present value of the company discounted at 9 percent would be $38.163 billion. At 10 percent growth for ten years and 5 percent thereafter, the value of Coca-Cola would be $32.497 billion. And if we assume only 5 percent throughout, the company would still be worth at least $20.7 billion [$828 million divided by (9% − 5 %)].

Tenet: Buy at Attractive Prices

In June 1988, the price of Coca-Cola was approximately $10 per share (split-adjusted). Over the next ten months, Buffett acquired 93.4 million shares, for a total investment of $1.023 billion (see Figure 5.17). His average cost per share was $10.96. At the end of 1989, Coca-Cola represented 35 percent of Berkshire's common stock portfolio. It was a bold move.

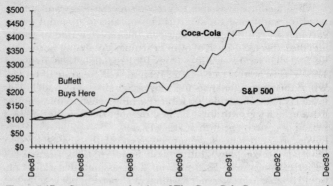

Figure 5.17. Common stock price of The Coca-Cola Company compared to the S&P 500 Index (indexed to $100 at start date).

From the time that Goizueta took control of Coca-Cola in 1980, the company's stock price has increased every year. In the five years before Buffett purchased his first shares of Coca-Cola, the average annual gain in share price was 18 percent. The company's fortunes were so good that Buffett was unable to purchase any shares at distressed prices. During this period, the Standard & Poor's 500 Index was gaining as well. Neither Coca-Cola nor the stock market presented Buffet an opportunity to buy shares at low prices. Still, Buffett charged ahead. Again, he says that price has nothing to do with value.

The stock market's value of Coca-Cola in 1988 and 1989, during Buffett's purchase period, averaged $15.1 billion. But by Buffett's estimation, the intrinsic value of Coca-Cola was anywhere from $20.7 billion (assuming 5 percent growth in owner earnings), $32.4 billion (assuming 10 percent growth), $38.1 billion (assuming 12 percent growth), to $48.3 billion (assuming 15 percent growth). So Buffett's margin of safety—the discount to intrinsic value—could be as low as a conservative 27 percent or as high as 70 percent. "Value" investors observed the same Coca-Cola that Buffett purchased and because its price to earnings, price to book, and price to cash flow were all so high, considered Coca-Cola overvalued.

Tenet: The One-Dollar Premise

Since 1988, the price performance of Coca-Cola has been extraordinary. From $10 per share, the stock reached $45 in 1992. During this same period, Coca-Cola has trounced the performance of the Standard & Poor's 500 Index (see Figure 5.17). Since 1987, the market value of Coca-Cola has risen from $14.1 billion to $54.1 billion. The company has produced $7.1 billion in earnings while paying out $2.8 billion in dividends to shareholders and retaining $4.2 billion for reinvestment. For every dollar the company has retained, it has created $9.51 in market value. Berkshire's $1.023 billion investment in Coca-Cola in 1988–1989 was worth $3.911 billion by 1992.

The dramatic price increase in Coca-Cola between 1988 and 1992 has reduced the margin of safety between Coca-Cola's market price and its intrinsic value. Some investors argue that Coca-Cola is overvalued and suggest that the company will find it difficult to repeat its outstanding economic and share price performance in the years ahead. Roberto Goizueta's goal for the company is to double Coca-Cola's output by the year 2000. Goizueta points out in *Coca-Cola, A Business System Toward 2000: Our Mission in the 1990s* that Coca-Cola is the only production and distribution business capable of bringing refreshments to every corner of the world. It is through increased per-capita consumption of Coca-Cola's beverages in Eastern Europe, the former Soviet Union, Indonesia, India, Africa, and China that the company will reach its goal of doubling sales. Although these countries may never match the per capita consumption of the United States (296 eight-ounce servings per person per year), any small improvement in consumption within these developing countries will translate into increased earnings. Half of the world's population consumes less than two eight-ounce servings per person per year. The opportunities in China, India, and Indonesia alone are capable of propelling Coca-Cola's fortunes into the next century.

Summary

The best business to own, Buffett says, is one that over time can employ large amounts of capital at very high rates of return. This description fits Coca-Cola. Coca-Cola is the most widely recognized and esteemed name brand in the world. It is easy to understand why Buffett considers Coca-Cola to be the most valuable franchise in the world.

PERMANENT RELATIONSHIPS

To reach the status of permanent holdings, a company must possess good economics and good management—people who are able and trustworthy and, equally important, people with whom Buffett enjoys associating. The Washington Post Company, GEICO, Capital Cities/ABC, and The Coca-Cola Company are companies with average and above-average economic potential. Over the years, the managers of these businesses have proven their trustworthiness. They have protected the interests of shareholders and summarily increased the value of their investments. Each manager has an aversion to corporate waste and a passion for higher profitability. They all understand the rational allocation of capital. Lastly, Buffett genuinely enjoys both his professional and personal relations with Katherine and Donald Graham, Lou Simpson and Bill Snyder, Tom Murphy and Dan Burke, and Roberto Goizueta and Donald Keough.

Buffett has found splendid business relations to be so rare and enjoyable that he intends never to sever his permanent common stock holdings. If a permanent holding were exchanged for another business, Buffett would have to develop a relation with a new management team. The prospect of ending a business relationship with any of these admired managers just to add a few percentage points to Berkshire Hathaway's return does not interest him.

SIX

Fixed-Income
Marketable
Securities

WARREN BUFFETT IS PERHAPS best known in the investment world for his decisions in common stocks (described in Chapter 7), but he also buys fixed-income securities
for Berkshire's insurance companies. In selecting fixed-income
investments, Buffett will consider short-term cash equivalents,
medium-term fixed-income securities, long-term fixed-income securities, and arbitrage positions. He admits he has no strong preference when it comes to investing in these different categories.
He simply seeks out, at any given time, those investments that provide the highest after-tax return.

It is important to understand that fixed-income securities represent a significantly smaller percent of Berkshire's insurance
investment portfolio compared to other insurance companies. In
1993, fixed-income securities—cash, bonds, and preferred stocks—
represented 17 percent of Berkshire's investment portfolio. With

most insurance companies, between 60 percent and 80 percent is more typical. Because of Berkshire's superior financial quality and disciplined insurance underwriting philosophy, Buffett has been able to invest a majority of Berkshire's assets in common stocks. Generally, he has little enthusiasm for bonds and considers them to be, at best, mediocre investments.

Buffett's aversion to bonds is twofold. First, because of his inflation bias, he expects that the future purchasing power of money will decline. Since bonds are denominated in money, Buffett will become more enthusiastic about bonds only when he becomes more confident about the long-term stability of our currency. Second, it is Buffett's opinion that bonds should be viewed from a businessperson's perspective, and most fixed-income contracts (interest rates) are set below investment returns a businessperson would demand. This "bond-as-a-business" approach to fixed-income investing is highly unusual.

If you invest $10 million in a business that earns 12 percent on equity and retains all of its earnings, Buffett explains, in thirty years that business would be worth $300 million, having earned $32 million in the last year. Now, Buffett says, if you purchase $10 million of bonds with an annual coupon of 12 percent, using the interest income to purchase more 12 percent bonds, at the end of thirty years you, too, would have $300 million in capital also earning $32 million in the final year. Knowing the long-term average return on equity of an American business is 12 percent, Buffett would say that the bond investment was a "businesslike" purchase.

Looking back at 1946, Buffett notes that a twenty-year AAA municipal bond traded at a 1 percent yield. The purchaser of these bonds, he says, was buying a business that earned 1 percent on book value and for the next twenty years could never earn a dime more than 1 percent. Now, he explains, probably no business in America, in 1946, was bought or sold at book value that the buyer believed was unable to earn more than 1 percent on book value, yet fixed-income investors snapped up these bonds despite these miserable economics. Furthermore, investors, in the following years, continued to purchase bonds that by business standards were totally inadequate.

By the late 1970s and early 1980s, bond interest rates began to rise as inflation increased. In 1981, the yield on long-term government bonds was 16 percent, and 14 percent on tax-exempt municipal bonds. During this period, insurance companies switched from issuing one-year automobile policies to six-month policies. Insurance executives argued convincingly that during a period of rapidly rising inflation, they were unable to estimate future costs associated with repairing automobiles. Ironically, notes Buffett, once they decided that in an inflationary world, one-year auto policies were unreasonable, insurance executives turned around and lent money (purchased bonds) at fixed rates for thirty years.

The long-term bond, says Buffett, has become the last fixed-priced, long-term contract in an inflationary world. The buyers of bonds can get a fixed price for their investment, twenty years into the next century. Buyers of insurance, office space, chocolate, or newsprint would be ridiculed if they requested a fixed price for thirty years. This financial inconsistency, Buffett points out, is lost on individuals who purchase long-term bonds.

Although interest rates in the late 1970s and early 1980s approximated the returns of most businesses, Buffett was not a net purchaser of long-term bonds. There always existed, in his mind, the possibility of runaway inflation. In this environment, common stocks would lose real value, but bonds outstanding would suffer far greater losses. An insurance company heavily invested in bonds in a hyperinflationary environment has the potential to wipe out its portfolio. Although the possibility of hyperinflation was remote and interest rates in the early 1980s incorporated expectations of high inflation, the risk of being wrong, Buffett explains, was unacceptable.

Even so, insurance companies, because of their obligation to policy holders, must invest some of their assets in fixed-income securities. Still, Buffett has limited Berkshire's fixed-income securities to convertible bonds, convertible preferred stocks, and short- and intermediate-term bonds with sinking funds. Before purchasing, Buffett requires long-term bonds to clear high financial hurdles. This includes a current interest rate return that approximates a business return and the possibility that the bond will post a capital gain. These unique bonds often have been mispriced by the market and trade significantly below par value.

BONDS

Washington Public Power Supply System

On July 25, 1983, the Washington Public Power Supply System (WPPSS; pronounced, with macabre humor, "woops") announced that it was in default of $2.25 billion of municipal bonds used to finance the uncompleted construction of two nuclear reactors known as Projects 4 and 5. The state ruled that the local power authorities were not obligated to pay WPPSS for power they had previously promised to buy but ultimately did not require. The court's decision led to the largest municipal bond default in U.S. history. The size of the default and the debacle that followed depressed the market for public power bonds for several years. Investors sold their utility bonds forcing prices lower and current yields higher.

The cloud over WPPSS Projects 4 and 5 cast a shadow over Projects 1, 2, and 3. Now, Buffett explains, there were significant differences between the terms and obligations of Projects 4 and 5 and those of Projects 1, 2, and 3. The first three were operational utilities that were also direct obligations of Bonneville Power Administration, a government agency. However, there existed the possibility the problems of Projects 4 and 5 were so severe that they could weaken the credit position of Bonneville Power.

Buffett evaluated the risks of owning municipal bonds of WPPSS Projects 1, 2 and 3. Certainly there was a risk that these bonds could default and a risk that the interest payments could be suspended for a prolonged period of time. Still another factor was the upside "ceiling" on what these bonds could ever be worth. Even though he could purchase these bonds at a discount to their par value, at the time of maturity they could only be worth one hundred cents on the dollar.

Shortly after Projects 4 and 5 defaulted, Standard & Poor's suspended its ratings on Projects 1, 2, and 3. The lowest coupon bonds of Projects 1, 2, and 3 sank to forty cents on the dollar and produced a current yield of 15–17 percent tax-free. The highest coupon bonds fell to eighty cents on the dollar and generated a similar yield. Undismayed, from October 1983 through June the following year, Buffett aggressively purchased bonds issued by WPPSS for Projects 1, 2, and 3. He purchased the low coupon bonds and the high coupon bonds. By the end of June 1984, Berkshire Hathaway owned $139 million of WPPSS Project 1, 2, and 3 bonds with a face value of $205 million.

With WPPSS, Buffett explains, Berkshire acquired a $139 million business that could expect to earn $22.7 million annually after tax (the cumulative value of WPPSS annual coupons), and pay those earnings to Berkshire in cash. Buffett points out there were few businesses available for purchase during this time that were selling at a discount to book value and earning 16.3 percent after tax on unleveraged capital. Buffett figured that to purchase an unleveraged operating company earning $22.7 million after tax ($45 million pretax), it would have cost Berkshire between $250 million and $300 million. Given a strong business that he understands and likes, Buffett would have happily paid that amount. But, he explains, Berkshire paid half that price for WPPSS bonds to realize the same amount of earnings. Furthermore, Berkshire purchased the business (the bonds) at a 32 percent discount to book value.

Looking back, Buffett admits that the purchase of WPPSS bonds turned out better than he expected. Indeed, the bonds outperformed most business acquisitions made in 1983. Buffett has since sold the WPPSS low coupon bonds. These bonds, which he purchased at a significant discount to par value, doubled in price while annually paying Berkshire a return of 15–17 percent tax-free. "Our WPPSS experience, though pleasant, does nothing to alter our negative opinion about long-term bonds," Buffett said. "It only makes us hope that we run into some other large stigmatized issue, whose troubles have caused it to be significantly misappraised by the market."[1]

RJR Nabisco Bonds

During the 1980s, a new investment vehicle, the high-yield bond, was introduced to the financial markets. Buffett considers these new high-yield bonds to be different from their predecessor *fallen angels*—Buffett's term for investment grade bonds that, having fallen on bad times, were downgraded by ratings agencies. The WPPSS bonds were fallen angels. The new high-yield bonds were a "bastardized" form of the fallen angels and were often referred to as junk bonds. These high-yield bonds, according to Buffett, were junk before they were issued.

Wall Street's securities salespeople were able to promote the legitimacy of junk-bond investing by quoting earlier research that indicated that higher interest rates compensated investors for the risk of default. Buffett, however, argued that earlier default statistics were meaningless, since the data were based on a group of bonds that were significantly different from the junk bonds currently issued. It was illogical, Buffett argued, to assume that junk bonds were identical to the fallen angels. "Beware of past performance proofs in finance," he said. "If history books were the key to riches, the Forbes 400 would consist of librarians."[2]

As the 1980s unfolded, high-yield bonds became "junkier" as new offerings flooded the market. "Mountains of junk bonds," noted Buffett, "were sold by those who didn't care to those that didn't think—and there was no shortage of either."[3] At the height of this debt mania, Buffett predicted that certain capital enterprises were guaranteed to fail when it became apparent that debt-laden companies were struggling to meet their interest payments. In 1989, Southmark Corporation and Integrated Resources both defaulted on their bonds. Even Campeau Corporation, a U.S. retailing empire created with junk bonds, announced it was having difficulty meeting its debt obligations. Then on October 13, 1989, UAL Corporation, the target of a $6.8 billion buyout led by management and unions that was to be financed with high-yield bonds, announced that it was unable to obtain financing. Arbitrageurs sold their UAL common stock position and the Dow Jones Industrial Average dropped 190 points in one day.

The disappointment over the UAL deal coupled with the losses in Southmark and Integrated Resources led many investors to question the value of high-yield bonds. Portfolio managers began dumping their junk-bond positions. Without any buyers, the price for high-yield bonds plummeted. After beginning the year with outstanding gains, Merrill Lynch's index of high-yield bonds returned a paltry 4.2 percent compared to investment grade bonds, which returned 14.2 percent. By the end of 1989, junk bonds were deeply out of favor with the market.

A year earlier, in 1988, Kohlberg Kravis & Roberts succeeded in purchasing RJR Nabisco for $25 billion, financed principally with bank debt and junk bonds. Although RJR Nabisco was meeting its financial obligations, when the junk bond market unravelled, RJR bonds declined along with other junk bonds. In 1989 and 1990, during the junk bond bear market, Buffett began purchasing RJR bonds.

While most junk bonds continued to look unattractive during this time, Buffett figured that RJR Nabisco was unjustly punished. The company's stable products were generating enough cash flow to cover its debt payments. Additionally, RJR Nabisco had been successful in selling portions of its business at very attractive prices, thereby reducing its debt-to-equity ratio. Buffett analyzed the risks of investing in RJR and concluded that the company's credit was higher than perceived by other investors who were selling their bonds. RJR bonds were yielding 14.4 percent (a businesslike return) and the depressed price offered the potential for capital gains.

In 1989 and 1990, Buffett acquired $440 million in discounted RJR Bonds. In the spring of 1991, RJR Nabisco announced it was retiring most of its junk bonds by redeeming the bonds at face value. The RJR bonds rose 34 percent, producing a $150 million capital gain for Berkshire Hathaway.

ARBITRAGE

Buffett sometimes holds medium-term tax exempt bonds as cash alternatives. He realizes that by substituting medium-term bonds for short-term Treasury bills, he runs the risk of principal loss if he is forced to sell at a disadvantageous time. Because these tax-free bonds offer higher after-tax returns than Treasury bills, Buffett figures that the potential loss is offset by the gain in income. However, this is not his only profitable alternative to Treasury bills. Confronted with more cash than investable ideas, Buffett occasionally turns to arbitrage.

Arbitrage, in its simplest form, involves purchasing a security in one market and simultaneously selling the same security in another market. The object is to profit from price discrepancies. For example, if stock in a company was quoted as $20 per share in the London market and $20.01 in the Tokyo market, an arbitrageur could profit from simultaneously purchasing shares of the company in London and selling the same shares in Tokyo. In this case, there is no capital risk. The arbitrageur is merely profiting from the inefficiencies that occur between markets. Because this transaction involves no risk, it is appropriately called riskless arbitrage. Risk arbitrage, on the other hand, is the sale or purchase of a security in hopes of profiting from some announced value.

The most common type of risk arbitrage involves the purchase of a stock that is at a discount to some future value. This future value is usually based on a corporate merger, liquidation, tender offer, or reorganization. The risk an arbitrageur confronts is the possibility that the future announced price of the stock will not be realized. To evaluate risk arbitrage opportunities, Buffett explains, you must answer four basic questions: "How likely is it that the promised event will indeed occur? How long will your money be tied up? What chance is there that something better will transpire—a competing takeover bid for example? What will happen if the event does not take place because of antitrust action, financing glitches, etc.?"[4]

To help shareholders understand the advantages of arbitrage, Buffett shares the story of Berkshire's arbitrage of Arcata Corporation.[5] In 1981, Arcata Corporation agreed to sell the company to the leveraged buyout firm, Kolhberg Kravis Roberts & Company (KKR). Arcata's current business included forest products and printing. In addition, in 1978, the U.S. government had by force acquired more than 10,000 acres of redwood timber from Arcata to expand the Redwood National Park. The government offered Arcata $98 million, to be paid in installments, plus 6 percent simple interest on the outstanding debt. Arcata argued that the purchase price for the land was unjustifiably low and the 6 percent simple interest was inadequate. In 1981, the value of Arcata was its operating business plus the potential settlement with the government. KKR offered to purchase Arcata for $37 per share plus two-thirds of any additional amount the government might be forced to pay.

Buffett analyzed the buyout of Arcata Corporation by KKR. He figured that KKR's track record in successfully obtaining financing for deals was good, and if KKR decided to walk away from the transaction, Arcata would locate another buyer. Arcata'a board of directors were determined to sell the company. The last question that needed to be answered was more difficult. What was the value of the redwood timber seized by the government? Buffett, who admittedly "couldn't tell an elm from an oak coolly evaluated the claim at somewhere between zero and a whole lot."[6]

Berkshire Hathaway began acquiring Arcata stock in the fall of 1981 at around $33.50 per share. By November 30, Berkshire owned 400,000 shares, roughly 5 percent of the company. A definitive agreement was signed between Arcata and KKR in January 1982, at which time Buffett added 255,000 shares to Berkshire's holdings at prices near $38 per share. Despite the complexities of the transaction, Buffett's willingness to pay more than KKR's $37 per share offer indicated his belief that the settlement with the government regarding the redwood timber was worth more than zero.

Weeks later, the deal began to unravel. First, despite Buffett's assumption, KKR was having trouble financing the acquisition. The housing industry was in a slump and lenders were being careful. Arcata's stockholder meeting was postponed until April. KKR, unable to arrange all of the financing, offered $33.50 per share for Arcata. The board of directors turned down KKR's offer. By March, Arcata accepted another competing bid and sold the company for $37.50 per share, plus one-half of the potential litigation settlement. Berkshire received $1.7 million above its $22.9 million investment, a very satisfactory 15 percent annualized return.

Years later, Berkshire received a long-awaited installment on the Arcata arbitrage investment. During litigation, the trial judge appointed two commissions, one to determine the value of the redwood timber and the second to decide a proper interest rate. In January 1987, the first commission announced that the redwood timber was worth not $97.9 million but $275.7 million, and the second commission announced that an appropriate interest rate should be 14 percent compounded, not 6 percent simple. The court ruled that Arcata was due $600 million. The government appealed but eventually settled for $519 million. In 1988, Berkshire received $19.3 million, or an additional $29.48 per Arcata share.

Buffett has practiced arbitrage for decades. Whereas most arbitrageurs might participate in fifty or more deals annually, Buffett seeks out only a few financially large transactions. He limits his participation to deals that are announced and friendly. He refuses to speculate about potential takeovers or the prospects for greenmail. Although he has never calculated his arbitrage performance over the years, Buffett reckons that Berkshire has averaged an annual return of about 25 percent pretax. Because arbitrage is often a substitute for short-term Treasury bills, Buffett's appetite for deals fluctuates with Berkshire's cash level. More importantly, he explains, arbitrage prevents him from loosening his rigid standards regarding the purchase of long-term bonds.

With Berkshire's success in arbitrage, shareholders might wonder why Buffett would ever need to stray from this strategy. Admittedly, Buffett's investment returns were better than he imagined, but by 1989 the arbitrage landscape was changing. The financial excesses brought about by the leveraged buyout market were creating an environment of unbridled enthusiasm. Buffett was not sure when lenders and buyers would come to their senses, but he always acted cautiously when others were giddy. Even before the collapse of the UAL buyout, Buffett was pulling back from arbitrage transactions. Berkshire's withdrawal from arbitrage was made easier with the advent of convertible preferred stocks.

CONVERTIBLE PREFERRED STOCKS

A convertible preferred stock is a hybrid security that possesses characteristics of both stocks and bonds. Generally, these stocks provide investors with higher current income than common stocks. This higher yield offers protection from downside price risk. If the common stock declines, the higher yield of the convertible preferred stock prevents it from falling as low as the common shares. In theory, the convertible stock will fall in price until its current yield approximates the value of a nonconvertible bond with a similar yield, credit, and maturity.

A convertible preferred stock also provides the investor with the opportunity to participate in the upside potential of the common shares. Since it is convertible into common shares, when the common stock rises, the convertible stock will rise as well. However, because the convertible stock provides high income and has the potential for capital gains, it is priced at a premium to the common stock. This premium is reflected in the rate at which the preferred is convertible into common shares. Typically, the conversion premium may be 20 percent to 30 percent. This means that the common must rise in price 20–30 percent before the convertible stock can be converted into common shares without losing value.

When Buffett began investing in convertible preferred stocks, many people were confused. Initially, it was not clear whether Buffett's actions were an endorsement of the company and its business or merely the reward he received for protecting these companies from unwanted suitors. In each case, Salomon, Gillette, Champion International, and USAir were being challenged by takeover groups. Salomon was faced with a potential takeover by Revlon Group's Ronald Perelman. Gillette was being hounded by Coniston Partners, and Michael Steinhardt threatened to take over USAir. Champion International was not in imminent danger, but by selling Berkshire $300 million of new convertible preferred stock, which represented 8 percent of the company, it was attempting to prevent a successful takeover. Buffett became known as a "white knight," rescuing companies from hostile invaders.

Salomon, Inc.

In 1987, shortly before the October stock market crash, Berkshire Hathaway announced it had purchased $700 million of newly issued shares of Salomon 9 percent preferred stock, convertible after three years into Salomon common stock at $38 per share. If Berkshire did not convert the preferred stock, Salomon would redeem it over five years, beginning October 1995. At the time, Salomon's common stock was trading around $33 per share. The preferred was issued at a 15 percent premium to its conversion parity. In other words, Salomon's common stock would have to rise 15 percent before Berkshire could convert its preferred into common without losing money.

In 1987, Ronald Perelman was attempting to take over Salomon. John Gutfreund, then CEO of Salomon, did not believe that it was in Salomon's best interest to sell the company to Perelman. "So I called Warren," said Gutfreund, "and we cut a deal very quickly."[7] Buffett and Gutfreund had known each other for years. In 1976, Gutfreund assisted GEICO in its recovery from near bankruptcy. Since that time, Buffett had observed on many occasions how

Gutfreund placed the interests of clients above the interests of his firm, ultimately denying the firm lucrative fees. Such behavior, commented Buffett, was unusual for Wall Street. Gutfreund was someone he trusted and admired.

From Buffett's standpoint, the Salomon preferred was a medium-term, fixed-income equivalent with interesting conversion possibilities. Admittedly, he had no special insight regarding the investment banking business. He could not predict with any confidence what the future cash flows of the business would be. This unpredictability, Buffett explains, was the reason Berkshire's investment was a convertible preferred issue rather than common stock. However, it was his belief that over time, "a leading, high-quality capital-raising and market-making operation can average good returns on equity." If he was correct, the "conversion right will eventually prove to be valuable."[8]

In 1986, Salomon's common stock had traded as high as $59— 55 percent above Berkshire's conversion option price. If Salomon reached its high again within three years, Berkshire's total return, if converted and including dividends, would be 88 percent or a 29 percent annualized return. If it took five years before Salomon's stock priced reached $59, Berkshire's annual return would be 17.6 percent. Although a 17 percent annual return was below what Berkshire had been able to achieve in its own common stock portfolio, it was decidedly better than the returns of most businesses and almost twice as high as long-term bond rates. Despite the conversion potential, the overwhelming portion of the preferred's value, explained Buffett, was its fixed-income characteristics. And it was those characteristics that salvaged the Salomon investment from two unseen disasters.

Less than a month after Buffett purchased the Salomon preferred stock, the 1987 October crash occurred (see Figure 6.1). Salomon's stock price sank to $16. If Buffett had invested in the common shares, he would have lost half his investment. By year end, 1987, Salomon struggled back to $19 per share. From here, Salomon needed to double in price before Berkshire could break even on its conversion. In 1988, Salomon's share price gained 23 percent, ending the year at $24 per share. The following year the stock edged up to $29 per share before sliding back to $23 after the October 13, 1989 market selloff. It was 1991 before Salomon again crossed over the $33 per share price, where Buffett first had

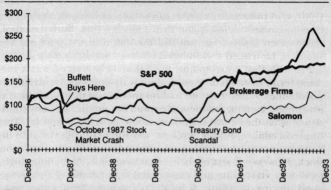

Figure 6.1. Common stock price of Salomon compared to the S&P 500 and brokerage firm indexes (indexed to $100 at start date).

purchased the convertible preferred. Finally, the stock was gaining strength. It reached $37 per share shortly before the company's August 1991 announcement that it had violated U.S. Treasury rules. What happened next tells more about Buffett the executive than the Salomon investment.

"On August 16, 1991, I got a call about quarter to seven in the morning," said Buffett. "It was the top officers of Salomon telling me that they were going to offer their resignation."[9] A week earlier, the company had admitted to violating Treasury auction rules when it controlled 95 percent of the two-year Treasury notes sold to bidders in May. Treasury rules state that a company cannot purchase in an auction more than 35 percent of the total offering. Not only had Salomon grossly exceeded this limit, it hid the violation from authorities for several months. Gutfreund was aware of the violation shortly after it was committed; he, along with other senior Salomon executives, was criticized for not informing authorities in timely fashion. The criticism was so severe that Gutfreund had no choice but to resign.

This was a small problem, Buffett facetiously admitted, since Salomon owed more money than any other company in the United States, except Citicorp, and half of it was due in several weeks. If Salomon failed, the financial repercussions for the country, as well as Berkshire Hathaway, would be dramatic. Seeing no choice but to assure government regulatory authorities, politicians, shareholders, and customers that Salomon was worth saving, Buffett offered to become interim chairman of Salomon until the crisis was resolved. It is fair to say that Buffett's presence and leadership during the investigation prevented Salomon from collapsing.

During the next ten months, Buffett named Deryck Maughan chairman and chief executive of Salomon Brothers, the company's investment banking unit. Maughan had previously run Salomon's profitable East Asian operations in Tokyo. Next he appointed Robert Denham, managing partner of Munger Tolles & Olson (Charlie Munger's law firm), as Salomon's top lawyer. Denham, along with Buffett, negotiated the company's $290 million settlement with federal regulators over the firm's bidding violations. Lastly, Buffett reorganized Salomon's management, compensation, and performance evaluations. When Buffett stepped down as interim chairman in June 1992, he nominated Robert Denham as chairman of Salomon Incorporated.

When Salomon announced its violations, its stock price dropped to $16 per share. After four years, the share price was back at the same level where it traded after the 1987 October crash. From the time Buffett took charge of Salomon in September 1991, Salomon's share price has risen steadily. By December 1993, twenty-eight months after the scandal was announced, the share price had risen 193 percent to $47 per share. Despite the miraculous recovery, Salomon's preferred stock has been a relative disappointment. Not only has the common share price, since 1987, failed to outperform the Standard & Poor's 500 Index (see Figure 6.1), it has also dramatically underperformed other brokerage firms. Berkshire's investment in Salomon's preferred, which includes dividends and conversion rights into common, has averaged 13 percent over the last six years. The return is less than what an average business might have returned, but demonstrably more than other medium-term, fixed-income securities.

Undoubtedly, part of Salomon's below-average growth was due in large part to the actions of management. This is the first case where one of Berkshire's primary investments has been damaged by the illegal behavior of senior executives. If he were to make a mistake in evaluating a business, Buffett always figured it would result from his misunderstanding of the company's future economics, not the ethical behavior of management. "In evaluating people," Buffett said, "you look for three qualities: integrity, intelligence, and energy. And if you don't have the first, the other two will kill you."[10] No financial statistics would have forecast Salomon's management problems. However, Buffett's realignment of Salomon's board of directors to include a nonexecutive chairman, whose priority is to protect the interest of shareholders, will help ensure that future problems in the company will be dealt with quickly and openly.

Between February 3, 1994 and March 4, 1994, Buffett, in a series of eighteen different transactions, purchased 5,519,800 shares of Salomon common stock. In addition to 495,200 common shares previously purchased in November 1993, Berkshire Hathaway currently owns 6,015,000 shares of Salomon common stock and 700,000 shares of preferred stock. By becoming an owner of common shares, Buffett's confidence in Salomon as a business has demonstrably increased. However, Salomon is still a trading company and thus its earnings are volatile by nature. But, as Buffett observes, See's Candy Shops's earnings are volatile as well. Its business results are terrific at Christmas and poor in July. There is, Buffett points out, more than one way to get to heaven.

Clearly, Buffett's confidence in Salomon has risen because of new management and the controls he has put in place. Deryck Maughan's executive compensation is tied to Salomon Brother's return on equity. If the company does well, and shareholders do well as a result, Maughan's compensation will increase. If shareholders suffer, so too will Maughan's salary. Buffett is also comforted in having Robert Denham as Salomon's nonexecutive chairman. "It's not a business as predictable as a Gillette or a Coca-Cola," Buffett says, "but we have some good people running Salomon."[11]

USAir Group

On August 7, 1989, Berkshire invested $358 million in USAir Group. In return, Berkshire received convertible preferred stock yielding 9.25 percent. It is convertible into common shares at $60 per share. If Berkshire does not convert into common, USAir must redeem the preferred in ten years. At the time Berkshire invested in USAir, the company's common stock price was trading at $50 per share. The purchase, confessed Buffett, "displayed exquisite timing. I plunged into the business at almost the exact moment that it ran into problems."[12]

When Buffett invested in USAir, he figured that the company would benefit from the synergies created by the acquisition of Piedmont Airlines. Furthermore, the airline industry was consolidating. In the past, USAir had demonstrated impressive economics. From 1981 to 1988 it averaged 14 percent return on equity. The pretax margins averaged between 8 percent and 12 percent, and the company's market value rose from $200 million to $1.5 billion.

Still, Buffett was unfamiliar with the airline industry. He had no knowledge of how to forecast the economics of this business. So rather than invest solely in the common shares, Buffett opted for preferred shares. "This does not mean that we predict a negative future for (USAir); we're agnostics, not atheists," wrote Buffett. "Our lack of strong convictions about (this business) means that we must structure our investment differently from what we do when we invest in a business appearing to have splendid economic characteristics."[13]

Nonetheless, Buffett believed that under tolerable industry conditions, USAir's common stock would do well, and thus Berkshire's convertible preferred would tag along with the appreciation of the common. What he learned was something else.

USAir's problems were caused by its difficult merger with Piedmont and by the airline industry's irrational behavior. Buffett admits that he should have expected the merger with Piedmont to be followed by turmoil. Mergers in general behave this way, and in the airline business, difficult mergers are prevalent. Fortunately, Ed Colodny, chairman of USAir, and Seth Schofield, vice chairman, soon corrected the merger complications. However, neither could prevent the debacle that soon engulfed the airline industry.

Airline service is a commodity product. Consumers choosing an airline often base their decision on price. As airlines fought for market share, they continually lowered prices. "The economics of the airline industry," explained Buffett, "have deteriorated at an alarming pace, accelerated by the kamikaze pricing tactics of certain carriers."[14] This pricing behavior was most prevalent among bankrupt carriers. Once an airline files for bankruptcy, it can continue to offer flights to customers while operating debt-free. Starved for cash, bankrupt airlines sold flights below cost just to generate cash. The problem in a commodity business, Buffett learned, is that you are only as smart as your dumbest competitor. Healthy airlines were being dragged down by the foolish behavior of bankrupt airlines. Nonetheless, Buffett figured that unless the airline industry was decimated, Berkshire's USAir investment could provide a reasonable return.

Unfortunately, in 1991, the airline industry had its worst year in history. Within a fourteen-month period, Midway, Pan Am, America West, Continental, and TWA all filed for bankruptcy. Under the protection and encouragement of the bankruptcy courts, all of these airlines continued to operate, charging fares below the costs of other marginal airlines that were struggling to stay profitable. The bankruptcy courts were creating a domino effect that threatened the entire airline industry. In 1991, the airline industry lost more money in one year than had been made in aggregate since the Wright brothers' first flight at Kitty Hawk. In 1991, Buffett reduced the market value of its USAir convertible preferred down to $232 million, $126 million less than it paid. "The low valuation that we have given USAir," said Buffett, "reflects the risk that the industry will remain unprofitable for virtually all participants in it, a risk that is far from negligible."[15]

Buffett admits that although he understood the competitive nature of the airline business, he never imagined the cutthroat behavior of airline executives. After enduring the economics of this industry, Buffett concluded that there was no worse business than the airline business. It is a commodity business with huge fixed costs and overcapacity. Despite the efforts of skilled management, the reward is survival, Buffett argues, not prosperity.

USAir's potential for survival increased measurably with British Air's minority investment in the company. British Air, for $300 million, purchased a 19.9 percent voting stake in USAir Group. This trans-Atlantic alliance is designed to funnel passengers to both airlines by linking flights between the carriers. USAir will fly American travelers to Heathrow, where they will connect with British Air for continuation of their overseas trip. Likewise, British Air will bring European travelers to the United States, who will change planes and continue their flights aboard USAir. Conceptually the alliance makes sense. Of course, merging airline service is never easy.

USAir's convertible investment was a mistake, "an unforced

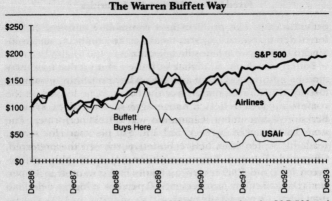

Figure 6.2. Common stock price of USAir compared to the S&P 500 and airline indexes (indexed to $100 at start date).

error," Buffett confesses. Like Salomon, USAir has not only underperformed the Standard & Poor's 500 Index (see Figure 6.2), it has also underperformed its peer group. A student at Columbia University asked Buffett why he invested in USAir. "My psychologist asks me that too," quipped Buffett. "Actually I have an 800 number now which I call if I ever get an urge to buy an airline stock. I say, 'My name is Warren, I'm an air-aholic' and they talk me down."[16]

Champion International

On December 6, 1989, Champion International sold 300,000 shares of convertible preferred stock to Berkshire Hathaway. Each preferred share was entitled to cumulative dividends at the annual rate of $92.50. In addition, the preferred is convertible into 26.3 shares of common at $38 per share. When Berkshire purchased the preferred, Champion's common stock was trading at $30 per share.

Andrew Sigler, chairman and chief executive of Champion International, has been a critic of hostile takeovers. Fearing that Champion might soon be the target of a takeover (in 1989 Georgia-Pacific was acquiring Great Northern Nekoosa), Sigler invited

Buffett to invest in the company. Berkshire's convertible preferred represents an 8 percent stake in the company and is intended to dissuade any hostile takeover.

Buffett was no more familiar with the forest products industry than he was the brokerage and the airline industries. Unable to forecast the future economics of the business, he looked on the convertible preferred as a hedge against uncertainty. Prior to Berkshire's investment, Champion was a dull performer. The stock had bounced between $22 and $40 per share for several years. In the ten years before Buffett purchased the preferred, Champion averaged 7 percent return on equity, although between 1987 and 1989 return on equity had improved to 12 percent. Debt to equity has averaged 60 percent, a higher debt load than Buffett is comfortable with.

The best thing that can be said about the company is that it is trading at a discount to its book value. This book value includes state-of-the-art paper mills and valuable timber holdings. The company owned 5.8 million acres of timber, on its books for $1.5 billion. Other transactions involving the sale of timber similar to Champion's holdings would price the company's acreage closer to $2.6 billion. At the time Berkshire invested in the convertible preferred, Champion had purchased 2.8 million of its shares under a 10-million-share buyback authorized by the board of directors. Although the economics of the paper and forest products business were unimpressive, Champion possessed unrecognized value in its timber holdings. If the company sold some of this timber and used the proceeds to buy back stock and reduce debt, Champion's common stock price would rise, as would Berkshire's preferred stock.

Despite the potential for improvement, Champion's progress has been sluggish. After fifteen years of consecutive positive earnings, the company lost money in 1991, 1992, and 1993. Weak demand for paper products coupled with overcapacity have resulted in price reductions of 25 percent. Profitability margins have been squeezed and the stock price has continued to languish (see Figure 6.3).

Although Champion's short-term economic performance has lagged behind both the Standard & Poor's 500 Index and the Paper/Forest Products Index (see Figure 6.3), its long-term value remains its timber holdings. For long-term investors, "lumber

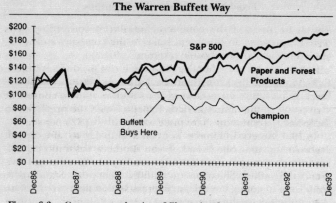

Figure 6.3. Common stock price of Champion International compared to the S&P 500 and forest products indexes (indexed to $100 at start date).

companies are a store of value against inflation. The record shows that wood on the stump tends to generate long-term total returns of 4 percent and 6 percent above inflation rates."[17] Over the years, Buffett has maintained a bias toward higher inflation. Possibly, Champion's timber holdings represent an inflation hedge for Berkshire Hathaway. For every one hundred shares of Champion International investors own, their proportional interest equals 5.5 acres of prime timber.

American Express

On August 1, 1991, Buffett invested $300 million in American Express. The American Express preferred was different from Berkshire's other convertible preferred stocks. Although it carries a 8.85 percent fixed dividend, the preferred must be converted three years after issuance into a maximum 12,244,898 shares of American Express common stock. If the value of American Express stock to Berkshire at the time of conversion is $414 million or greater, the conversion ratio will be adjusted downward to limit the value of common stock Berkshire receives.

Unlike other convertible preferreds, the American Express preferred has an upside ceiling. Berkshire is allowed to extend the conversion period by one year if the price of American Express is $24.50 per share or below—Berkshire's breakeven price—on the third anniversary of the preferred issue. Although the agreement allows Berkshire to extend the conversion date by one year, there is no downside limit to American Express's share price. If the stock price is $20 the following year, Berkshire must convert at that price. At the time American Express issued the preferred to Berkshire, its common share price was trading at $25 per share.

In 1991, American Express went on a campaign to raise capital. Its brokerage unit, Shearson Lehman Brothers, was thinly capitalized after a series of writeoffs. American Express's credit card division was funding Shearson's shortfalls. That year, Standard & Poor's downgraded American Express senior debt from AA to AA−, an immediate embarrassment to James Robinson, chairman and chief executive of American Express. Jack Byrne, former chairman of GEICO and now member of the board of directors at American Express, suggested that Robinson contact Buffett about an equity investment that would immediately raise capital. "I told Jack that I would be interested," Buffett recalls, "and he had Jim Robinson call me."[18] A week later, Buffett invested $300 million in a private issue of American Express preferred stock.

It is not clear why Buffett accepted American Express's restrictions. The upside ceiling limited Berkshire's capital gain to 37 percent. If American Express's stock price reaches $37.53, the company has the option to redeem the shares on a sliding scale down to $33.79. Still, despite the restrictions, Buffett wanted to invest. He would have invested $500 million, he admits, but Robinson only wanted to issue $300 million in preferred stock. Buffett cautions readers that they should not analyze his latest move as portent. "For me, it's what's available at the time."[19] The fixed-income alternatives available were Treasury bills at 6 percent and Treasury bonds at 7.5 percent.

In October 1991, two months after Buffett invested in American Express, the company announced a $265 million charge and 93 percent decline in third-quarter earnings. American Express's common stock sank to $18 (see Figure 6.4). Since then, the stock price has grudgingly moved higher. In 1992, the company sold a 46 percent interest in First Data, the company's information service subsidiary, raising $975 million. In 1993, the company sold its Shearson brokerage for $1 billion to Primerica. It has retained the

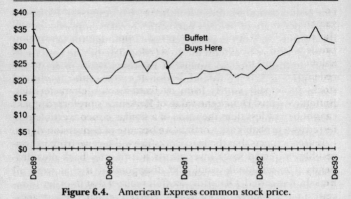

Figure 6.4. American Express common stock price.

Lehman Brothers investment banking and trading division but plans to spinoff this subsidiary to American Express shareholders in 1994. What will remain after the spinoffs is the company's Travel Related Services Division (credit card division), IDS Financial Services (a financial planning and investment subsidiary), American Express Bank, and a 54 percent interest in First Data Corporation.

By year end 1993, American Express's common stock reached $31 per share. If Berkshire had been able to convert to common at this price, Berkshire would have gained $80 million on its investment. Including dividends received, Berkshire's two-year average annual return on its American Express investment has been 21 percent.

The Real Value of Convertibles

It is important to remember that Buffett thinks of convertible preferred stocks first as fixed-income securities and second as vehicles for appreciation. Much attention has been paid to the underlying common stock performance of each preferred, ignoring the inherent advantages of the preferreds themselves. For example, when Salomon common stock traded at $22 per share, several members of the press figured that Salomon preferred, convertible into common at $38, was worth 60 percent of its face value. This reasoning, Buffett points out, "must conclude that all the value of a convertible preferred resides in the conversion privilege and that the value of a nonconvertible preferred of Salomon would be zero, no matter what its coupon or terms for redemption."[20] The value of Berkshire's convertible preferred stocks principally comes from its fixed-income characteristics, Buffett explains. Hence the value of Berkshire's preferred stocks cannot be any less than the value of a similar nonconvertible preferred and probably are worth more because of conversion rights.

Buffett expects that the least Berkshire will receive from its convertible preferred stock investments is its money back plus dividends. He admittedly would be disappointed if that were all Berkshire received. Of course, Buffett realizes that in order to receive a return better than a fixed preferred return, the investees' common stock must do well. "Good management and at least tolerable industry conditions will be needed if that is to happen," Buffett says.[21] The financial services industry appears more favorable than the airline industry, suggesting that the common stock returns for Salomon and American Express should exceed USAir. Although Champion International has performed poorly since Berkshire's investment, the potential for improvement remains. As a group, Buffett never expected the returns of Berkshire's convertible preferreds to match the economics of a wonderful business. However, he does expect that the returns will outperform the results of most fixed-income portfolios.

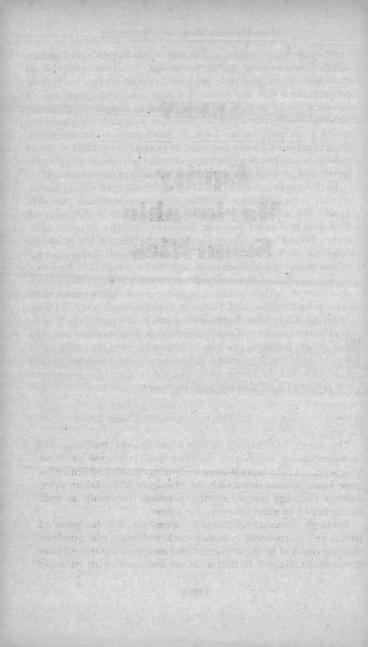

SEVEN

Equity
Marketable
Securities

IN ADDITION TO ITS permanent common-stock holdings, described in Chapter 5, Berkshire Hathaway owns significant positions in five other stocks. As of 1993, Berkshire owned 14 percent of General Dynamics Corporation, 11 percent of The Gillette Company, 12 percent of Wells Fargo & Company, 7 percent of Federal Home Loan Mortgage Corporation, and 2 percent of Guinness plc.

The primary difference between permanent holdings and "nonpermanent" holdings is one of personal relationships. As we have seen, over the years Warren Buffett has developed not only a close business association with the managers of Berkshire's permanent holdings but a heartfelt personal friendship as well, strengthened by many years of interaction.

Although personal relationships affect the sell discipline of Berkshire's permanent common-stock holdings, the purchase characteristics of both permanent and nonpermanent stocks are the same. In all cases, Buffett seeks out companies with attractive economics, run by shareholder-oriented managers, that are also available at attractive prices. Once he purchases these companies, Buffett is "quite content to hold a security indefinitely, so long as the prospective return on equity capital of the underlying business is satisfactory, management is competent and honest, and the market does not overvalue the business."[1]

THE GILLETTE COMPANY

The Gillette Company (Gillette) is an international consumer products company. Its businesses include the manufacturing and distribution of blades and razors, toiletries and cosmetics, stationary products, electric shavers, small household appliances, and oral care appliances and products. The company has manufacturing operations in 28 countries and distributes its products in more than 200 countries and territories. Foreign operations account for more than 60 percent of Gillette's sales and earnings.

Tenet: Favorable Long-Term Prospects

The company was founded by King C. Gillette at the turn of the century. As a young man, Gillette contemplated how he would make his fortune. A friend suggested that he should invent a product that consumers would use once, throw away, and replace with another. While working as a salesperson for Crown Cork & Seal, Gillette hit upon the idea of a disposable razor blade. In 1903, his fledgling company began selling the Gillette safety razor with twenty-five disposable blades for five dollars.

Today, Gillette is the world's leading manufacturer and distributor of blades and razors. Its marketshare is 64 percent, miles ahead of the number-two product, Warner-Lambert's Schick, which has 13 percent of the market. Gillette is so dominant worldwide that in many languages its name has become the word for "razor blade." In Europe, the company has a 70 percent market share, 80 percent in Latin America. Sales are just beginning to grow in Eastern Europe, India, and China. For every one blade Gillette sells in the United States, it sells five overseas. While razor blades account for approximately one-third of the company's sales, it contributes two-thirds of its profits.

Tenet: Consistent Operating History

Few companies have dominated their industry as long as Gillette. It was the leading brand of razors and blades in 1923 and the leading brand in 1993. Maintaining that position for so many years has required the company to spend hundreds of millions of dollars inventing new, improved products. Even though Wilkinson, in 1962, developed the first coated stainless steel blade, Gillette bounced back quickly and has since worked hard to remain the world's leading innovator of shaving products. In 1972, Gillette developed the popular twin-blade Trac II. In 1977, the company introduced the Atra razor with its pivoting head. Most recently, in 1989, the company developed the popular Sensor, a razor with independently suspended blades. Gillette's consistent success is a result of its innovation and patent protection of its new products.

Despite this enviable company profile, Gillette suffered through a difficult financial period in the early 1980s. Unlike other successful companies that often become bloated by their good fortune, Gillette has always been a well-managed company. Colman Mockler, chief executive of Gillette in the 1980s, ran a lean business. He cut costs, reduced the workforce, and closed poorly performing businesses. Productivity increased 6 percent annually under Mockler's leadership.

The company's temporary woes were a result of inexpensive disposable razors that immediately cut into profit margins. In 1974, Bic introduced its disposable razor in Greece. Initially, it was thought that disposable razors would capture only 10 percent of the shaving market. Instead they captured 50 percent. Gillette, having been surprised once by the introduction of Wilkinson's coated blades in the 1960s, reacted immediately to Bic's threat and countered with its own disposable razor. With heavy promotion, Gillette quickly took the lead in this market segment. However, even though Gillette's disposable was priced higher, the company's profit margins were being squeezed.

Gillette eventually overcame Bic's stiff competition by introducing the Sensor. Gillette figured that half of the shaving market, consisting of males forty-five years and older, would pay a higher price for a razor that guaranteed a closer, smoother shave and no razor performed as well as a Sensor. Rather than lose the company's image as the maker of quality shaving products, the company stopped advertising disposables altogether and committed its advertising and marketing resources to the Sensor razor. It was a risky strategy but it paid off.

In the 1980s, Gillette was a vibrant and innovative consumer products company. This was evident more so from inside the company, where research and development teams were inventing exciting new products, than from the outside, where investors were observing something else. Because of competition from lower margin disposable razors, Gillette began to look like a mature slow-growing consumer company ripe for a takeover. From 1981 through 1985, pretax profit margins hovered between 9 percent and 11 percent. Return on equity (see Figure 7.1), although respectable at 20 percent, flattened out with no sign of improvement. Gillette's income growth was anemic as well. Between 1981 and 1985, annual income grew at a 5.2 percent rate (see Figure 7.2), while sales hardly budged, rising less than 1 percent per year. In short, the company appeared stagnant.

Mockler fought off four takeover attempts during this time,

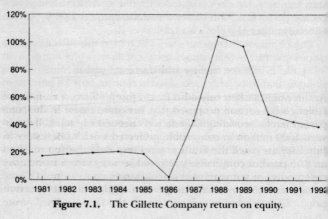

Figure 7.1. The Gillette Company return on equity.

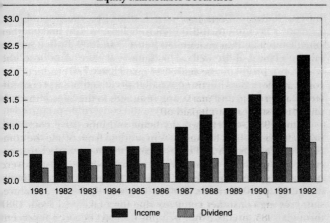

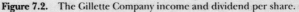

Figure 7.2. The Gillette Company income and dividend per share.

culminating in a hotly contested battle against Coniston Partners in 1988. Gillette barely won the proxy vote, garnering only 52 percent of the votes. But in doing so, the company obligated itself to buy back 19 million shares of Gillette stock at $45 per share. Institutional holdings of Gillette shares dropped from 55 percent outstanding to 35 percent. Between 1986 and 1988, the company replaced $1.5 billion in equity with debt, and, for a short period, Gillette had a negative net worth.

Tenet: Simple and Understandable

At this point, Buffett called his friend Joseph Sisco, a member of Gillette's board, and proposed that Berkshire invest in the company, thereby providing Gillette with needed capital. Gillette issued $600 million in convertible preferred stock to Berkshire in July 1989 and used the funds to pay down debt. Buffett received an 8.75 percent convertible preferred security with a mandatory redemption in ten years and the option to convert into Gillette common at $50 per share, 20 percent higher than the current price. "Gillette's business is very much the kind we like," wrote

Buffett. "Charlie (Munger) and I think we understand the company's economics and therefore believe we can make a reasonable intelligent guess about its future."[2] In 1989, Buffett joined Gillette's board of directors. That same year they introduced the Sensor, two profitable coincidences (see Figure 7.3).

The terms of the Gillette convertible preferred stock prevented Buffett from converting to common for two years. However, Gillette retained the right to redeem the convertible preferred at par and force conversion if the common stock price exceeded $62.50 for at least twenty consecutive trading days. After the introduction of the Sensor, Gillette's prosperity magnified. Earnings per share began growing at a 20 percent annual rate. Pretax margins increased from 12 percent to 15 percent and return on equity reached 40 percent, twice its return in the early 1980s.

In February 1991, the company announced a 2-for-1 stock split. Gillette's share price was then $73. Since it had exceeded $62.50 for more than twenty consecutive trading days, the company announced it was going to redeem Berkshire's convertible preferred stock. Berkshire converted its preferred and received 12 million common shares, or 11 percent of Gillette's shares outstanding. In less than two years, Berkshire's $600 million investment in Gillette had grown to $875 million, a 45 percent gain excluding dividends.

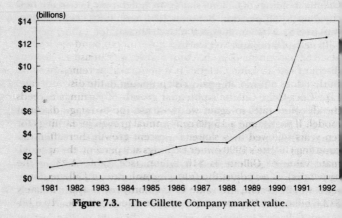

Figure 7.3. The Gillette Company market value.

Tenet: Determine the Value

Now that Berkshire owned Gillette common yielding 1.7 percent versus the convertible preferred yielding 8.75 percent, its investment in Gillette was no longer a fixed-income security with appreciation potential but a straight equity commitment. If Berkshire were to retain its common stock, Buffett needed to be convinced that Gillette was a good investment. We know Buffett understood the company and that the company's long-term prospects were favorable. Gillette's financial characteristics including return on equity and pretax margins were improving. The ability to increase prices, thereby boosting return on equity to above-average rates, signaled the company's growing economic goodwill. Mockler was purposely reducing Gillette's long-term debt and working hard to increase shareholder value. In short, the company met all the prerequisites for purchase. What remained for Buffett was to determine the company's value, thereby assuring himself that Gillette was not overpriced.

Gillette's owner earnings at year end 1990 were $275 million (see Table A.22 in the Appendix). Between 1987 and 1990, owner earnings grew at a 16 percent annual rate. Although this is too short a period to fully judge a company's growth, we can begin to make certain assumptions. In fact, in 1991, Buffett compared Gillette to Coca-Cola. "Coca-Cola and Gillette are two of the best companies in the world," Buffett wrote, "and we expect their earnings to grow at hefty rates in the years ahead."[3]

In early 1991, the thirty-year U.S. government bond was trading at a 8.62 percent yield. To be conservative, we can use a 9 percent discount rate to value Gillette. It is important to remember that Buffett does not add an equity risk premium to the discount rate. Like Coca-Cola, Gillette's potential growth of earnings exceeds the discount rate, so again we must use the two-stage discount model. If we assume a 15 percent annual growth in earnings for ten years followed by a slower 5 percent growth thereafter, discounting Gillette's 1990 owner earnings at 9 percent, the approximate value of Gillette is $16 billion (see Table A.23 in the Appendix). If we adjust the future growth rate of Gillette downward to 12 percent, the value of the company is approximately $12.6 billion; at 10 percent growth, the value would be $10.8 billion. At 7 percent growth in owner earnings, the value of Gillette is at least $8.5 billion.

Tenet: Buy at an Attractive Price

From 1984 through 1990, the average annual gain in Gillette's share was 27 percent. In 1989, the share price gained 48 percent (see Figure 7.4), and in 1990, the year before Berkshire converted its preferred to common, Gillette's share price rose 28 percent. In February 1991, Gillette's share price reached $73 per share (presplit), then a record high. At that time, the company had 97 million shares outstanding. When Berkshire converted, total shares increased to 109 million. Gillette's stock market value was $8.03 billion.

Depending on your growth assumptions for Gillette, at the time of conversion, the market price for the company was at a 50 percent discount to value (15 percent growth), 37 percent discount to value (12 percent growth), or a 25 percent discount to value if you assumed at 10 percent future growth for Gillette's owner earnings. At 7 percent growth, the value of Gillette, at $8.5 billion, was roughly equal to its market price. In any case, in 1991, Gillette was no overpriced relative to its assumed value.

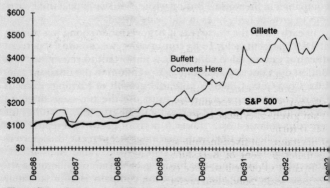

Figure 7.4. Common stock price of Gillette compared to the S&P 500 Index (indexed to $100 at start date).

Tenet: The One-Dollar Premise

By the end of 1992, the share price of Gillette reached $56 ($112 presplit). Berkshire's unrealized capital gain was $765 million, a 127 percent return on its original $600 million investment. From 1988 to 1992, the market value of Gillette increased by $9.3 billion. During this time, the company earned $1.6 billion, distributed $582 million to shareholders, and retained $1.011 billion for reinvestment. For every dollar it retained, the market value of the company increased $9.21. This above-average performance is reflected in Gillette's common stock price performance relative to the Standard & Poor's 500 Index (see Figure 7.4). Gillette's razor blade business is a prime beneficiary of globalization. Unit sales growth of blades in developing countries is 30 percent and should continue to grow at that rate as the company infiltrates India and China. Operating margins for the razor blade business in developing countries are not as high as the 40 percent margins in the United States but are closer to the company's 20 percent average. Typically, Gillette begins with low-end blades that have lower margins and, over time, introduces improved shaving systems with higher margins. The company stands to benefit not only from increasing unit sales but steadily improving profit margins as well. In short, Gillette's future appears bright. "It's pleasant to go to bed everynight," says Buffett, "knowing there are 2.5 billion males in the world who will have to shave in the morning."[4]

GENERAL DYNAMICS

General Dynamics operates in two distinct businesses. It is the nation's leading designer and builder of nuclear submarines and the manufacturer of armored vehicles including the U.S. Army's M1A1 and M1A2 battle tanks. In 1990, General Dynamics was the country's second largest U.S. Defense contractor behind McDonnell Douglas Corporation. General Dynamics has provided missile systems (Tomahawk, Sparrow, Stinger, and other advanced cruise missiles), air defense systems, space-launched vehicles, and fighter planes (F-16) for American armed forces. In 1990, the company had combined sales of more than $10 billion. By 1993, the company's sales were $3.5 billion. Despite the drop in sales, shareholder value during this period increased seven fold.

In 1990 the Berlin Wall crumbled, signaling the beginning of the end of America's long and expensive Cold War. The following year, communism collapsed in the Soviet Union. With each hard-earned victory, from World War I to the Vietnam War, the United States has had to reshape the massive concentration of its defense resources. Now that the Cold War is over, the U.S. military industrial complex is in the midst of another reorganization.

In January 1991, General Dynamics appointed William Anders as chief executive of the company. At the time, General Dynamics' share price was at a decade low of $19 per share. Initially, Anders attempted to convince Wall Street that General Dynamics, even with a shrinking defense budget, could earn higher valuations. He began to restructure the company, hoping to remove any financial uncertainty that would prejudice analysts. He cut capital expenditures and research development by $1 billion, cut employment by the thousands, and instituted an executive compensation program that was based on the performance of General Dynamics' share price.

It was not long before Anders began to realize the defense industry had fundamentally changed and that to be successful, General Dynamics would have to take more dramatic steps than just pinching pennies. Despite initial reorganization, the defense industry was still confronted with massive overcapacity. There simply was not enough defense business to go around. A smaller defense budget would ultimately require companies to either become smaller, diversify into nondefense businesses, or dominate what little defense business was available.

Tenet: The Institutional Imperative

In October 1991, Anders commissioned a consultant's study of the defense industry. This study concluded that when defense companies acquired nondefense businesses, failure occurred 80 percent of the time. The study also pointed out that as long as the defense industry was burdened with overcapacity, none of the defense companies would achieve efficiencies. Anders concluded that in order for General Dynamics to be successful, it would have to rationalize its business. He decided that General Dynamics would keep only those businesses that (1) demonstrated a market acceptance of its franchiselike product and (2) could achieve "critical mass," the balance between research and development and production capacity that produces economies of scale and financial strength. Where critical mass could not be achieved, Anders said, the business would be sold.

Initially, Anders believed that General Dynamics would focus on its four core operations: submarines, tanks, aircraft, and space systems. These businesses were market leaders, and Anders figured they would remain viable in a shrinking defense market. The rest of General Dynamics' businesses would be sold. In November 1991, General Dynamics sold its Data Systems to Computer Sciences for $200 million. The next year the company sold Cessna Aircraft to Textron for $600 million, and later sold its missile business to Hughes Aircraft for $450 million. In less than six months, the company raised $1.25 billion by selling noncore businesses. Anders' actions woke up Wall Street. General Dynamics' share price in 1991 rose 112 percent. What Anders did next got Buffett's attention.

Tenet: Rationality

With the cash holdings, Anders declared that the company would first meet its liquidity needs and then bring down debt to ensure financial strength (see Figure 7.5). After reducing its debt, General Dynamics was still generating cash well in excess of its needs. Knowing that adding capacity to a shrinking defense budget did not make sense, and that diversification into nondefense businesses invited failure, Anders decided to use the excess cash to benefit shareholders. In July 1992, under the terms of its Dutch auction, General Dynamics purchased 13.2 million shares at prices between $65.37 and $72.25, reducing its shares outstanding by 30 percent (see Figure 7.6).

On the morning of July 22, 1992, Buffett called Anders to tell him that Berkshire's insurance subsidiaries had purchased 4.3 million shares of General Dynamics (see Figure 7.9). Buffett told Anders that he was impressed with General Dynamics' strategy and that he bought the shares for investment purposes. In September, Buffett granted General Dynamics' board a proxy to vote Berkshire's shares as long as Anders remained chief executive of the company.

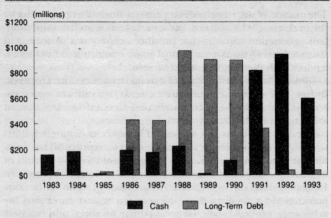

Figure 7.5. General Dynamics cash equivalents and long-term debt.

Of Berkshire's most recent common stock purchases, none has caused as much confusion as General Dynamics. It had none of the traditional markings of Buffett's earlier purchases. It was not a company that was simple and understandable, it was not a consistent performer, and it did not have favorable long-term prospects.

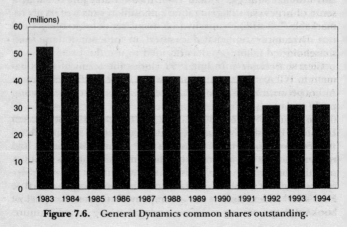

Figure 7.6. General Dynamics common shares outstanding.

The company was in an industry that not only was controlled by the government (90 percent of General Dynamics' business came from government contracts), but the industry was shrinking in size. General Dynamics had pitiful profit margins and below-average returns on equity. Furthermore, its future cash flows were unknown, so how could Buffett determine its value? The answer is, Buffett did not initially purchase General Dynamics as long-term common stock holding. He purchased General Dynamics as an arbitrage opportunity.

"We were lucky in our General Dynamics purchase," Buffett wrote. "I had paid little attention to the company until last summer, when it announced it would repurchase about 30 percent of its shares by way of Dutch tender. Seeing an arbitrage opportunity, I began buying the stock for Berkshire, expecting to tender our holdings for a small profit."[5] Because it was first purchased for arbitrage, General Dynamics escaped the financial and business tenet requirements that exist in Berkshire's other common stock holdings.

Still, Buffett became a long-term holder of General Dynamics. The plan was to tender Berkshire's shares at the Dutch auction "but then I began studying the company," said Buffett, "and the accomplishments of Bill Anders in the brief time he'd been CEO. And what I saw made my eyes pop. Bill had a clearly articulated and rational strategy; he had been focused and imbued with a sense of urgency in carrying it out; and the results were truly remarkable."[6] Buffett abandoned his thoughts of arbitraging General Dynamics and instead decided to become a long-term shareholder.

Clearly, Buffett's investment in General Dynamics is a testament to Bill Anders's ability to resist the institutional imperative. Although critics have argued that Anders liquidated a great company, Anders argues he simply monetized the unrealized value of the company. When he took charge in 1991, the price of General Dynamics was trading at a 60 percent discount to its book value (see Figure 7.7). In the ten previous years, General Dynamics had returned to its shareholders a compounded annual return of 9.1 percent compared to the 17.1 percent return for ten other defense companies, and a 17.6 percent return for the Standard & Poor's 500 Index. Buffett saw a company that was trading below book value, generating cash flow, and embarking on a divestiture

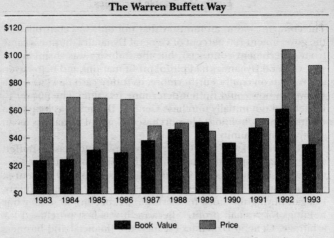

Figure 7.7. General Dynamics book value and price per share.

program. Additionally, and most importantly, management was shareholder-oriented.

Although General Dynamics had earlier thought that the aircraft and space systems divisions would remain core holdings, Anders decided to sell these businesses. The aircraft business was sold to Lockheed. General Dynamics, Lockheed, and Boeing were one-third partners in the development of the next generation of tactical fighter, the F-22. Now, Lockheed has acquired General Dynamics' mature F-16 business and become a two-thirds partner with Boeing on the F-22 project. The space systems division was sold to Martin Marietta, maker of the Titan family of space launch vehicles. The sale of the aircraft and space systems businesses provided General Dynamics with $1.72 billion.

Flush with cash, the company again returned the money to its shareholders. In April 1993, the company issued a $20 per share special dividend to shareholders. In July the company issued an $18 special dividend, and in October gave $12 per share to its owners. In 1993, the company returned $50 in special dividends and raised the quarterly dividend from $.40 to $.60 per share (see Figure 7.8). From July 1992 through the end of 1993, for its investment of $72 per share, Berkshire has received $2.60 in common

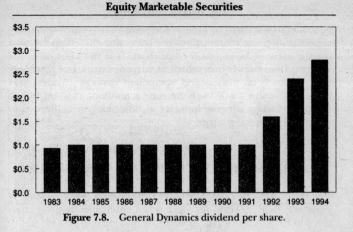

Figure 7.8. General Dynamics dividend per share.

dividends, $50 in special dividends, and a share price that rose to $103. Since Anders started to monetize the value of General Dynamics and return the money to its shareholders, General Dynamics has not only outperformed its peer group, it has soundly beaten the Standard & Poor's 500 Index (see Figure 7.9).

How long will Buffett hold General Dynamics? He tells us that

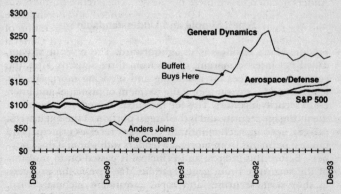

Figure 7.9. Common stock price of General Dynamics compared to the S&P 500 and aerospace/defense indexes (indexed to $100 at start date).

he will hold a security as long as the prospective return on equity is satisfactory, the market does not overvalue the company, and management is honest and competent. It is not clear whether General Dynamics is overvalued at current prices, but it is clear that Anders is an honest and competent manager. Anders and General Dynamics will likely become a textbook case on how a company facing adverse industry conditions can achieve outstanding economic returns.

FEDERAL HOME LOAN MORTGAGE CORPORATION

The Federal Home Loan Mortgage Corporation (Freddie Mac) is a publicly held, government-sponsored enterprise that was chartered by Congress in 1970. Its statutory mission is to provide stability in the secondary market for residential mortgages. Freddie Mac buys mortgages from lenders, pools the mortgages, and packages them into securities. These securitized mortgages are then sold to investors. By linking the capital markets with mortgage lenders, Freddie Mac is able to lower the cost of secondary mortgages to lenders and investors. This lower cost is ultimately passed on to home buyers in the form of affordable mortgage credit.

Tenet: Simple and Understandable

Freddie Mac's business is straightforward. The revenue stream, called net interest margin, comes from three sources. First, the company earns fees for managing and servicing mortgages for lenders and for guaranteeing the payment of principal and interest to security investors. This fee income is earned over the life of the mortgage security and is the largest portion of the net interest margin. Second, each month the company receives principal and interest payments from mortgage lenders with whom it does business. Before this interest and principal is passed on to investors of the securitized mortgage, Freddie Mac invests the proceeds in short-term securities and earns investment income. Third, Freddie Mac keeps a small portion of mortgages for its own portfolio and, just like any other traditional financial institution, earns the difference between the investment yield and the associated debt financing cost. The combined income from these three sources of business creates an annuitylike stream of income for the company.

Tenet: Favorable Long-Term Prospects

Of the $700 billion conventional single-family mortgages that were originated in 1992, 64 percent of that amount was sold and securitized by Freddie Mac and its sibling, Fannie Mae. Fannie Mae (Federal National Mortgage Corporation) is also a government-sponsored enterprise that, like Freddie Mac, provides funds for residential mortgages. Both companies have similar structures and the same business lines. Although the two compete directly, they operate as a duopoly in a fast-growing market with high barriers to entry. A duopoly, says Buffett, "is the next best thing to a monopoly."[7] Because of the breadth and magnitude of their activities, and because of their government-sponsored status, Freddie Mac and Fannie Mae have competitive advantages that have prevented significant penetration by other companies into the secondary market for mortgages. It is reasonable to assume that this competitive advantage will continue into the future.

In addition to their duopoly status, both companies enjoy the prospects of a growing market. The share of conventional single-family mortgages sold into the secondary market has increased over the last decade and is expected to grow. In 1990, revisions in the savings and loan laws forced savings banks to maintain larger reserves for loan losses than would be otherwise required if they owned a diversified portfolio of securitized mortgages. In essence, the new law forced traditional mortgage lenders to give both Freddie Mac and Fannie Mae more business, as demonstrated by the increase in securitized mortgage lending from 33 percent in 1988 to 60 percent in 1992.

In 1984, Freddie Mac issued preferred stock to the Federal Home Loan Board member savings and loans. It was, after all, the savings and loans that provided the seed money for Freddie Mac. However, ownership of the stock was restricted to board members.

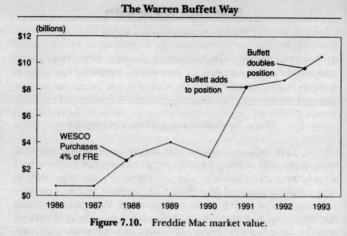

Figure 7.10. Freddie Mac market value.

After a few years, because the stock was not reflecting the potential value of the company, it was decided that Freddie Mac stock would be offered to the public and listed on the New York Stock Exchange. In 1988, for the first time, stockholders other than savings and loans could own Freddie Mac. In 1988, Wesco's Mutual Savings increased its position in Freddie Mac to 4 percent of the shares outstanding (see Figure 7.10). Because Berkshire Hathaway owns 80 percent of Wesco Financial, it is indirectly the beneficiary of Freddie Mac stock.

Tenet: Return on Equity

Charlie Munger, chairman of Mutual Savings, correctly figured that Freddie Mac was a superior business compared to the traditional savings and loan. Because Freddie Mac earns handsome fees and spreads while simultaneously avoiding interest rate risk (the company retains a very small mortgage portfolio), it is a much better business than the top 10 percent savings and loans, he noted. This evidence can be found in Freddie Mac's high returns on equity. These returns, compared to most savings and loans, can be maintained in part because Freddie Mac does not have to pay deposit insurance premiums.

Tenet: Determine the Value

In April 1992, Freddie Mac split its shares 3 for 1. There were now 180 million shares outstanding. In 1991, Berkshire had added to its Freddie Mac position. In 1992, Buffett began to accumulate additional shares and, by year end, Berkshire owned 16,196,700 (postsplit shares) of the company, doubling its position (see Figure 7.10). This was a meaningful purchase. Buffett added $337 million to a company whose share price had already risen 182 percent the year before. Berkshire now owned 9 percent of Freddie Mac. To make that commitment, Buffett obviously saw value.

In 1986, Freddie Mac's net income was $247 million. By 1991, income had grown to $555 million (see Figure 7.11). In five years, owner earnings grew at a rate of 17 percent. The value of Freddie Mac was not only the discounted value of its current earnings, but the future growth of the company's earnings as well. We know that Buffett thought highly of Freddie Mac's long-term potential. The company earned high returns on equity. It was in a growing industry where it was one of only two major players. The management of Freddie Mac had worked to keep risks low by limiting interest rate risk and diligently checking the credit risk of its mortgage applicants. Management believed that Freddie Mac would continue to generate annual earnings growth in the midteens for the next several years.

Freddie Mac is another company that is best valued using the

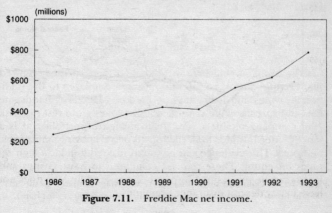

Figure 7.11. Freddie Mac net income.

two-stage discount model. If we assume that Freddie Mac will be able to grow its earnings at 15 percent for the next ten years followed by a slower 5 percent growth thereafter, discounting 1991 earnings of $555 million by 9 percent (the average yield of a thirty-year U.S. government bond), the value of Freddie Mac in 1992 was $32 billion (see Table A.24 in the Appendix). If we assume 12 percent growth in the first stage, Freddie Mac's value was $25 billion; at 10 percent growth, the value was $21 billion, and at 7 percent growth—half the rate at which management believed it could grow earnings—Freddie Mac was worth $17 billion. At this lowest valuation, Buffett, in 1992, purchased shares in Freddie Mac at a 57 percent discount to the company's value.

Why did Freddie Mac, in 1992, trade at prices that were substantially below the company's value? Perhaps investors thought that the company would not be able to grow its earnings in the future. Possibly they suspected management would increase the interest rate risk of the company by retaining more mortgages in its own portfolio or increase credit risk by relaxing its underwriting requirements. But there was no evidence to confirm these suspicions. Maybe because Freddie Mac's share price had already risen 182 percent in 1991 (see Figure 7.12), investors thought there was no more upside price potential. Whatever the reasons, there is no escaping the fact that in 1992, Freddie Mac was undervalued.

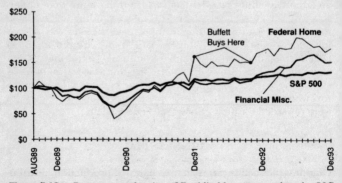

Figure 7.12. Common stock price of Freddie Mac compared to the S&P 500 and financial miscellaneous indexes (indexed to $100 at start date).

Even if we assumed that Freddie Mac would grow its earnings at only 4 percent per year, the average rise in the U.S. Gross Domestic Product, the value of Freddie Mac in 1992 was $11.1 billion.

Tenet: The One-Dollar Premise

In the four years between 1989 and 1992, Freddie Mac earned $2.028 billion. After distributing common and preferred dividends, the company retained $1.539 billion. During this time, the market value of the company increased from $4.033 billion to $8.723 billion. For every dollar the company retained, its market value increased by $3.04.

Summary

Freddie Mac has an unusual history. Its quasigovernment status confused many investors. The conversion from a closely held preferred stock owned only by savings and loans to a publicly held corporation was perplexing. For a short time, some mistakenly thought that Federal Home Loan Mortgage and the Federal Savings and Loan Insurance Corporation (FSLIC) were destined for the same fate. Buffett saw through the confusion. No doubt Wesco's ownership of Freddie Mac in the earliest years gave him an advantage. But that advantage was nothing more than understanding what was taking place. This understanding was available to anyone who took the time to investigate the business. "Great investment opportunities," Buffett said, "come around when excellent companies are surrounded by unusual circumstances that cause the stock to be misappraised."[8] Freddie Mac was an unusual stock. The stock market misappraised the company. Those investors who investigated the company and understood its economics were rewarded for their efforts (see Figure 7.12).

GUINNESS PLC

Guinness plc (Guinness) is an international production, distribution, and marketing company of premium brand alcoholic beverages. Guinness is the fourth largest net exporter and eleventh largest company in the United Kingdom. By profitability, Guinness is the world's largest alcoholic beverage company. The company has two principal operating companies: United Distillers (spirits) and Guinness Brewing Worldwide (brewing).

United Distillers is the world leader in sales of Scotch whiskey. It produces the world's best-selling Scotch, Johnnie Walker, and also produces other popular Scotch brands including Bell's (the best-selling Scotch whiskey in the United Kingdom), Dewar's White Label (the best-selling Scotch whiskey in the United States, fifth in the world), and White Horse Fine Old (the best-selling Scotch whiskey in Japan, seventh largest in the world). Guinness also produces the world's leading gin, Gordon's Gin, selling more than 50 percent more volume than its nearest competitor. It also produces the popular U.S. imported gin, Tanqueray. By operating profits, Guinness/United Distillers earned, in 1992, £769 million compared to Grand Met, £509 million, Seagram, £470 million, and Allied Lyons, £409 million.

Guinness Brewing Worldwide is the seventh largest brewer in the world by volume and third largest by operating profit. The Guinness brands are brewed in 44 countries and sold in more than 130 countries. The company's premium brands include Guinness stout, the world's leading stout brand, accounting for 40 percent of the company's beer volume. Guinness also produces Harp Lager, Cruzcampo Lager, Smithwick's Ale, and Kaliber. The brewing company is organized into four operating regions: Ireland, Europe, Africa & Americas, and Asia-Pacific. Annual sales of Guinness plc in 1992 were £4.36 billion and operating profits were £795 million. Of operating profits, 15 percent come from the United Kingdom, 19 percent from the United States, 20 percent from Asia-Pacific, 29 percent from Europe, and 17 percent from the rest of the world.

Tenet: Simple and Understandable

Guinness plc is Berkshire's first significant investment in a foreign company. However, Guinness is very much the same type of company as Coca-Cola and Gillette, says Buffett, and his experience with those two companies made him very comfortable with Guinness. Both Coca-Cola and Gillette, although based in the

United States, earn the majority of their profits from international operations just as Guinness does. "Indeed," Buffett explains, "in the sense of where they earn their profits—continent by continent—Coca-Cola and Guinness display strong similarities."[9] However, Buffett is quick to point out, he will never get the drinks of these two companies confused. He remains a devout Cherry Coke fan.

Still, as an investor, the similarities between Coca-Cola and Guinness are striking. Both companies sell beverages. Coca-Cola sells the world's number one nonalcoholic beverage. Guinness sells the world's number one Scotch whiskey and gin alcoholic beverages. Both companies recognize that their home markets are mature and that the best chance for increasing earnings is investing in new and emerging countries. Lastly, both companies' beverages are esteemed brand names that are recognized worldwide. They are franchise products, so they have not only the potential for international unit volume growth but, because of pricing flexibility, the potential for above-average profitability.

Tenet: Favorable Long-Term Prospects

It is puzzling how the long-term prospects for liquor companies can be so favorable when people are drinking less. In the United States, consumption of spirits has been decreasing at an annual rate of 3 percent for much of the last decade. Worldwide consumption is declining as well. In 1991, the year that Berkshire first purchased Guinness, liquor sales dropped 1 percent in the free world to 525 million cases. However, "Consumption is not actually a very good indicator in any business of whether there are opportunities there," said Anthony Tennant, chief executive officer of Guinness, in 1991.[10]

The liquor industry accepts the fact that consumption is declining in mature markets like the United States, Britain, and Northern Europe. Knowing that their customers are drinking less, they try to persuade them to drink better and more expensive liquor. The process is called "trading up." The worldwide marketing message of the liquor industry is "drinking better is a part of living better." This message is sold universally to both mature industrialized markets as well as developing countries. The booming profits earned by spirits companies is the byproduct of sophisticated marketing meeting affluence in developing countries. As their standard of living increases, people in Thailand, Brazil, and Eastern Europe order Johnnie Walker, Chivas Regal, Gordon's Gin, and Courvoisier to signal their arrival to success. "Guinness has the remarkable ability to sell liquor as a status symbol," said Charlie Munger. "The higher the price, the greater the status."[11]

The only market where this strategy is weak is in the United States. The recession has forced consumers to consider "value" brands over the higher-priced premium brands. But industry specialists predict that this buying pattern will be short-lived. Unlike cigarettes, most liquor purchases are periodical. Consumers of spirits are not confronted with pricing pressures that daily cigarette purchases cause.

Liquor companies grasped three important concepts long before most other consumer products companies.[12] First, they understood that their global brands were highly profitable. Johnnie Walker contributes approximately $500 million a year to Guinness's operating profit. Name-brand products have a tendency to increase in value over time and new brands find it almost impossible to break through. The last hot new liquor brand to penetrate the spirits market was Bailey's Original Irish Cream in 1980.

The second concept grasped by liquor companies was the importance of controlling the pricing and distribution of their products in foreign markets. Companies soon learned they lost control of their valuable name-brand products when the bottles were exported and left sitting on the docks. As liquor companies acquired additional brands, they acquired the distribution companies as well. From 1986 through 1991, Guinness acquired and/or displaced 700 distributors worldwide.

Lastly, liquor companies were not shy about cooperating with their competitors. Lacking the financial muscle of a Coca-Cola and the distribution system and assets to penetrate a new market, liquor companies would form joint ventures. The partnership would then spread the fixed costs and later split the profits. Guinness has more than thirty-five joint ventures, including a venture with Bacardi, which sells Guinness products in South America. Most recently, Guinness has formed a 25 percent corporate partnership with LMVH Moet Hennessy. Although the partnership has struggled lately, LMVH has a stable of valuable, premium international brand products including Dom Perignon, Moet & Chandon, Veuve Clicquot, Pommery, Mercier, Canard-Duchene, Ruinart, and Hennessy and Hine Cognac.

Tenet: Profit Margins

The manufacture of beverage products, alcoholic or nonalcoholic, is a very profitable business. Guinness plc is not only the most profitable alcoholic beverage company in the world, it is the next most profitable beverage company in the world, second only to Coca-Cola. The company's pretax margins (see Figure 7.13) have risen steadily since Guinness acquired United Distillers in 1986. Before the acquisition, Guinness, then solely a brewery company, posted profit margins similar to the margins earned by Anheuser-Busch. When Guinness acquired United Distillers' high margin spirits business, pretax margins doubled.

Guinness has been responsible with its debt. After the 1986 United Distiller's acquisition, Guinness's long-term debt as a percent of capital was 48 percent. The company aggressively paid down this debt in the following years. By 1988, long-term debt as a per-

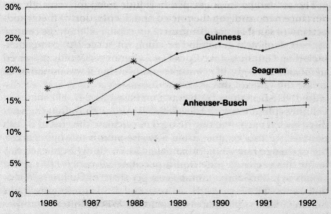

Figure 7.13. Pretax profit margins of Guinness plc, Seagram, and Anheuser-Busch.

cent of capital was 18 percent. The ratio rose to 29 percent in 1992 but is still comparatively lower than Seagram and Anheuser-Busch.

Not only has Guinness been able to keep its debt low, but it has continually grown its net income at a 20 percent plus annual rate over the last seven years. Since acquiring United Distillers, Guinness has consistently grown earnings better than its competitors. However, sales growth during this period has averaged less than 9 percent, indicating that much of the growth in income has been the result of rising margins. In 1992, profit growth, before restructuring changes, fell to a lowly 6 percent. The decline in income growth was due to the global recession, particularly the poor performance of Guinness's 25 percent stake in LMVH Moet Hennessy. Despite the recession, the company anticipated that it would be able to increase income in the following year by raising prices on its premium spirits.

Tenet: Determine the Value

One of the attractions of the beverage business, and it is true in the spirits and brewery business, is the relatively low need for capital expenditures and working capital compared to the cash flow generated by the business. There is little need for research and development, and production costs are comparatively low as a percent of sales. Hence, the returns on capital of beverage companies are high and generally are rising for successful companies, including Guinness. Like Coca-Cola, Guinness not only possessed significant amounts of economic goodwill, but it was poised to increase the value of this asset as well.

In 1991, Berkshire Hathaway purchased 31,247,000 shares of Guinness plc at a cost of $264,782,000. Although Buffett does not discuss what exchange rate he used to calculate the cost in British pounds, we can assume, using a twelve-month moving average, the exchange rate was approximately $1.76. Conversely, each dollar at this exchange rate would purchase 56 pence (100 pence equals £1). Berkshire's average cost per share of Guinness in U.S. dollars was $8.47, or £4.81. At year end 1991, there were 1.952 billion Guinness plc shares outstanding. When Buffett considers purchasing a stock, he thinks in terms of purchasing the entire company. Although he purchased only 1.6 percent of Guinness, theoretically he would have been willing to purchase the entire company at similar prices. In 1991, Buffett purchased Guinness plc at £4.81 per share. With 1.952 billion shares outstanding, Buffett's purchase was equivalent to purchasing the entire company for £9.389 billion.

In 1991, Guinness's net income was £636 million. The company had depreciation and amortization charges of £122 million and capital expenditures of £224 million. Owner earnings thus equalled £534 million. The average thirty-year U.S. government bond yield in 1991 was near 8.5 percent. We do know that Buffett's tendency is be cautious using current government bond yields as interest rates are declining. To remain conservative, a 9 percent discount rate will be used in this valuation. If we discount Guinness' owner earnings by 9 percent, the value of Guinness is £5.933 billion (£534 divided by 9 percent). But like Coca-Cola and Gillette, much of the value of Guinness is not the discounted value of its current earnings but the discounted value of its current earnings plus the growth of its future earnings.

After the acquisition of United Distillers in 1986, Guinness's earnings grew an average 25 percent annual rate. However, between 1990 and 1991, earnings slowed to a modest 13 percent annual rate and have since declined from this level. When Buffett made the decision to purchase Guinness in 1991, he knew that the earnings growth of the company was slowing from its 25 percent rate and would probably match a more realistic 10–15 percent rate in the future. Using the two-stage discount model, we can calculate the value of Guinness plc. If we assume that Guinness will grow for the next ten years at a slower 10 percent average annual rate followed by 5 percent growth thereafter, discounting the owner earnings of the company by 9 percent, the value of the company is £20.983 billion (see Table A.25 in the Appendix). At this assumed growth rate, Buffett purchased Guinness plc at a 56 percent discount to its value.

If we assume an even slower 5 percent growth rate for the company over the next several years, the value of Guinness plc in 1991 was £13.350 billion [£534 divided by (9% – 5%)]. At this below historical average growth rate, Buffett purchased Guinness plc at a 30 percent discount to its value.

Summary

Several years ago, Buffett admitted that he would have no interest in purchasing a foreign company because of the difficulties in behaving like an owner. Communications between companies and foreign shareholders are not as ideal as the link between companies domiciled in the same country as their owners. Nevertheless, he made the exception. Of course Buffett is comforted knowing that Guinness is in a business similar to Berkshire's largest holding, Coca-Cola. Understanding how Coca-Cola's business operates and how it profits in the world economy, Buffett more easily understands how Guinness will achieve its goals. He has also learned that companies with valuable franchises, such as Coca-Cola, Gillette, and Guinness, can afford to be loosely managed and still remain above-average investments. Hence the need to be an intimate shareholder in a company like Guinness was less important. Buffett is probably more confident being a foreign shareholder of this company than he would be owning many other foreign companies that lack Guinness's economic appeal.

WELLS FARGO & COMPANY

If General Dynamics was the most confusing investment Buffett ever made, then Wells Fargo & Company (Wells Fargo) would certainly qualify as the most controversial. In October 1990, Buffett announced that Berkshire had purchased 5 million shares of Wells Fargo, investing $289 million in the company at an average $57.88 per share (see Figure 7.14). Berkshire Hathaway was now the largest shareholder of the bank, owning 10 percent of the shares outstanding.

Earlier in the year, Wells Fargo had traded as high as $86 per share until investors began abandoning California banks and thrifts. They feared the recession that was gripping the West Coast would soon cause wide loan losses in the commercial and residential real estate market. Since Wells Fargo had the most commercial real estate of any California bank, investors sold their stock and short sellers added to the downside pressure. The short interest in Wells Fargo's stock jumped 77 percent in the month of Oc-

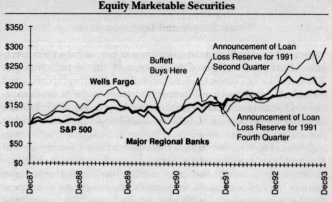

Figure 7.14. Common stock price of Wells Fargo compared to the S&P 500 and regional bank indexes (indexed to $100 at start date).

tober, about the same time that Buffett began purchasing shares in the company.

In the months following the announcement that Berkshire had become a major shareholder of the bank, the battle for Wells Fargo resembled a heavyweight fight. In one corner, Buffett was the bull, betting $289 million that Wells Fargo would increase in value. In the other corner, short sellers were the bears, betting that Wells Fargo, already down 49 percent for the year, was destined to fall further. The Feshbach brothers, the nation's biggest short sellers, were betting against Buffett. "Wells Fargo is a dead duck," said Tom Barton, a Dallas money manager for the Feshbach brothers. "I don't think it's right to call them a bankruptcy candidate but I think it's a teen-ager."[13] By that, Barton meant he thought that Wells Fargo would trade down into the teens. Buffett "is a famous bargain hunter and long-term investor," said George Salem, an analyst with Prudential Securities, but "California could become another Texas."[14] Salem was referring to the bank failures that had occurred in Texas during the decline in energy prices. Buffett "won't have to worry about who spends his fortune much longer," said John Liscio at Barron's, "not if he keeps trying to pick a bottom in bank stocks."[15]

Tenet: Simple and Understandable

Buffett is very familiar with the business of banking. In 1969, Berkshire Hathaway purchased 98 percent of the Illinois National Bank and Trust Company. Before the Bank Holding Act required Berkshire to divest its interest in the bank in 1979, Buffett reported the sales and earnings of the bank each year in Berkshire's annual reports. The bank took its place beside Berkshire's other controlled holdings.

Just as Jack Ringwalt helped Buffett understand the intricacy of the insurance business, Gene Abegg, who was chairman of Illinois National Bank, taught Buffett about the banking business. What Buffett learned was banks were profitable businesses if management issued loans responsibly and curtailed costs. "Our experience has been that the manager of an already high-cost operation frequently is uncommonly resourceful in finding new ways to add to overhead," said Buffett, "while the manager of a tightly-run operation usually continues to find additional methods to curtail costs, even when costs are already well below those of its competitors. No one has demonstrated this latter ability better than Gene Abegg."[16]

Tenet: Favorable Long-Term Prospects

Wells Fargo is not Coca-Cola, Buffett says. Under most any circumstances, it is hard to imagine how Coca-Cola could fail as a business. But the banking business is different. Banks can fail and have, on many occasions. Most bank closures can be traced to managerial mistakes, Buffett points out. In most cases, banks fail when management foolishly issues loans that a rational banker would never have considered. When assets are twenty times equity, which is common in the banking industry, any managerial foolishness involving even a small amount of assets can destroy a bank's equity.

Still, it is not impossible for banks to be good investments, Buffett says. If management does its job, banks can generate a 20 percent return on equity. Although this is below what a Coca-Cola or Gillette might earn, it is above the average return for most businesses. It is not necessary to be number one in your industry if you are a bank, Buffett explains. What counts is how you manage your assets, liabilities, and costs. Like the insurance business, banking is very much a commodity business. And as we know, in a commoditylike business, the actions of management are frequently the most distinguishing trait of that business. In this respect, Buffett picked the best management team in banking. "With Wells Fargo," he states, "we think we have obtained the best managers in the business, Carl Reichardt and Paul Hazen. In many ways, the combination of Carl and Paul reminds me of another—Tom Murphy and Dan Burke at Capital Cities/ABC. Each pair is stronger than the sum of its parts."[17]

Tenet: Rationality

When Carl Reichardt became chairman of Wells Fargo in 1983, he began to transform the sluggish bank into a profitable business. From 1983 through 1990, Wells Fargo averaged returns of 1.3 percent on assets and 15.2 percent on equity. By 1990, Wells Fargo had become the tenth largest bank in the country with $56 billion in assets. Reichardt, like many managers that Buffett admires, is rational. Although Reichardt has not yet instigated stock buy-back programs or passed along special dividends, all of which reward shareholders, he does run Wells Fargo for the benefit of its owners. Like Tom Murphy at Capital Cities/ABC, he is legendary when it comes to controlling costs. Once costs were under control, Reichardt never let up. He constantly searches for ways to improve Wells Fargo's profitability.

When measuring a bank's operating efficiency, an analyst can compare the company's noninterest expense as a percent of net interest income.[18] This ratio measures the operating expenses of the bank to its net-interest income. Wells Fargo's operating efficiencies are 20–30 percent better than First Interstate or Bank of America (see Figure 7.15). Reichardt manages Wells Fargo as other entrepreneurs would manage their operations. "We try to run this company like a business," said Reichardt. "Two and two is four. It's not seven or eight."[19]

When Buffett was buying Wells Fargo in 1990, the bank ended that year with the highest percentage of commercial real estate loans of any major bank in the country. Wells Fargo's $14.5 billion in commercial loans was five times its equity. Because California's

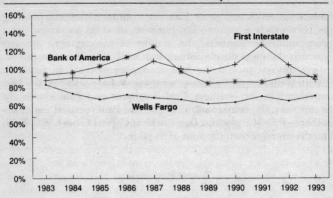

Figure 7.15. Noninterest expense as a percentage of net interest income for Bank of America, First Interstate, and Wells Fargo.

recession was worsening, analysts figured that a large portion of the bank's commercial loans would sour. It was this reason that caused Wells Fargo's share price to decline in 1990 and 1991.

In the wake of the FSLIC debacle, bank examiners rigorously reviewed Wells Fargo's loan portfolio. They pressured the bank to set aside $1.3 billion in reserves for bad loans in 1991 and another $1.2 billion the following year. Because reserves were set aside every quarter, investors began to feel squeamish with each subsequent announcement. Instead of taking one large charge for loan loss reserves, the bank strung out the charges over a period of two years. Investors began to wonder whether the bank would ever reach the end of its problem loans.

After Berkshire announced its ownership of Wells Fargo in 1990, the stock price climbed briefly. In early 1991, the share price reached $98, providing Berkshire with a $200 million profit. But then, in June 1991, the bank announced another charge to reserves and the stock price fell thirteen points in two days to $74. Although the stock price recovered slightly in the fourth quarter of 1991, it became clear that Wells Fargo would have to take yet another charge against earnings for additions to its loan loss reserves. At year end 1991, Wells Fargo's stock price closed at $58 per share. After a roller coaster ride, Berkshire's investment in

Wells Fargo was break-even. "I underestimated the severity of both the California recession and the real estate troubles of the company," Buffett confessed.[20]

Tenet: Determine the Value

In 1990, Wells Fargo earned $711 million, an 18 percent increase over 1989. In 1991, because of loan loss reserves, Wells Fargo earned $21 million. In 1992, earnings increased slightly to $283 million but still were less than half what the company earned two years earlier. Not surprisingly, there is an inverse relationship between a bank's earnings and its loan loss provisions (see Figure 7.16). But if you remove Wells Fargo's loan loss provisions from the company's income statement, you uncover a company with dynamic earnings power (see Figure 7.17). Since 1983, the bank's net interest income has grown at an 11.3 percent rate, and its noninterest income (investment fees, trust income, deposit charges) has grown at a 15.3 percent rate. If you exclude the unusual loan loss provisions in 1991 and 1992, the bank would have had approximately $1 billion in earnings power.

The value of a bank is the function of its net worth plus its projected earnings as a going concern. When Berkshire Hathaway

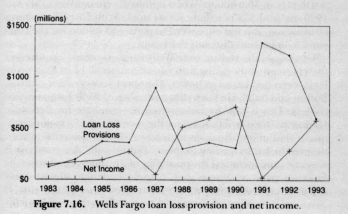

Figure 7.16.   Wells Fargo loan loss provision and net income.

215

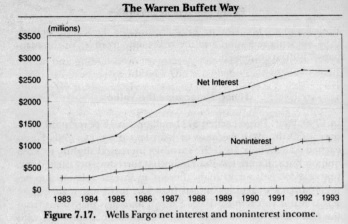

Figure 7.17. Wells Fargo net interest and noninterest income.

began purchasing Wells Fargo in 1990, the company, in the previous year, had earned $600 million. The average yield on the thirty-year U.S. government bond in 1990 was approximately 8.5 percent. To remain conservative, we can discount Wells Fargo's 1989 earnings of $600 million by 9 percent and value the bank at $6.6 billion. If the bank never earned another dime over $600 million in annual earnings during the next thirty years, it was worth at least $6.6 billion. When Buffett purchased Wells Fargo in 1990, he paid $58 per share for its stock. With 52 million shares outstanding, this was equivalent to paying $3 billion for the company, a 55 percent discount to its value.

Of course, the debate over Wells Fargo centered on whether the company, after taking into consideration all of its loan problems, even had earnings power. The short sellers said it did not; Buffett said it did. He knew that ownership of Wells Fargo was not riskless. This is how he rationalized his purchase for Berkshire Hathaway. "California banks face the specific risk of a major earthquake that might wreak enough havoc on borrowers to in turn destroy the banks lending to them," Buffett said. "A second risk is systemic [and includes] the possibility of a business contraction or financial panic so severe that it would endanger almost every highly-leveraged institution, no matter how intelligently run."[21] Now the possibility of these two events occurring, in Buffett's judgment, was low. But there still remained one viable risk, he said. "The market's major fear," he explained, "is that West Coast real estate values will tumble because of overbuilding and deliver huge losses to banks that have financed the expansion. Because it is a leading real estate lender, Wells Fargo is thought to be particularly vulnerable."[22]

Buffett knew that Wells Fargo earned $1 billion pretax annually after expensing an average $300 million for loan losses. He figured if 10 percent of the bank's $48 billion in loans, not just commercial real estate loans but all of the bank's loans, were problem loans in 1991 and produced losses, including interest, averaging 30 percent of the principal value of the loan, Wells Fargo would break even. In his judgment, the possibility of this occurring was low. Even if Wells Fargo earned no money for a year, the thought would not be distressing. "At Berkshire," Buffett said, "we love to acquire businesses or invest in capital projects that produced no return for a year, but that could be then expected to earn 20 percent on growing equity."[23] The attraction of Wells Fargo intensified when Buffett was able to purchase shares at a 50 percent discount to its value.

"Banking doesn't have to be a bad business, but it often is," Buffett said, adding that "bankers don't have to do stupid things, but they often do."[24] Buffett describes a high risk loan as any loan made by a stupid banker. When Buffett purchased Wells Fargo, he bet that Reichardt was not a stupid banker. "It's all a bet on management," said Charlie Munger. "We think they will fix problems faster and better than other people."[25] Berkshire's bet has paid off. By the end of 1993, Wells Fargo's price per share reached $137.

While regulators forced Reichardt to stockpile more than $2 billion in reserves for bad loans, it now appears that the bank is over-reserved by $1 billion. They call it the revenge of Carl Reichardt. "There is no bank where regulators missed the boat more than Wells Fargo," said Thomas Brown, an analyst with Donaldson, Lufkin & Jenrette.[26] With this excess equity ($19 per share) in the form of unnecessary loan loss provisions, Wells Fargo has the option to buy back shares and/or dramatically raise the dividend.

Summary

Warren Buffett's confidence in Wells Fargo continues to grow. In 1992, Berkshire purchased more shares of the bank, raising its holdings to 6.3 million shares, representing 11.5 percent of the bank. He asked and received clearance from the Federal Reserve to buy up to 22 percent of the bank. In November 1993, Berkshire added shares of Wells Fargo to its position at prices between $106 and $110 per share. "I don't want to start touting Wells Fargo's stock or anything," Buffett said. "I just think it is a very good business, with the best management, at a reasonable price. And usually when that is the case, there is more money to be made."[27]

EIGHT

A Few More Good Stocks

DESPITE THE DISMAL RETURNS in the stock market, 1994 was a relatively busy year for Buffett. In fact, when markets appear uninspiring is precisely the time when Buffett's interest begins to focus. Berkshire Hathaway made four distinct and significant purchases in the second half of the year. Buffett, with his continued appreciation of the economics surrounding the media and publishing industry, purchased 4.9 percent of Gannett, the nation's largest newspaper publisher. He also purchased 8.3 percent of PNC Bank, a major regional bank headquartered in Pittsburgh.

In a more surprising move, Buffett added 6.6 million common shares of Salomon to Berkshire's already substantial $700 million convertible preferred investment in that company. Finally, during the summer of 1994, Berkshire converted its American Express preferred shares into common. Buffett then continued to purchase shares of American Express throughout the remainder of the year and well into the first quarter of 1995. In total, Buffett invested $1.36 billion in the company. It was Berkshire's first billion-dollar investment since Buffett's purchases of Coca-Cola in 1988 and 1989.

The Walt Disney Company's acquisition of Capital Cities/ABC created a wonderful opportunity for Warren Buffett. Berkshire's 20 million shares of Cap Cities, with a cost basis of $17.25 per share, are worth more than $120 per share. Although the terms of the acquisition allow holders of Cap Cities to receive more shares of Disney or more cash, depending on availability, Berkshire stands to gain at least $65 per share and one share of Disney for every share of Cap Cities it owns. Buffett now has become the second largest shareholder of The Walt Disney Company with $1.3 billion in additional cash.

GANNETT COMPANY *

Gannett Company is a $7.7 billion diversified news and media company. Its businesses include newspaper publishing, broadcasting stations, and outdoor advertising. Gannett is the country's largest newspaper group with eighty-two daily newspapers, fifty nondaily publications, and the popular *USA Today* and *USA Weekend*. The *USA Today* publication is quickly becoming our nation's daily newspaper. In 1994, total average paid daily circulation for Gannett newspapers exceeded 6.3 million copies.

Gannett owns and operates ten television stations in Phoenix, Denver, Washington, D.C., Atlanta, Jacksonville, and other cities. The company also operates six FM and five AM radio stations in Los Angeles, San Diego, Tampa–St. Petersburg, Chicago, Dallas, and Houston. In addition, Gannett is the largest outdoor advertising group in North America, with operations in eleven states and Canada.

Tenet: Simple and Understandable

Newspapers and television stations are businesses that Buffett easily understands. He has owned The Washington Post Company

---

*Robert G. Hagstrom, Jr., is the portfolio manager of the Focus Trust. This mutual fund owns shares of common stock in Gannett Company. Furthermore, the Focus Trust may, from time to time, purchase additional shares of the company.

and Buffalo News for more than twenty years, and Capital Cities/ ABC since 1985. That experience not only heightens his qualifications as a knowledgeable owner of Gannett, but also neatly falls within his circle of competence.

Tenet: Favorable Long-Term Prospects

From 1973 through 1987, newspapers and television stations enjoyed an exceptionally prosperous period. Newspapers, grasping that they were a primary source for both local and national advertising, leveraged this advantage by regularly increasing lineage rates. When the economy slowed, ultimately affecting circulation and revenues from classified advertising, newspapers could count on a slight increase in advertising lineage rates to help manage earnings growth. During this period, television stations were also the beneficiaries of limited competition. Although the audience base for cable television continued to expand, network television was still the way to reach the majority of television viewers.

Then, in the late 1980s, the picture began to change. Companies were noticeably shrinking their advertising budgets because of the slowing economy. In addition, companies also began experimenting with putting their ad dollars into other media. Direct mail, inserts, and target marketing began diverting dollars away from traditional newspaper advertising, and cable advertising had the same effect on television broadcasters.

At first, analysts and media companies were not sure how to attribute the shifts. Was it a result of a contracting economy, or was this a more permanent shift in advertising dollars signaling that advertisers had found more cost-effective ways to reach consumers? In either case, newspaper and broadcast companies, realizing they no longer dominated their markets, had no choice but to moderate their rate increases and begin to compete more vigorously for advertising dollars.

Competition inevitably puts pressure on returns and profitability. Newspapers were not excluded from this pressure. Mr. Market, as so often happens, vacillated between euphoria and despair. Not surprisingly, as newspapers and media companies began to report lower relative returns, Mr. Market's enthusiasm began to deflate and the prices of these businesses summarily declined. But just as

Mr. Market has a tendency to overact on the upside, so too does he overact on the downside.

Tenet: Return on Equity

Although the profitability of newspaper companies had diminished, the attractiveness of these businesses was not as bad as stock prices indicated. True, returns on equity for the newspaper industry as a whole were generally higher in the mid-1980s, averaging close to 19 percent, and began to decline during the 1990s (see Figure 8.1). However, even then the returns on equity for the industry were still superior to the economic returns of most other businesses, averaging 13 percent compared to 10 percent. Gannett's return on equity, like its peer group, did decline. However, unlike its peer group, the company quickly regrouped and by 1993 increased its return on equity to record levels of 23 percent.

Tenet: Profit Margins

One reason Gannett has enjoyed a return to higher profitability has been management's tenacious attack on costs in both good

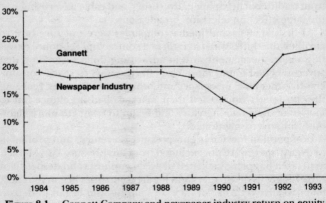

Figure 8.1. Gannett Company and newspaper industry return on equity.

times and in bad. Jack Curley, chairman and chief executive of Gannett, began slashing corporate expenses soon after he took control in 1986. During the late 1980s, Gannett's corporate expenses as a percentage of total sales were close to 2.3 percent. By 1993, that figured had declined to 1.8 percent. Management's attention to financial controls can easily be seen when comparing Gannett's profit margin with the newspaper industry (see Figure 8.2). Today, Gannett enjoys 11 percent profit margins, four percentage points higher than the industry average.

Tenet: Rationality

Much of Gannett's recent success can be attributed to Curley. His predecessor, Al Neuharth, had been responsible for Gannett's expansion. Neuharth unabashedly used Gannett's equity as a means to acquire other newspapers. Indeed, Gannett's average shares outstanding from 1974 through 1987 ballooned from 94 million shares to 162 million shares. Since assuming the chief executive duties in 1986, Curley has demonstrated more sensitivity, focusing on shareholder returns rather than expansion. In 1994, Gannett invested $399 million in itself, buying back eight million shares of stock at an

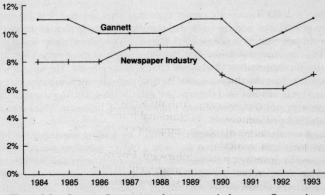

Figure 8.2. Gannett Company and newspaper industry profit margins.

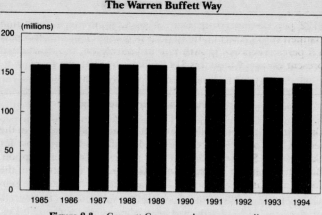

Figure 8.3. Gannett Company shares outstanding.

average price of $50 per share (see Figure 8.3). "Compared to the asking prices for other media companies," said Curley, "we believe our own shares represent compelling value."[1]

Tenet: Determine the Value

Since 1985, Gannett's owner earnings (net income less capital expenditures adding back depreciation) have grown at 12 percent per year. At year end 1993, Gannett's owner earnings stood at $474 million. We know that Buffett discounts owner earnings at the then prevailing thirty-year U.S. Treasury bond. He will, however, adjust the discount rate during periods when interest rates are cyclically low, and this was the case in 1994. During the fourth quarter of 1994, long bond rates hovered between 7.5 percent and 8.0 percent.

If we discount the owner earnings by a more conservative 10 percent and assume that Gannett's owner earnings would continue to grow by 12 percent for the next ten years followed by a slower 5 percent thereafter, the discounted present value of Gannett's future owner earnings is approximately $17 billion, or

$122 per Gannett share (see Table A.26). If we assume that Gannett could grow at only 10 percent going forward followed by a 5 percent residual growth rate in year eleven, the discounted present value of Gannett is $14.6 billion, or $104 per share.

Tenet: Buy at an Attractive Price

Gannett's stock price traded between $45 and $50 per share in the second half of 1994 (see Figure 8.4) Buffett's average cost for Gannett was $48 per share. At a 12 percent growth assumption, Buffett purchased Gannett at a 60 percent discount to the company's intrinsic value. At a 10 percent growth rate, the pur-

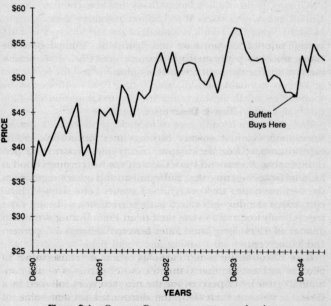

Figure 8.4. Gannett Company common stock price.

chase was a 54 percent discount to its intrinsic value. In either case, the margin of safety was present.

Gannett is a classic Buffett investment. He bought an easily understandable business with favorable underlying economics, managed by responsible and rational managers. And he purchased shares at sensible prices. While others dumped their investments in newspaper companies sensing the business economics were heading nowhere but down, Buffett set about to calculate what Gannett was worth despite its more economically competitive position. Mr. Market's emotional pendulum had swung too far, and once again Buffett picked up another jewel.

PNC BANK CORPORATION

PNC Bank is the twelfth largest bank holding company in the United States, with assets of $64 billion and shareholder's equity of $4.4 billion. PNC Bank is a result of the 1983 merger of Pittsburgh National Corporation and Provident National Bank located in Philadelphia. Since the merger, PNC has steadily increased its banking presence by acquisitions and the formation of various nonbank subsidiaries. Today, PNC's offices can be found as far north as Massachusetts, west to Ohio, south to Kentucky, and east to New Jersey.

PNC delivers a broad range of financial products and services to customers via four separate business lines. Retail banking provides customary lending, deposit, and payment system access to individuals and small businesses. Corporate banking provides traditional financing, treasury management, and other financial services to businesses and government bodies. The bank's typical corporate customer specializes in industries such as health care, natural resources, real estate, and telecommunications, and has annual sales anywhere from $5 million to $250 million or more. Combined, corporate banking and retail banking provide the bulk of PNC's business earnings: 70 percent of total earnings in 1993, more than 90 percent in 1994.

PNC's third business is investment management and trust (IM&T), which provides investment advice, asset management, and administrative and custodial services to individuals, institutions, and mutual funds. PNC's IM&T division is one of the largest providers of bank-sponsored investment research in the country, and its research is sold to more than 245 other financial institutions. PNC is the second largest bank manager of mutual funds, the ninth largest U.S. bank investment manager, and the thirty-second largest manager among all investment managers. Assets under management continue to grow. In the first quarter of 1995, PNC completed the acquisition of BlackRock Financial Management L.P., a New York investment management firm with more than $24 billion in assets under management.

Recently, analysts, who study the banking industry, have begun to focus on a bank's fee-based business. Fee business is a more predictable source of earnings and typically helps smooth the irregular earnings that come from a bank's loan portfolio. Despite PNC's attractive IM&T division, this business segment provided only 7 percent of the bank's earnings in 1993 and 9 percent in 1994.

Investment banking, PNC's fourth business, provides asset/liability management functions for the bank, which includes the management of the bank's security positions. Investment banking also provides brokerage services for more than 200 licensed brokers, venture capital investments, and corporate and public finance. PNC's investment banking is one of the largest bank underwriters of revenue bonds for the health-care industry, colleges, and universities. It was the investment bank's stumble in 1994 that ultimately caught Buffett's eye.

PNC, relative to other banks, has always had a large securities portfolio. The reason for this can be found in Pittsburgh's cyclical steel industry. The bank, to offset the inevitable effects of a slowing economy, traditionally relied on its securities portfolio when loan demand faltered. Today, despite Pittsburgh's more diversified economy and its lessening dependence on the steel industry, PNC continues to have a significant securities portfolio. In 1994, the bank's securities portfolio represented 39 percent of PNC's assets and loans were 59 percent of its assets. These figures are in marked contrast to PNC's regional peer group, which averages 20 percent and 75 percent, respectively.

A large securities portfolio is not necessarily bad. In fact, when responsible bankers are able to match assets and liabilities, the results can be profitable. In a large bond portfolio, however, risk is always present because of interest rate changes. When interest rates change, a bank's assets and liabilities can easily become "mismatched."

By 1994, PNC found itself in this delicate position. The bank had purposely mismatched assets and liabilities in order to benefit from falling interest rates. Indeed, this strategy worked splendidly for the prior three years. But in 1994, interest rates began to rise. Despite economists' predictions, the Federal Reserve increased rates seven times during the year, and the bond market witnessed its worst performance since the Depression. The relative losses in the bond market eclipsed even the 1987 stock market sell-off. PNC's investment banking division reported a $136 million loss for the year.

When interest rates rise, financial stocks, banks in particular, fall in price. After outpacing the Standard & Poor's 500 Index from 1991 through 1993, major regional banks began a steep decline in 1994 (see Figure 8.5) More disheartening for PNC shareholders, PNC stock relative to their industry group fell even further. In fact, PNC was one of the worst performing bank stocks in 1994, down almost 30 percent compared to the average bank stock that lost about 4 percent.

Despite the earnings shortfall attributed to the rise in interest rates, PNC has always been a well-managed bank. Management separates the financial results of each division (corporate banking, retail banking, investment management and trust, and investment banking) and reports to shareholders as if each segment were operated as a stand-alone business. Each division reports after-tax profit margins, expressed as earnings as a percentage of revenues, as well as overhead ratios that are the percentage of noninterest expenses to revenues. In addition, capital is assigned to each business unit based on management's own assessment of risk.

The corporate banking and retail banking divisions, during 1993 and 1994, earned 18 percent and 20 percent return on equity. Investment management and trust generates returns on equity greater than 40 percent, while investment banking has the potential for even higher returns. After-tax profit margins for retail banking and IM&T are a respectable 20 percent. Corporate banking and investment banking, because they are not retail oriented require fewer employees, bricks, and mortar; thus they generate after-tax profit margins between 40 percent and 50 percent.

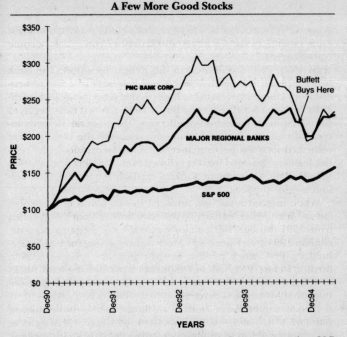

Figure 8.5. Common stock price of PNC Bank Corp. compared to S&P 500 and major regional bank indexes (indexed to $100 at start date).

These consistently high profitability returns can easily be appreciated when we observe the growth of PNC's net interest income and noninterest income (see Figure 8.6). In 1984, net interest income was $400 million. By 1993, it had grown to $1.9 billion, a growth rate of 19 percent. Noninterest income had grown at a 16 percent rate during this period, rising from $200 million to $822 million.

Tenet: Determine the Value

In 1993, PNC earned $610 million, down from $745 million the year before. During the fourth quarter of 1994, Buffett began

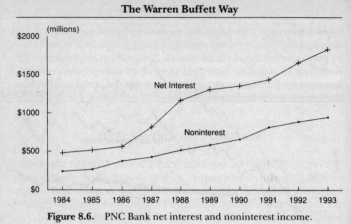

Figure 8.6. PNC Bank net interest and noninterest income.

acquiring shares in PNC at an average price of $25.85 per share (see Figure 8.5). At that price, the market value of PNC with 235 million shares outstanding was approximately $6.1 billion. If we merely discounted PNC's 1993 earnings of $610 million by 10 percent, which, although higher than the thirty-year U.S. Treasury bond yield, is nonetheless a conservative rate, the bank, if it never earned a dime more than $610 million annually over the next decade, would have been worth $6.1 billion. But, given the quality of the bank, the attention of management, and the potential growth of the bank's net interest income and noninterest income, it is likely that PNC, going forward, will earn more than $610 million annually. As such, a margin of safety existed between the market price of PNC and its calculated intrinsic value.

Over the years, Buffett has mastered the ability to ignore macro events that he believes are having a temporary effect on a company. He overcame the pessimism surrounding Wells Fargo and has seen Berkshire's investment in that bank triple. PNC is not Wells Fargo nor is it facing anywhere near the financial dilemma that confronted Carl Reichardt and Paul Hazen. Buffett has simply made a bet that the negative impact to PNC of rising interest rates is temporary. Because other investors bailed out of the stock thus forcing the price to unreasonably low levels, Buffett was able to pick up shares at bargain prices. "Indeed" writes Buffett, "we have usually made our best purchases when apprehensions about some macro event were at a peak. Fear is the foe of the faddist, but the friend of the fundamentalist."[2]

SALOMON INCORPORATED

"Frustrating." It is the word that easily comes to mind when you analyze Berkshire's investment in Salomon. Buffett has invested considerable time, energy, and money in this company and yet, on the surface at least, the results thus far have been less than gratifying. But frustration is not synonymous with failure.

Failure implies that you lost; that you were unable to achieve your desired return. Berkshire's investment in USAir is a failure; a mistake that even Buffett admits to shareholders in Berkshire's 1994 annual report. USAir suspended the payment of its preferred dividend to Berkshire. The company's stock price, once $50, has declined to single digits, and Buffett has written-down his investment to twenty-five cents on the dollar.

Salomon, on the other hand, has not suspended the payment of its 9 percent preferred dividend to Berkshire Hathaway. Each year, since 1987, Salomon has dutifully sent $63 million to Berkshire in return for its $700 million investment. Although Salomon's stock price did not outperform its peer group during the early 1990s (see Figure 8.7), neither has it reached such depressed levels that one might question the company's viability.

Also, it is worth noting that Berkshire's total return from its investment in Salomon includes the preferred dividend income and the option to convert to common shares at $38. Although there is, at this time, little profitability in converting preferred shares into common, the income picture is positive. Since corporations are able to exclude from taxes 70 percent of the dividend income they receive from other corporations, Berkshire's net after-tax return from Salomon's preferred shares is close to 8.1 percent, substantially better than U.S. Treasuries and other corporate securities of similar maturity and credit ratings.

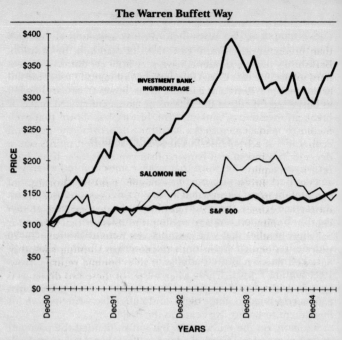

Figure 8.7. Common stock price of Salomon Inc. compared to S&P 500 and investment banking/brokerage indexes (indexed to $100 at start date).

Tenet: Favorable Long-Term Prospects

Investment banking firms are not airlines but neither are they beverage companies. That is to say, Salomon as a business has certain economics that are more favorable than USAir's. But make no mistake, investment banking does not, nor will it, have long-term economics that match Coca-Cola's economics.

Buffett, as far back as 1987, admitted the investment banking business, in general, lacked the basic investment tenets found in Berkshire's other core investments. Trying to predict the future cash flows of stable businesses such as Coca-Cola, Gillette, Capital

Cities/ABC, and The Washington Post Company is far simpler than predicting the future cash flows of Salomon. In addition, Berkshire's core investments have very little economic risk. It is hard to imagine that Coca-Cola or The Washington Post could fail as businesses. Investment banking firms, however, can and do fail as businesses. Whereas the actions of management can make or break an investment banking firm, history has shown that even mediocre management has a hard time destroying the powerful economics of a franchise business. Still, as Buffett points out, a decently run investment banking firm can earn, over time, high returns on equity.

Salomon Brothers, the investment banking portion of Salomon, is in two distinct businesses. The customer-driven institutional investment banking has the potential to earn 12–15 percent on equity. Proprietary trading, the division that trades for Salomon Brother's own account, has the potential to earn 15–20 percent on equity. When both divisions are running smoothly, Salomon has produced above average economic returns. However, as Buffett has learned, when either of these two divisions is not producing up to its potential, Salomon's economic returns can be shocking.

Tenet: Rationality

As an industry, Wall Street is not known for rationality. Indeed, many have questioned Buffett's strategy of investing in an industry that so often demonstrates irrationality. Salomon in particular has for years acted with little regard for its shareholders and seemed to lack any sense of rational behavior. Even despite the introduction of outside shareholders, Salomon has always acted more like a private partnership than a public company.

Consider, for example, the compensation system. With most private partnerships, it is the net profits of the business that are paid to its partners. The greater the profits, the greater the dollars paid to the partners. When Salomon became a public company, the outside shareholders (the owners of the company) expected, quite naturally, that in exchange for their capital, they would receive a profit on their investment. Salomon has demonstrated its ability to generate substantial profits from its business. However, the former partners, now employees, continued to expect that the lion's share of Salomon's gross profits would come to them.

When Buffett became an owner of Salomon, not surprisingly, he became very interested in the company's method of allocating capital. What he found out, to his dismay, was Salomon had an imbedded method of giving huge bonuses and salaries to an ever increasing number of managing directors despite the mediocre net returns then available to shareholders.

It was not until Buffett installed Robert Denham and Deryck Maughan as chairman and chief executive of Salomon that he was able to advance a compensation system based on rationality. The idea was to pay individual directors according to their contribution after shareholders achieved a reasonable return on their investment. For the first time, employees of Salomon were compensated on their ability to generate respectable returns for the owners first.

Such a system seemed quite rational to Buffett, who for years, has set hurdle rates for Berkshire's businesses. But of course, Wall Street is not Main Street. What has worked so well for Buffett and Berkshire for decades has worked poorly at Salomon. Ever since the new compensation system was introduced, employees of Salomon have become bitter and disenchanted. Many managing directors have quit.

This seemingly endless turmoil over employee compensation has created a wave of doubters who regard Salomon's future with suspicion. But Buffett holds fast. He has neither succumbed to nor inflamed the controversy that surrounds Salomon. What he has done is add 6.6 million shares of common stock to his convertible preferred investment, giving Berkshire slightly more than 20 percent of the voting power of Salomon.

Tenet: Buy at Attractive Prices

Berkshire bought 6.6 million common shares at approximately $49 per share (see Figure 8.8). There are 105 million shares of Salomon outstanding. Thus, at the time Buffett was purchasing Salomon, the market value of the company was $5.1 billion. For a

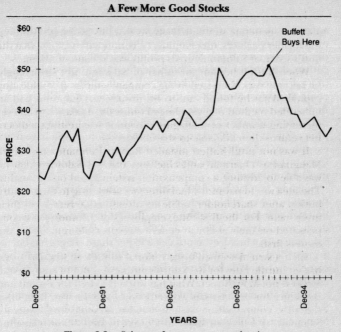

Figure 8.8. Salomon Inc. common stock price.

company to be worth $5.1 billion discounted at 10 percent, which is a higher interest rate than what was then the current yield of a thirty-year U.S. Treasury bond, it would need to earn at least $510 million annually. Since 1984, Salomon has earned an average $380 million annually, including its record $864 million gain in 1993 followed by its record $399 million loss in 1994. If Salomon could grow its $380 million base by 5 percent annually, the company would be worth $7.9 billion. However, even such a conservative growth rate of 5 percent can be difficult for Salomon to achieve because its business is so unpredictable.

Still, the idea that Salomon's earnings would lend itself to such predictability is suspect. In many ways, the business of Salomon is similar to another Berkshire's business: writing catastrophe insurance. In any one year, the damage from a hurricane could wipe out Berkshire's premium income for the year and force Buffett to dip into reserves to pay out several million dollars in claims. Of course, there is also the possibility that no catastrophes will occur in a particular year and Berkshire will book all the premium income as profits. Most likely, the average experience will be that Berkshire from time to time will pay out some modest losses and net some modest profits. It is as difficult to predict when catastrophes occur as it is difficult to predict when Salomon will have that exceptionally profitable or disastrous year. What you come to learn is that over a longer time horizon, risk is reduced and earnings begin to smooth.

Starting in October 1995, Salomon must begin to redeem Berkshire's convertible preferred investment at a rate of $140 million per year for the next five years. Buffett has the option to redeem for cash or convert into 3.68 million common shares of Salomon with a break-even price of $38 per share. There has been a great deal of speculation over what Buffett's strategy will be come October. Will Buffett convert for cash, for stock, or some combination thereof?

One of the more insightful analyses of Buffett's investment in Salomon comes from Robert Coleman, at Combined Capital Management. Coleman figures that even if Buffett converts the entire preferred issue into common stock, he will have earned a decent return from his investment in Salomon and furthermore positioned Berkshire fortuitously. The way Coleman figures it, Berkshire's $1 billion investment in Salomon thus far has netted $504 million in dividend income. After dividends, Buffett's net cash investment stands at approximately $500 million. Coleman figures Berkshire's investment is worth more than $700 million considering Berkshire owns 20 percent of a company with a stated book value of $3.5 billion that has the potential to earn above-average returns on equity.

Salomon has endured and overcome incredible challenges since the mid-1980s: an attempted takeover of the company by Ron Perelman, the 1987 Stock Market Crash, the Treasury Bond Scandal, 1994 Bond Market Crash, and now a controversial compensation program. Considering its responses to those challenges, it is hard to define Salomon as a failure. Granted, Salomon has not produced the gratification apparent in so many other Berkshire stocks. But as Buffett likes to remind Berkshire's shareholders, "There is more than one way to get to heaven." Salomon may yet prove to be that investment which ultimately found its own distinct path to profitability.

AMERICAN EXPRESS COMPANY*

"I find that a long-term familiarity with a company and its products is often helpful in evaluating it," confesses Buffett.[3] With the exception of Coca-Cola, GEICO, and The Washington Post Company, Buffett has had a longer history with American Express than with any other company Berkshire owns. In the mid-1960s, the Buffett Limited Partnership invested 40 percent of its assets in American Express shortly after the company's salad oil scandal. At the time, American Express had issued warehouse receipts certifying the existence of a huge batch of salad oil. In fact, the salad oil never existed and American Express soon found itself liable for millions of dollars in claims. The stock price soon dropped to half, at which time Buffett purchased 5 percent of the company for $13 million. In the intervening thirty years, Berkshire has accumulated 10 percent of the shares of American Express at a cost of $1.4 billion.

Tenet: Consistent Operating History

Although the company has weathered a cycle of changes, American Express is essentially in the same business it was when Buffett first purchased the company three decades ago. There are three divisions. Travel Related Services (TRS), which issues the American Express charge card and American Express Travelers Cheques, contributes 72 percent of American Express's sales. American Express Financial Advisors (formerly IDS Financial Services), a finan-

---

*Robert G. Hagstrom, Jr., is the portfolio manager of the Focus Trust. This mutual fund owns shares of common stock in American Express Company. Furthermore, the Focus Trust may, from time to time, purchase additional shares of the company.

cial planning, insurance, and investment product division contributes 22 percent of sales. American Express Financial Advisors has more than 3,600 financial advisors responsible for $106 billion in assets, making this division one of the largest money managers in the country. American Express Bank contributes a modest 5 percent of sales for the company, but the bank has long been the local representative for the American Express card with a network of eighty-seven offices in thirty-seven countries worldwide.

American Express Travel Related Services continues to be a predictable provider of profits. The division has always generated substantial owner earnings and easily has funded its own growth. But when a company generates more cash than it requires for operations, it often becomes a test of management to responsibly allocate this capital. Some managers pass this test by investing only that capital which is required and returning the balance to the company's owners either by increasing the dividend or by repurchasing shares. Other managers, unable to resist the institutional imperative, constantly find ways to spend cash and expand the corporate empire. Unfortunately, this was the fate of American Express for several years under the leadership of James Robinson.

Robinson's plan was to use TRS's excess cash to acquire related businesses and thus build American Express into a financial services powerhouse. IDS proved to be a profitable purchase. Shearson-Lehman, however, was a disappointment. Not only was Shearson unable to fund itself, it required increasing amounts of TRS's excess cash for its own operation. Over time, Robinson invested $4 billion in Shearson. It was this financial drain that prompted Robinson to contact Buffett. Berkshire purchased $300 million in preferred shares. Although Buffett was willing to invest in American Express at that time via preferred shares, it was not until rationality finally surfaced at the company that he felt confident to become a common shareholder.

Tenet: Rationality

It is no secret that the company's crown jewel is the famed American Express Card. What seemed to be lacking at American Express was a management team that recognized and appreciated the economics of this business. Fortunately, this realization occurred in 1992, when Robinson unceremoniously resigned and Harvey Golub became chief executive. Golub, striking a familiar tone with Buffett, began to use terms such as "franchise" and "brand value" when he referred to the American Express Card. Golub's immediate task was to strengthen the brand awareness of TRS and shore up the capital structure at Shearson-Lehman to ready it for sale.

Over the next two years, Golub began the process of liquidating American Express's underperforming assets and restoring profitability and high returns on equity for the company. In 1992, Golub initiated a public offering for First Data Corporation (the company's information data service division), which netted American Express over $1 billion. The following year, the company sold The Boston Company, its money management division, to Mellon Bank for $1.5 billion. Soon after, Shearson-Lehman was separated into two businesses. Shearson's retail accounts were sold and Lehman Brothers was spun-off to American Express shareholders via a tax-free distribution, but not before Golub had to pump a final $1 billion into Lehman.

By 1994, American Express was beginning to show signs of its old profitable self. The resources of the company were now firmly behind TRS. The goal of management was to build the American Express Card into the "world's most respected service brand." Every communication from the company emphasized the franchise value of the name American Express. Even IDS Financial Services was renamed American Express Financial Advisors.

Now that everything was in place, Golub set the financial targets for the company: to increase earnings per share by 12–15 percent annually and to achieve 18–20 percent return on equity. Then American Express, in September 1994, issued a statement that demonstrated clearly the rationality of the company's new management. Subject to market conditions, the board of directors authorized management to repurchase 20 million shares of its common stock. That was music to Buffett's ears.

During the summer of 1994, Buffett had converted Berkshire's preferred issue in American Express. Soon thereafter, he began to acquire even more shares of common stock (see Figure 8.9). By year-end, Berkshire owned 27 million shares at an average

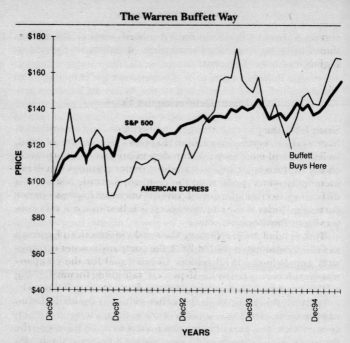

Figure 8.9. Common stock price of American Express compared to the S&P 500 index (indexed to $100 at start date).

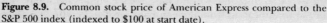

price of $25 per share. With the completion of the stock repurchase plan it had announced in the fall of 1994, the following spring American Express announced it would repurchase an additional 40 million shares, representing 8 percent of the total stock outstanding.

Clearly, American Express is a very different company today than it was even a few years ago. After jettisoning Shearson-Lehman with its massive capital needs, American Express had a powerful ability to generate excess cash. For the first time, the company had more capital and more shares than needed. Buffett, appreciating the economic changes that were underway at American Express, dramatically increased Berkshire's position in the company. By March 1995, Buffett added another 20 million shares bringing Berkshire's ownership of American Express to slightly less than 10 percent.

Tenet: Determine the Value

Since 1990, the noncash charges, depreciation, and amortization have roughly equaled American Express's acquisition of land, buildings, and equipment. When depreciation and amortization charges approximate capital spending, owner earnings equals net income. However, because of the company's erratic history, it is difficult to ascertain the growth rate of American Express's owner earnings. Under these circumstances, it is best to use a very conservative growth projection.

By the end of 1994, reflecting the results of American Express's net of the subsidiaries sold in 1993, the company's owner earnings were approximately $1.4 billion. Golub's goal for the company was to grow earnings at a 12–15 percent rate going forward. Using a 10 percent growth in earnings for the next ten years followed by a 5 percent residual growth thereafter (which is decidedly below management's forecast), and discounting the earnings by 10 percent (which is a conservative discount factor considering the thirty-year U.S. Treasury bond was yielding 8 percent) the intrinsic value of American Express is $43.4 billion, or $87 per share (see Table A.27). If the company is able to grow its earnings at 12 percent, the intrinsic value of American Express is closer to $50 billion, or $100 per share. At the more conservative valuation, Buffett was purchasing American Express at a 70 percent discount to the company's intrinsic value. That figure represents a significant margin of safety.

Tenet: Favorable Long-Term Prospects

For some investors, it is difficult to appreciate the franchise qualities of American Express. Today, the general-purpose credit card market is dominated by Visa and MasterCard. Because both of these companies issue cards with no annual fee and customers can use their cards at most locations, how can American Express compete? First, American Express is becoming accepted by a growing list of merchants. The American Express Card is now accepted at 80 percent of U.S. retail outlets, 86 percent of gasoline stations, and close to 100 percent of the very important worldwide travel and entertainment market. Second, and more important, American Express cardholders spend more than MasterCard or Visa users: an average of $4,000 a year compared to $1,500. For merchants, spending volume is a key selling point, and so American Express is having no trouble signing up more and more merchants.

Many investors, observing the boom in consumer spending, constantly search out stocks in restaurants, casinos, and entertainment complexes. Buffett has eliminated the risk of having to buy any one of these businesses while still profiting from this industry phenomenon. No matter which form of leisure or entertainment the consumer chooses, many are paying for the experience by using an American Express Card. By owning 10 percent of the company, Buffett has picked up a royalty on the multitude of purchases occurring everyday.

THE WALT DISNEY COMPANY*

"I do not have blanket enthusiasm for all mergers," confessed Buffett. "But this deal makes more sense to me than any deal I've seen, with the possible exception of Capital Cities and ABC."[1] Thus kicked-off the largest corporate merger since the acquisition of RJR Nabisco by Kolberg Kravis Roberts & Company in 1989. In a stunning move, The Walt Disney Company, led by Michael Eisner, offered to purchase Capital Cities/ABC for $19 billion. This "new" Walt Disney Company thus becomes the largest media and entertainment company in the world.

---

*Robert G. Hagstrom, Jr., is the portfolio manager of the Focus Trust. This mutual fund owns shares of Capital Cities/ABC and shares of the Walt Disney Company. Furthermore, the Focus Trust may, from time to time, purchase additional shares of these companies.

As much as people were amazed by Eisner's boldness, they were equally awed by Tom Murphy's final act as head of Capital Cities/ ABC. Perhaps no other CEO ever demonstrated so well the ability to steer a company through such a fast-changing business landscape. Capital Cities' initial public offering occurred in 1957 at a price of $5.75 per share. Today, that single share, adjusted for stock splits, is 80 shares worth approximately $10,000. That is an incredible 22 percent average annual rate of return over the past thirty-eight years.

In turning over Capital Cities/ABC to Disney, Murphy left behind the number one television network, ABC; eight television and twenty-one radio stations; seven daily and seventy-one weekly newspapers; sixty-one specialty magazines; 80 percent ownership of ESPN, America's largest cable network; and stakes in two other cable networks: A&E and Lifetime. In addition, Capital Cities/ ABC formed alliances and purchased equity interests in several international television and film production companies as well as international television broadcasters.

Murphy also left $400 million, net of all debt, in the company safe. This, alone, is an admirable feat in an industry littered with companies that, by overpaying for acquisitions, have hobbled themselves with enormous debt. It is all the more remarkable when you consider Murphy started, in 1954, with one television station and one AM radio station in Albany, New York.

The combined Walt Disney and Capital Cities/ABC company is indeed impressive. To Capital Cities/ABC's list of assets, Disney brings theme parks (Disneyland, Disney World, and Epcot Center), film and television production companies (Touchstone and Walt Disney Pictures), animation division ("Aladdin," "Lion King," "Pocahontas"), film distribution (Miramax and Buena Vista), and the Disney Channel. It owns more than 350 Disney stores worldwide that sell a broad range of consumer products. Disney also has interests in Euro Disney, Hyperion Press, the Mighty Ducks hockey team, the California Angels baseball team, and a theater company that recently produced the widely acclaimed stage version of "Beauty and the Beast." This new combined company has a market value well over $40 billion and should generate $16.5 billion in annual revenues.

243

Tenet: Favorable Long-Term Prospects

The media business is often defined in two parts: content and conduit. Content is product—namely, films and television programs. Conduit refers to the channels of distribution or how the product is delivered to the consumer. The dynamic part of the Disney–Cap Cities marriage is the merger of "the number one content company in the world [Disney] with the number one distribution company [Cap Cities]," explains Buffett.[5]

In the past, investors have valued content more highly than distribution. Although the economics of a media distribution company are very appealing, the returns on successful programming can be enormous. Lately, both content and distribution companies have been circling each other in what can best be described as a furious mating dance. The strategy of combining a programmer with a distributor appears rather obvious. Because of a change in federal law, networks are no longer banned from owning companies that develop programs. They can now own, as well as distribute, programming, thereby increasing their overall profitability. Programmers, in turn, by aligning with a distributor, help guarantee placement for their programs.

But to judge the Disney–Cap Cities merger as a convenient arrangement between a programmer and distributor appears to miss the point. "When we acquired Capital Cities/ABC, we weren't buying a network," claims Eisner, "The company's more than that."[6] Indeed, it appears that the most enticing part of the Cap Cities arsenal is none other than ESPN, the Entertainment Sports Programming Network. ESPN reaches 66 million households in the United States and an additional 95 million households located in more than 150 countries worldwide. Murphy was asked whether ESPN was the most valuable asset of the acquisition: "To Disney," Murphy replied, "I think that's true."[7]

The merger between Cap Cities and Disney is not about cutting costs. Nor is it singularly about ensuring the placement of programs. The merger between Cap Cities and Disney is about increasing revenues, and the only way to increase revenues, both meaningfully and lastingly, is to expand overseas.

The networks' constant jostling for number one position is, over the long term, a zero-sum game. There are, after all, only 500 million eyeballs in this country and that number is not growing very fast. The way to sustain revenue growth is not by playing musical chairs with the network's programming line-up, but to reach more eyeballs. Just as Coca-Cola, Gillette, and Wrigley have come to understand the way to increase sales is through expanding consumption of their products, so, too, have media companies begun to appreciate this lesson. The goal in the entertainment business is to capture more eyeballs, and the number of eyeballs overseas compared to the number in the United States is staggering.

The two types of programming that easily travel worldwide are sports and animated entertainment. Both are universally appealing, easy to translate into different languages, and apolitical in content. By owning the Disney Channel and ESPN, Disney is now able to expand overseas in a very strong fashion. Although the Disney brand name is recognized throughout the world, its programming reach does not begin to match the penetration of ESPN because ESPN began international distribution of sports programming years before the Disney Channel signed up its first subscriber. Today, ESPN not only delivers popular international sports, such as basketball, football, baseball, and soccer, but it has cemented its relationship with individual countries by interspersing its programming with favorite local sporting events tailored to each country. For example, in India, an NFL football game might be followed by a local cricket match, whereas in China that same football game might precede a table tennis tournament. Now, the Disney Channel will be able to piggyback ESPN's physical reach as well as its two decades of worldwide experience to accelerate the distribution of its animated programming. By understanding the value of ESPN, you begin to appreciate that the Disney–Cap Cities merger is not solely about buying a U.S. network.

Tenet: Rationality

Michael Eisner's reputation as an effective corporate manager is often overshadowed by his extravagant compensation arrangement with The Walt Disney Company and his dominating personality. But no one has ever claimed that Eisner does not passionately care about Disney nor can anyone dispute the value he has created for

Disney's shareholders. Since the mid-1980s, Eisner has helped create $22 billion in market value for Disney's shareholders. For every dollar Eisner retained for the company, he created almost $4 in market value. That testament alone indicates the market's appreciation for Eisner's management approach.

Still, the most fundamental indication of rationality is most often found in a manager's attitude toward issuing company shares and the ultimate dilution of individual shareholder value. Here Michael Eisner has scored extremely well. In fact, his reluctance to issue additional shares of Disney stock for acquisition purposes nearly scuttled the Cap Cities deal. Murphy and Eisner had discussed the potential of merging the two companies over the years and more earnestly over the past few months. In each case, talks broke off after Eisner refused to issue new Disney shares for Cap Cities. Murphy, understandably, wanted an exchange of company shares to eliminate the significant capital gains tax that would have to be paid in an all-cash offer, and to allow Cap Cities' shareholders to continue to prosper in the future of the new company. Eventually, Murphy and Eisner were able to come to terms by compromising. Eisner offered to exchange one share of Disney stock and $65 for every share of Cap Cities. Murphy agreed.

Tenet: Determine the Value

The challenge facing investors now is not to determine whether Disney's offer for Cap Cities is fair and reasonable, but, rather, to ascertain the value of owning or purchasing shares in this new company. Although there are always financial uncertainties associated with merging two companies, let alone two companies of this size operating in a dynamic worldwide marketplace, we can still make a fair estimate of the intrinsic value of the new Disney company by using the methodology outlined in this book.

The intrinsic value of the new Disney company can be best understood by evaluating the operating results of the two individual companies on a pro forma basis. Using a conservative estimate of both companies' 1995 operating results, we can then make adjustments to these results to reflect the costs of the merger. By year-end 1995, Disney will have earned approximately $1.37 billion.

Depreciation charges for the year will total $495 million and the company will have spent $1.1 billion on capital expenditures. Disney's owner earnings (net income plus depreciation less capital expenditures) will approximate $765 million. Cap Cities is expected to earn $785 million this year, take $175 million in depreciation charges and spend $125 million on capital expenditures. Its 1995 owner earnings will approximate $835 million.

On a combined basis, the new Disney company, in 1995, will generate owner earnings of $1.6 billion. But this new company will also have an additional $10 billion in debt—the funds used to pay for the merger. Stephen Bollenbach, chief financial officer of Disney, estimates that the cost of this debt, of which half will be at a fixed rate and half will be at an adjustable rate, will be 7 percent annually. This new debt load means Disney will be charged $700 million annually in borrowing costs. Considering Disney will likely be paying a 40 percent corporate tax rate, the annual net after-tax cost to Disney will be approximately $420 million. Net owner earnings of the new Disney company after merger costs should equal $1.18 billion ($1.6 billion less $420 million).

We know Buffett discounts owner earnings by the then-prevailing thirty-year U.S. Treasury bond yield. But we also know that when interest rates are cyclically low, as they are now, he is hesitant to discount at such low rates and instead adjusts the discount rate higher. If we assume that this new company will be able to grow its owner earnings at a conservative 15 percent annual rate for ten years followed by an even more conservative 5 percent rate thereafter, and then discount those earnings at an adjusted 10 percent rate, the intrinsic value of the new Disney company is approximately $53.8 billion (see Table A.28).

Tenet: Buy at Attractive Prices

When Disney merges with Cap Cities, the company will issue an additional 154 million shares of stock that represent the total number of Cap Cities shares outstanding. Disney's total shares outstanding will then become 675 million. If Disney can grow its owner earnings at a 15 percent rate for the next ten years followed by a slower 5 percent rate thereafter, the intrinsic value per share of

Disney is approximately $80. At Disney's current market price of $60 per share, it appears the company is selling at a 25 percent discount to its intrinsic value. This is not a large margin of safety compared to most of Buffett's purchases, but it does indicate the owners of Disney stock as well as owners of Cap Cities stock who will receive Disney stock are not holding an overvalued investment.

It is easy to increase the intrinsic value of a company simply by increasing the rate at which you estimate its owner earnings will grow. For example, if you believe that Disney will be able to grow its owner earnings at a 17 percent rate, the intrinsic value of Disney is $93 per share. If you believe Disney will be able to meet its goal of growing the company at a 20 percent rate, the intrinsic value of the company is well over $100 per share.

However, Buffett cautions investors not to inflate the growth assumptions used in their analysis. The margin of safety is meant to protect the investor from unseen circumstances that might affect a company and its owner earnings. You cannot simply enlarge the margin of safety and think you are protecting yourself by arbitrarily increasing growth rates. Still, our economic assumptions do not reflect the obvious synergies that will occur between Disney and Cap Cities. "The synergies go on and on," said Eisner. In fact, he claims that discussions in which the parties attempted to put a fair value on the merger were often interrupted by the realization of yet another opportunity that the merger presented.

The Disney–Cap Cities merger has not been without its critics. Some have questioned the wisdom of vertically integrating a media company. Others have suspiciously eyed the profitability of buying a network at its economic peak. Even a few skeptics wonder how this new company will ever be able to combine two contrasting corporate cultures. Still, there is the sense that an exceptional new business has been formed.

Often when a company announces it is purchasing another company, the acquired company's share price goes up and the purchaser's share price drops a few points. The immediate effect of a higher takeover price naturally forces the acquired company's share price higher to reflect the takeover. However, Wall Street customarily punishes purchasers, reasoning, either rightly or wrongly, they have taken on more risk by increasing debt or by merging two separate entities. Buffett, as so often is the case, saw things differently. He reasoned that by merging Cap Cities and Disney, a stronger company was indeed being created. While some executives were concerned about how Disney's share price would react on the day of the announced merger, Buffett bet one particular Disney executive $100 that Disney's share price would buck conventional wisdom and actually close higher by the end of the day. On Monday morning July 31, 1995, Eisner and Murphy announced the acquisition of Capital Cities/ABC by Disney, and, by the time the stock market closed at 4:00 p.m., Disney's share price had actually gained $1.25 on the day, finishing at $58.62.

The way the merger agreement was orchestrated, Cap Cities shareholders can either opt for more cash or more stock depending on availability. Berkshire, by owning 20 million shares of Capital Cities/ABC, now becomes by default the second largest shareholder, behind the Bass family, of the world's largest media and entertainment company. It is unclear whether Buffett will decide to take more shares of Disney and less cash or whether he will further purchase Disney's shares. The Disney–Cap Cities merger is still in its embryonic stage. Nevertheless, this new company appears to have many of the same investment tenets found in Berkshire's other holdings. Therefore, "the odds are extremely high," says Buffett, "that we will have a very large amount of Disney stock."[9]

NINE

An Unreasonable
Man

"THE REASONABLE MAN adapts himself to the world,"
wrote George Bernard Shaw. "The unreasonable one persists in trying to adapt the world to himself. Therefore all progress depends on the unreasonable man."[1] Shall we conclude that Warren Buffett is "the unreasonable man"? To do so presumes that his investment approach represents progress in the financial world, an assumption I freely make. For when we look at the recent achievements of "reasonable" men, we see, at best, unevenness; at worst, disaster.

The 1980s are likely to be remembered as the "future shock" decade of financial management. Program trading, leveraged buyouts, junk bonds, derivative securities, and index futures have, not surprisingly, frightened many investors. The distinctions between money managers have faded. The grind of fundamental research has been replaced by the whirl of computers. Black boxes have replaced management interviews and investigation. Automation has replaced intuition. Today, the average investor has become disenchanted and estranged from the financial marketplace. With most money managers unable to add value to client portfolios, it is easy to understand how passive index investing has gained popularity.

Throughout the last few decades, investors have flirted with many different investment approaches. Periodically, small capitalization, large capitalization, growth, value, momentum, thematic, and sector rotation have proven financially rewarding. At other times, these approaches have stranded their followers in periods of mediocrity. Buffett, the exception, has not suffered periods of mediocrity. His investment performance, widely documented, has been consistently superior. As investors and speculators alike have been distracted by esoteric approaches to investing, Buffett has quietly amassed a multi-billion-dollar fortune. Throughout, businesses have been his tools, common sense his philosophy.

How did he do it?

Given the documented success of Buffett's performance, coupled with the simplicity of his methodology, the more appropriate question is not how did he do it but why did not other investors apply his approach? The answer may lie in how individuals perceive investing.

When Buffett invests, he sees a business. Most investors see only a stock price. They spend far too much time and effort watching, predicting, and anticipating price changes and far too little time understanding the business they partly own. Elementary as this may be, it is the root that distinguishes Buffett. His hands-on experience owning and managing a wide variety of businesses while simultaneously investing in common stocks separates Buffett from all other professional investors.

Owning and operating businesses has given Buffett a distinct advantage. He has experienced both success and failure in his business ventures and has applied to the stock market the lessons he learned. The professional investor has not been given the same beneficial education. While other professional investors were busy studying capital asset pricing models, beta, and modern portfolio theory, Buffett studied income statements, capital reinvestment requirements, and the cash-generating capabilities of his companies. "Can you really explain to a fish what it's like to walk on land?" Buffett asks. "One day on land is worth a thousand years of talking about it and one day running a business has exactly the same kind of value."[2]

According to Buffett, the investor and the businessperson should look at the company in the same way, because they both want essentially the same thing. The businessperson wants to buy the entire company and the investor wants to buy portions of the company. If you ask a businessperson what he thinks about when purchasing a company, the answer most often given is: "How much cash can be generated from the business?" Finance theory dictates that, over time, there is a direct correlation between the value of a company and its cash-generating ability. Theoretically, the businessperson and the investor, in order to profit, should be looking at the same variables.

If adapting Buffett's investment strategy required only a change in perspective, then probably more investors would become proponents. Unfortunately, applying Buffett's approach requires changing not only perspective but also changing how performance is evaluated and communicated. The traditional yardstick for measuring performance is price change: the difference between the purchase price of the stock and the market price of the stock. In the long run, the price of a stock should approximate the change in value of the business. However, in the short run, prices can gyrate widely above and below a company's value, dependent on factors other than the progress of the business. The problem remains that most investors use short-term changes to gauge the success or failure of their investment approach. However, these short-term price changes often have little to do with the changing economic value of the business and much to do with anticipating the behavior of other investors.

In addition, professional investors are required by their clients to report performance in quarterly periods. Frequently, clients become impatient while waiting for the price of their portfolio to advance at some predetermined rate. If their portfolios do not show short-term performance gains, clients become dissatisfied and skeptical of the investment professional's ability. Knowing that they must improve short-term performance or risk losing clients, professional investors become obsessed with chasing stock prices.

Buffett believes it is foolish to use short-term prices to judge a company's success. Instead, he lets his companies report their value to him by their economic progress. Once a year, he checks several variables:

- Return on beginning shareholder's equity.
- Change in operating margins, debt levels, and capital expenditure needs.
- The company's cash generating ability.

If these economic measurements are improving, he knows the share price, over the long term, should reflect this. What happens to the stock price in the short run is inconsequential.

The difficulty of using economic measurements as yardsticks for success is that communicating performance in this manner is not customary. Clients and investment professionals alike are programmed to follow prices. The stock market reports price change daily. The client's account statement reflects price change monthly and the investment professional, using price change, is measured quarterly. The answer to this dilemma may lie in employing Buffett's concept of "look-through" earnings. If investors use look-through earnings to evaluate their portfolio's performance, perhaps the irrational behavior of solely chasing price might be tempered.

If you believe the probability of employing economic variables in lieu of short-term price changes is too far fetched, consider the growing institutional acceptance of "relationship investing."

RELATIONSHIP INVESTING

As the 1990s unfold, it is evident that a "new" investment strategy is beginning to emerge. Institutional investors, once the paragons of short-term trading, have begun to act like owners of the companies they have purchased. This idea has come to be called *relationship investing*, reflecting the notion that a long-term relationship is built between the investor and the company. With the support of the Securities and Exchange Commission, institutional investors are being encouraged to buy larger stakes in companies so they can behave more like long-term owners.

The logic of relationship investing is straightforward. Investors provide patient capital, which in turn allows management to pursue longer-term corporate goals. Neither investor nor management worries about short-term price changes. The value of relationship investing appeals to institutional investors because of its potential rewards. Whereas in the 1980s passive index investing provided ample returns, the 1990s may prove to be a more difficult environment.

Today, pension funds hold nearly 55 percent of all U.S. equities. In the past, when investors became disenchanted with a company and its management, the answer was to sell the stock and seek another investment. But when a large pension fund decides to move out of a certain position, even though the fund may be selling only 1 percent of its assets, that 1 percent may represent a very large portion of one company's stock. In one move, millions of dollars of stock are sold, a move that can be disruptive and unprofitable. Instead, institutional investors are learning that holding a common stock for the long term and working with management to improve corporate performance might be more profitable than simply selling shares.

Relationship investing is still evolving. In its most radical form, it includes confrontation between management and investor. But unlike the 1980s, when corporate raiders would seek to oust management and break apart the company, relationship investors would rather work with management to strengthen the business. In the least radical cases, relationship investing includes nothing more than providing patient capital and monitoring the company, which allows management to continue its corporate policies without worrying about potential takeovers or disgruntled investors. It is this style of relationship investing that Buffett employs.

It is not Buffett's intention to first purchase a company and then seek major changes. On the contrary, he avoids companies in need of major overhauls. Furthermore, because he will only purchase companies that possess shareholder-oriented managers, the idea of confronting management to improve shareholder returns is unthinkable. In most cases, Buffett will assign voting rights of his shares to management. Although this sometimes earns him a place on a company's board of directors, it is not universal. With both General Dynamics and Wells Fargo, Buffett assigned voting rights and did not take a board seat.

Buffett supported the notion of relationship investing even before it had a name, and long before it became fashionable. When Berkshire purchases a large block of stock in a company, Buffett assures management that they are free to do their job without worry. "That kind of certainty, combined with a good manager and a good business," he said, "provides excellent soil for a rich financial harvest. That's the economic case for our arrangements."[3]

We know that Buffett's investment approach, tested over time, has been successful. Buffett's methodology is not beyond comprehension and his relationship investing style, once unique, is now gathering proponents. At this point you may be wondering how you can adopt his investment strategies. The answer can be found in The Warren Buffett Way.

THE WARREN BUFFETT WAY

The major goal of this book is to help investors understand and employ the investment strategies that have made Buffett successful. It is my hope that, having learned from his past experiences, you will be able to go forward and apply his methods. Perhaps in the future you may see examples of Buffettlike purchases and, having understood what Buffett did in similar cases, will profit from his teachings.

Ideally, the greatest benefit from this book will go to the investor who, observing a future investment opportunity, might identify a stock as a Washington Post type purchase, or a Wells Fargo type purchase, or a Coca-Cola type purchase, or possibly a General Dynamics type purchase. When the stock market forces the price of a good business downward (as it did to Washington Post), or when specific risk temporarily punishes a business (as it did to Wells Fargo), or when investor indifference allows a superior business (such as Coca-Cola) to be priced at half of its intrinsic value, or when the actions of a manager rise above the institutional imperative (as did General Dynamics' Bill Anders), investors will be rewarded by thinking and behaving as Buffett would.

The Warren Buffett Way

Step 1. Turn off the stock market.
Step 2. Don't worry about the economy.
Step 3. Buy a business, not a stock.
Step 4. Manage a portfolio of businesses.

The Warren Buffett Way is deceptively simple. There are no computer programs to learn or two-inch thick investment banking manuals to decipher. There is nothing scientific about valuing a business and then paying a price that is below this business value. "What we do is not beyond anybody else's competence," says Buffett. "It is just not necessary to do extraordinary things to get extraordinary results."[1]

The irony is that Buffett's success is as much the failure of others as any innate superior ability he may possess. "It has been helpful to me," he explains, "to have tens of thousands (students) turned out of business schools taught that it didn't do any good to think."[5] I do not mean to imply that Buffett is average, far from it. He is unquestionably brilliant. But the gap between Buffett and other professional investors is widened by their own willingness to play a loser's game, a game Buffett chooses not to play. Readers of this book are given the same choice.

Whether you are financially able to purchase 10 percent of a company or merely one hundred shares, "The Warren Buffett Way" can help you achieve profitable investment returns. But "The Warren Buffett Way" will help only those investors who are willing to help themselves. To be successful, you must be willing to do some thinking on your own. If you are in need of constant affirmation, particularly from the stock market, that your investment decisions are correct, the probability of benefiting from "The Warren Buffett Way" is diminished. But if you can think for yourself, apply relatively simple methods, and have the courage of your convictions, the chance for profit is greatly increased.

Whenever people try something new, there is initial apprehension. Adopting a new and different investment strategy will naturally evoke some uneasiness. In "The Warren Buffett Way," the first step is the most challenging. If you can master this first step, the rest of the way is easy.

Step One: Turn Off the Stock Market

Remember that the stock market is manic-depressive. Sometimes it is wildly excited about future prospects and at other times it is unreasonably depressed. Of course, this behavior creates opportunities, particularly when shares of outstanding businesses are available at irrationally low prices. But just as you would not take direction from an advisor who exhibited manic-depressive tendencies, neither should you allow the market to dictate your actions. The stock market is not a preceptor; it exists merely to assist you with the mechanics of buying or selling shares of stock. If you believe that the stock market is smarter than you are, give it your money by investing in index funds. But if you have done your homework and understand your business and are confident that you know more about your business than the stock market does, turn off the market.

Buffett does not have a stock quote machine in his office, and he seems to get by just fine without it. If you plan on owning shares in an outstanding business for a number of years, what happens in the market on a day-to-day basis is inconsequential. You will be surprised that your portfolio weathers nicely without you constantly looking at the market. If you don't believe so, give yourself a test. Try not to look at the market for forty-eight hours. Don't look at a machine, don't check the newspaper, don't listen to a stock market summary, don't read a market diary. If after two days your companies are well, try turning off the market for three days, and then for a whole week. Pretty soon you will be convinced that your investment health has survived and that your companies are still operational, despite your inattention to their stock quotes.

"After we buy a stock, consequently, we would not be disturbed if markets closed for a year or two," says Buffett. "We don't need a daily quote on our 100 percent position in See's or H. H. Brown to validate our well being. Why, then, should we need a quote on our 7 percent interest in Coke?"[6] Very clearly, Buffett is telling us that he does not need the market's prices to validate Berkshire's common stock investments. The same holds true for individual investors. You know you have approached Buffett's level when your attention turns to the stock market and the only question on your mind is: "Has anybody done anything foolish lately that will allow me an opportunity to buy a good business at a great price?"

Step Two: Don't Worry About the Economy

Just as people spend fruitless hours worrying about the stock market, so too do they worry needlessly about the economy. If you find yourself discussing and debating whether the economy is poised for growth or tilting toward a recession, whether interest rates or moving up or down, or whether there is inflation or disinflation, STOP! Give yourself a break. Except for his preconceived notions that the economy inherently has an inflation bias, Buffett dedicates no time or energy analyzing the economy.

Often investors begin with an economic assumption and then go about selecting stocks that fit neatly within this grand design. Buffett considers this thinking foolish. First, no one has economic predictive powers any more than they have stock market predictive powers. Second, if you select stocks that will benefit by a particular economic environment, you inevitably invite turnover and speculation. Whether you correctly predict the economy or not, your portfolio is continuously adjusted to benefit in the next economic scenario. Buffett prefers to buy a business that has the opportunity to profit regardless of the economy. Of course, macroeconomic forces may affect returns on the margin, but overall, Buffett's businesses are able to profit nicely despite vagaries in the economy. Time is more wisely spent locating and owning a business that has the ability to profit in all economic environments than by renting a group of stocks that do well only if a guess about the economy happens to be correct.

Step Three: Buy a Business, Not a Stock

Let's pretend that you have to make a very important decision. Tomorrow you will be given an opportunity to pick one business in which to invest. To make it interesting, let us also pretend that once you have made your decision, it cannot be changed and, furthermore, you have to hold the investment for ten years. Ultimately, the wealth generated from this business ownership will support you in your retirement. Now, what are you going to think about? Probably many questions will run through your mind, initially causing a great deal of confusion. But if Buffett were given the same test, he would methodically begin with:

Business Tenet: Is the business simple and understandable?

You cannot make an intelligent guess about the future of your business unless you understand how it makes money. Too often individuals invest in stocks without a clue as to how a company generates sales, incurs expenses, and produces profits. If you can understand this economic process, you have the ability to intelligently proceed further in your investigation.

Business Tenet: Does the business have a consistent operating history?

If you are going to invest your family's future in a company, you will need to know whether the company has stood the test of time. It is unlikely that you will bet your future on a new company that has not experienced different economic cycles and competitive forces. You should be assured that your company has been in busi-

---

Buffett's Tenets

Business Tenets

- Is the business simple and understandable?
- Does the business have a consistent operating history?
- Does the business have favorable long-term prospects?

Management Tenets

- Is management rational?
- Is management candid with its shareholders?
- Does management resist the institutional imperative?

Financial Tenets

- Focus on return on equity, not earnings per share.
- Calculate "owner earnings."
- Look for companies with high profit margins.
- For every dollar retained, make sure the company has created at least one dollar of market value.

Market Tenets

- What is the value of the business?
- Can the business be purchased at a significant discount to its value?

---

ness long enough to demonstrate an ability, over time, to earn significant profits. However, a company can have an interrupted period of profitability, like Wells Fargo and GEICO, and still have a consistent operating history. Often this interrupted period affords you a one-time opportunity to purchase a good business at an exceptionally low price.

Business Tenet: Does the business have favorable long-term prospects?

The best business to own, the one with the best long-term prospects, is a franchise. A franchise is a business that sells a product or service that is needed or desired, that has no close substitute, and whose profits are not regulated. A franchise also possesses a great amount of economic goodwill that allows the company to better withstand the effects of inflation. The worst business to own is a commodity business. A commodity business sells products or services that are indistinguishable from competitors. Commodity businesses have little or no economic goodwill. The only distinction in a commodity business is price. The difficulty of owning a commodity business is that sometimes competitors, using price as weapon, will sell their product below the cost of business to temporarily attract customers in hopes that they will remain loyal. If you compete against other businesses that occasionally sell their products below cost, you are doomed.

Generally, most businesses fall somewhere in between: They are either weak franchises or strong commodity businesses. A weak franchise has more favorable long-term prospects than a strong commodity business. Even a weak franchise still has some pricing power that allows it to earn above-average returns on invested capital. Coca-Cola would be considered a weak franchise in this country. But internationally, particularly in markets where there is no close substitute, Coca-Cola has a strong franchise. Gillette possesses the same franchise qualities as Coca-Cola.

Conversely, a strong commodity business will earn above-average returns only if it is the lowest-cost supplier. GEICO, Freddie Mac, and Wells Fargo operate in a commodity market but generate above-average returns because they remain low-cost providers. One advantage to owning a franchise is that a franchise can endure management incompetence and still survive, whereas in a commodity business, management incompetence is lethal.

Management Tenet: Is management rational?

Since you do not have to watch the stock market or the economy, watch your company's cash instead. How management reinvests cash earnings will determine whether you will achieve an adequate return on your investment. If your business generates more cash than is needed to remain operational, which is the kind of business you want, observe closely the actions of management. A rational manager will only invest excess cash in projects that produce earnings at rates higher than the cost of capital. If those rates are not available, the rational manager will return the money to shareholders by increasing dividends and buying back stock. Irrational managers constantly look for ways to spend excess cash rather than return the money to shareholders. They are ultimately revealed when they invest below the cost of capital.

*Management Tenet: Is management candid with
its shareholders?*

Although you may never have the opportunity to sit down and talk to the chief executive officer of your business, you can tell much about CEOs by the way they communicate to their shareholders. Does your manager report the progress of your business in such a way that you understand how each operating division is performing? Does management confess its failures as openly as it trumpets its success? Most important, does management forthrightly proclaim that the company's prime objective is to maximize the total return of their shareholder's investment?

*Management Tenet: Does management resist the
institutional imperative?*

There is a powerful unseen force that allows managers to act irrationally and supersede the interests of its owners. That force is the *institutional imperative*—mindless, lemminglike imitation of other managers, no matter how irrational their actions may be. Beware of managers who justify their actions based on the logic that if other companies are doing it, it must be all right. One measure of managers' competence is how well they are able to think for themselves and avoid the herd mentality.

Financial Tenet: Focus on return on equity, not earnings per share.

Most investors judge a company's annual performance by earnings per share, watching to see if they set a record or make a big increase over the previous year. But since companies continually add to their capital base by retaining a portion of their previous year's earnings, growth in earnings (which automatically increases earnings per share) is really meaningless. When companies loudly report "record earnings per share," investors are misled into believing that management has done a superior job year after year. A truer measure of annual performance, because it takes into consideration the company's ever growing capital base, is return on equity—the ratio of operating earnings to shareholder's equity.

Financial Tenet: Calculate "owner earnings."

The cash-generating ability of a business determines its value. Buffett seeks out companies that generate cash in excess of their needs as opposed to companies that consume cash. But when determining the value of a business, it is important to understand that not all earnings are created equal. Companies with high fixed assets to profits will require a larger share of retained earnings to remain viable than companies with lower fixed assets to profits, because some of the earnings must be earmarked to maintain and upgrade those assets. Thus accounting earnings need to be adjusted to reflect the cash-generating ability.

A more accurate picture is provided by what Buffett calls "owner earnings." To determine owner earnings, add depreciation, depletion, and amortization charges to net income and then subtract the capital expenditures your company needs to maintain its economic position and unit volume.

Financial Tenet: Look for companies with high profit margins.

High profit margins reflect not only a strong business but management's tenacious spirit for controlling costs. Buffett loves managers who are cost-conscious and abhors managers who allow costs to escalate. Indirectly, shareholders own the profits of the business. Every dollar that is spent unwisely deprives the owners of the business a dollar of profit. Over the years, Buffett has observed that companies with high-cost operations typically find ways to sustain or add to their costs, whereas companies with below-average costs pride themselves on finding ways to cut expenses.

Financial Tenet: For every dollar retained, make sure the company has created at least one dollar of market value.

This is a quick financial test that will tell you not only about the strengths of the business but how well management has rationally allocated the company's resources. From a company's net income subtract all dividends paid to shareholders. What is left is the company's retained earnings. Now, add the company's retained earnings over a ten-year period. Next, find the difference between the company's current market value and its market value ten years ago. If your business has employed retained earnings unproductively over this ten-year period, the market will eventually catch up and will set a low price on the business. If the change in market value is less than the sum of retained earnings, the company is going backward. But if your business has been able to earn above-average returns on retained capital, the gain in market value of the business should exceed the sum of the company's retained earnings, thus creating more than one dollar of market value for every dollar retained.

Market Tenet: What is the value of the business?

The value of a business is determined by the estimated cash flows expected to occur over the life of the business, discounted at an appropriate interest rate. The cash flows of a business are the company's owner earnings. By measuring owner earnings over a long period, you will understand whether they are consistently growing at some average rate or merely bobbing around some constant value.

If the company has bob-around earnings, you should discount these earnings by the long-term interest rate. If owner earnings show some predictable growth pattern, the discount rate can be reduced by this rate of growth. Don't become overly optimistic about a company's future growth rate. It is better to use a conservative estimate for the company's future growth than allow enthusiasm to inflate the value of the business.

Buffett uses the thirty-year U.S. Treasury bond rate to discount expected cash flows. He does not add an equity risk premium to this rate. He will, however, cautiously adjust the discount rate higher when interest rates are declining.

*Market Tenet: Can the business be purchased
at a significant discount to its value?*

Once you have determined the value of a business, the next step is to look at the price. Buffett's rule is, purchase the business only when its price is at a significant discount to its value. Take note: Only at this final step does Buffett look at the stock market price.

Calculating the value of a business is not mathematically complex. However, problems arise when an analyst wrongly estimates a company's future cash flow. Buffett deals with this problem in two ways. First, he increases his chances of correctly predicting future cash flows by sticking with businesses that are simple and stable in character. Second, he insists that with each company he purchases, there must be a margin of safety between the company's purchase price and its determined value. This margin of safety helps create a cushion that will protect him—and you—from companies whose future cash flows are changing.

Step Four: Manage a Portfolio of Businesses

Now that you are a business owner as opposed to a renter of stocks, the composition of your portfolio will change. Because you are no longer measuring your success solely by price change or comparing annual price change to a common stock benchmark, you have the liberty to select the best businesses available. There is no law that says you must include every major industry within your portfolio, nor do you have to include twenty, thirty, forty, or fifty stocks in your portfolio to achieve adequate diversification. If a business owner would be comfortable owning ten different businesses, why should it be any different for the owner of common stocks?

Buffett believes that wide diversification is only required when investors do not understand what they are doing. If these "know-nothing" investors want to own common stocks, they should own a large number of equities and space out their purchases over time.

In other words, the "know-nothing" investor should use an index fund and dollar cost average purchases. There is nothing shameful about becoming an "index investor." In fact, Buffett points out, the index investor will actually outperform the majority of investment professionals. "Paradoxically," he notes, "when 'dumb' money acknowledges its limitations, it ceases to be dumb.[7]

"On the other hand," Buffett says, "if you are a know-something investor, able to understand business economics and to find five to ten sensibly-priced companies that possess important long-term competitive advantages, conventional diversification makes no sense to you."[8] Buffett asks you to consider: If the best business you own presents the least financial risk and has the most favorable long-term prospects, why would you put money into your twentieth-favorite business rather than add money to the top choices?

Investors can measure the economic progress of their business portfolio by calculating their look-through earnings, just as Buffett does. Multiply the earnings per share by the number of shares you own to calculate the total earnings power of your companies. The goal of the business owner, Buffett explains, is to create a portfolio of companies that, in ten years, will produce the highest level of look-through earnings.

Because growth of look-through earnings, not price changes, now becomes the highest priority in your portfolio, many things begin to change. First, you are less likely to sell your best businesses just because you have a profit. Ironically, corporate managers understand this when they focus on their own business operation. "A parent company," Buffett explains, "that owns a subsidiary with superb long-term economics is not likely to sell that entity regardless of price."[9] A CEO wanting to increase the value of his business will not sell the company's "crown jewel." Yet this same CEO will impulsively sell stocks in his personal portfolio with little more logic than "you can't go broke taking a profit." "In our view," Buffett explains, "what makes sense in business also makes sense in stocks: An investor should ordinarily hold a small piece of an outstanding business with the same tenacity that an owner would exhibit if he owned all of that business."[10]

Now that you are managing a portfolio of businesses, not only will you avoid selling your best businesses, you will pick new businesses for purchase with much greater care. As the manager of a portfolio of businesses, you must resist the temptation to purchase a marginal company just because you have cash reserves. If the company does not pass your tenet screen, do not purchase it. Be patient and wait for the right business. It is wrong to assume that if you are not buying and selling, you are not making progress. In Buffett's mind, it is too difficult to make hundreds of smart decisions in a lifetime. He would rather position his portfolio so he only has to make a few smart decisions.

THE ESSENCE OF WARREN BUFFETT

The driving force of Warren Buffett's investment strategy is the rational allocation of capital. Determining how to allocate a company's earnings is the most important decision a manager will make; determining how to allocate one's savings is the most important decision an investor will make. Rationality—displaying rational thinking when making that choice—is the quality Buffett most admires. Despite its underlying vagaries, there is a line of reason that permeates the financial markets. Buffett's success is a result of locating that line of reason and never deviating from its path.

Buffett has had his share of failures and no doubt will have a few more in the years ahead. But investment success is not synonymous with infallibility. Rather, it comes about by doing more things right than wrong. The Warren Buffett Way is no different. Its success as an investment approach is as much a result of eliminating those things you can get wrong, which are many and perplexing (predicting markets, economies, and stock prices), as requiring you to get things right, which are few and simple (valuing a business). When Buffett purchases stocks, he is focusing on two simple variables: the price of the business and its value. The price of a business can be found by looking up its quote. Determining value requires some calculation, but it is not beyond the ability of those willing to do some homework.

Because you no longer worry about the stock market, the economy, or predicting stock prices, you are now free to spend more time understanding your businesses. More productive time can be spent reading annual reports and business and industry articles that will improve your knowledge as a owner. In fact, the degree to which you are willing to investigate your own business lessens your dependency on others who make a living advising people to take irrational action.

Ultimately, the best investment ideas will come from doing your own homework. However, you should not feel intimidated. The Warren Buffett Way is not beyond the comprehension of most serious investors. You do not have to become an MBA-level authority on business valuation to use it successfully. Still, if you are uncomfortable applying these tenets yourself, nothing prevents you from asking your financial advisor these same questions. In fact, the more you enter into a dialogue on price and value, the more you will begin to understand and appreciate The Warren Buffett Way.

Over his lifetime, Buffett has tried different investment gambits. At a young age he even tried his hand at stock charting. He has studied with the brightest financial mind of our century, Benjamin Graham, and managed and owned a host of businesses with his partner, Charlie Munger. Over the last four decades, Buffett has experienced double-digit interest rates, high inflation, and stock market crashes. Through all the distractions, he found his niche, that point where all things make sense: where investment strategy cohabits with personality. "Our (investment) attitude," Buffett says, "fits our personalities and the way we want to live our lives."[11]

This harmony is easily found in Buffett's attitude. He is always upbeat and supportive. He is genuinely excited about coming to work every day. "I have in life all I want right here," he says. "I love every day. I mean, I tap dance in here and work with nothing but people I like.[12] There is no job in the world that is more fun than running Berkshire and I count myself lucky to be where I am."[13]

APPENDIX

Table A.1 Berkshire Hathaway 1977 Common Stock Portfolio

No. of Shares	Company	Cost	Market Value	Percentage of Portfolio	Industry	Business
934,300	The Washington Post Company	$ 10,628	$ 33,401	18.4	Consumer cyclical	Publishing
1,969,953	GEICO Convertible Preferred	19,417	33,033	18.2	Finance	Insurance
592,650	Interpublic Group of Companies	4,531	17,187	9.5	Consumer cyclical	Advertising
220,000	Capital Cities Communications, Inc.	10,909	13,228	7.3	Consumer cyclical	Broadcasting
1,294,308	GEICO Common Stock	4,116	10,516	5.8	Finance	Insurance
324,580	Kaiser Aluminum and Chemical Corp.	11,218	9,981	5.5	Basic materials	Metals and mining
226,900	Knight-Ridder Newspapers	7,534	8,736	4.8	Consumer cyclical	Publishing
170,800	Ogilvy & Mather International	2,762	6,960	3.8	Consumer cyclical	Advertising
1,305,800	Kaiser Industries, Inc.	778	6,039	3.3	Basic materials	Metals and mining
	Total	$ 71,893	$139,081	76.8		
	All other common stocks	34,996	41,992	23.2		
	Total common stocks	$106,889	$181,073	100.0		

Source: Berkshire Hathaway 1977 Annual Report.
Note: Dollar amounts are in thousands.

271

Table A.2 Berkshire Hathaway 1978 Common Stock Portfolio

No. of Shares	Company	Cost	Market Value	Percentage of Portfolio	Industry	Business
934,000	The Washington Post Company	$ 10,628	$ 43,445	19.7	Consumer cyclical	Publishing
1,986,953	GEICO Convertible Preferred	19,417	28,314	12.8	Finance	Insurance
953,750	SAFECO Corporation	23,867	26,467	12.0	Finance	Insurance
592,650	Interpublic Group of Companies	4,531	19,039	8.6	Consumer cyclical	Advertising
1,066,934	Kaiser Aluminum and Chemical Corp.	18,085	18,671	8.5	Basic materials	Metals and mining
453,800	Knight-Ridder Newspapers	7,534	10,267	4.6	Consumer cyclical	Publishing
1,294,308	GEICO Common Stock	4,116	9,060	4.1	Finance	Insurance
246,450	American Broadcasting Companies	6,082	8,626	3.9	Consumer cyclical	Broadcasting
	Total	$ 94,260	$163,889	74.2		
	All other common stocks	39,506	57,040	25.8		
	Total common stocks	$133,766	$220,929	100.0		

Source: Berkshire Hathaway 1978 Annual Report.
Note: Dollar amounts are in thousands.

Table A.3 Berkshire Hathaway 1979 Common Stock Portfolio

No. of Shares	Company	Cost	Market Value	Percentage of Portfolio	Industry	Business
5,730,114	GEICO Corp. (common stock)	$ 28,288	$ 68,045	20.3	Finance	Insurance
1,868,000	The Washington Post Company	10,628	39,241	11.7	Consumer cyclical	Publishing
1,007,500	Handy & Harman	21,825	38,537	11.5	Basic materials	Metals and mining
953,750	SAFECO Corporation	23,867	35,527	10.6	Finance	Insurance
711,180	Interpublic Group of Companies	4,531	23,736	7.1	Consumer cyclical	Advertising
1,211,834	Kaiser Aluminum and Chemical Corp.	20,629	23,328	7.0	Basic materials	Metals and mining
771,900	F.W. Woolworth Company	15,515	19,394	5.8	Consumer cyclical	Retail
328,700	General Foods, Inc.	11,437	11,053	3.3	Consumer staples	Food
246,450	American Broadcasting Companies	6,082	9,673	2.9	Consumer cyclical	Broadcasting
289,700	Affiliated Publications	2,821	8,800	2.6	Consumer cyclical	Publishing
391,400	Ogilvy & Mather International	3,709	7,828	2.3	Consumer cyclical	Advertising
282,500	Media General, Inc.	4,545	7,345	2.2	Consumer cyclical	Publishing
112,545	Amerada Hess	2,861	5,487	1.6	Energy	Oil
	Total	$156,738	$297,994	89.0		
	All other common stocks	28,675	36,686	11.0		
	Total common stocks	$185,413	$334,680	100.0		

Source: Berkshire Hathaway 1979 Annual Report.
Note: Dollar amounts are in thousands.

Table A.4 Berkshire Hathaway 1980 Common Stock Portfolio

No. of Shares	Company	Cost	Market Value	Percentage of Portfolio	Industry	Business
7,200,000	GEICO Corporation	$ 47,138	$105,300	19.9	Finance	Insurance
1,983,812	General Foods	62,507	59,889	11.3	Consumer staples	Food
2,015,000	Handy & Harman	21,825	58,435	11.0	Basic materials	Metals and mining
1,250,525	SAFECO Corporation	32,062	45,177	8.5	Finance	Insurance
1,868,600	The Washington Post Company	10,628	42,277	8.0	Consumer cyclical	Publishing
464,317	Aluminum Company of America	25,577	27,685	5.2	Basic materials	Metals and mining
1,211,834	Kaiser Aluminum and Chemical Corp.	20,629	27,569	5.2	Basic materials	Metals and mining
711,180	Interpublic Group of Companies	4,531	22,135	4.2	Consumer cyclical	Advertising
667,124	F.W. Woolworth Company	13,583	16,511	3.1	Consumer cyclical	Retail
370,088	Pinkerton's, Inc.	12,144	16,489	3.1	Transport/services	Professional service
475,217	Cleveland-Cliffs Iron Company	12,942	15,894	3.0	Basic materials	Metals and mining
434,550	Affiliated Publications, Inc.	2,821	12,222	2.3	Consumer cyclical	Publishing
245,700	R.J. Reynolds Industries	8,702	11,228	2.1	Consumer staples	Tobacco
391,400	Ogilvy & Mather International	3,709	9,981	1.9	Consumer cyclical	Advertising
282,500	Media General	4,545	8,334	1.6	Consumer cyclical	Publishing
247,039	National Detroit Corporation	5,930	6,299	1.2	Finance	Banking
151,104	The Times Mirror Company	4,447	6,271	1.2	Consumer cyclical	Publishing
881,500	National Student Marketing	5,128	5,895	1.1	Finance	Financial services
	Total	$298,848	$497,591	93.9		
	All other common stocks	26,313	32,096	6.1		
	Total common stocks	$325,161	$529,687	100.0		

Source: Berkshire Hathaway 1980 Annual Report.
Note: Dollar amounts are in thousands.

Table A.5 Berkshire Hathaway 1981 Common Stock Portfolio

No. of Shares	Company	Cost	Market Value	Percentage of Portfolio	Industry	Business
7,200,000	GEICO Corporation	$ 47,138	$199,800	31.3	Finance	Insurance
1,764,824	R.J. Reynolds Industries	76,668	83,127	13.0	Consumer staples	Tobacco
2,101,244	General Foods	66,277	66,714	10.4	Consumer staples	Food
1,868,600	The Washington Post Company	10,628	58,160	9.1	Consumer cyclical	Publishing
2,015,000	Handy & Harman	21,825	36,270	5.7	Basic materials	Metals and mining
785,225	SAFECO Corporation	21,329	31,016	4.9	Finance	Insurance
711,180	Interpublic Group of Companies	4,531	23,202	3.6	Consumer cyclical	Advertising
370,088	Pinkerton's, Inc.	12,144	19,675	3.1	Transport/services	Professional service
703,634	Aluminum Company of America	19,359	18,031	2.8	Basic materials	Metals and mining
420,441	Arcata Corporation	14,076	15,136	2.4	Basic materials	Paper
475,217	Cleveland-Cliffs Iron Company	12,942	14,362	2.2	Basic materials	Metals and mining
451,650	Affiliated Publications, Inc.	3,297	14,114	2.2	Consumer cyclical	Publishing
441,522	GATX Corporation	17,147	13,466	2.1	Capital goods	Machinery
391,400	Ogilvy & Mather International	3,709	12,329	1.9	Consumer cyclical	Advertising
282,500	Media General	4,545	11,088	1.7	Consumer cyclical	Publishing
	Total	$335,615	$616,490	96.4		
	All other common stocks	16,131	22,739	3.6		
	Total common stocks	$351,746	$639,229	100.0		

Source: Berkshire Hathaway 1981 Annual Report.
Note: Dollar amounts are in thousands.

Table A.6 Berkshire Hathaway 1982 Common Stock Portfolio

No. of Shares	Company	Cost	Market Value	Percentage of Portfolio	Industry	Business
7,200,000	GEICO Corporation	$ 47,138	$309,600	32.7	Finance	Insurance
3,107,675	R.J. Reynolds Industries	142,343	158,715	16.8	Consumer staples	Tobacco
1,868,600	The Washington Post Company	10,628	103,240	10.9	Consumer cyclical	Publishing
2,101,244	General Foods	66,277	83,680	8.8	Consumer staples	Food
1,531,391	Time, Inc.	45,273	79,824	8.4	Consumer cyclical	Publishing
908,800	Crum & Forster	47,144	48,962	5.2	Finance	Insurance
2,379,200	Handy & Harman	27,318	46,692	4.9	Basic materials	Metals and mining
711,180	Interpublic Group of Companies	4,531	34,314	3.6	Consumer cyclical	Advertising
460,650	Affiliated Publications, Inc.	3,516	16,929	1.8	Consumer cyclical	Publishing
391,400	Ogilvy & Mather International	3,709	17,319	1.8	Consumer cyclical	Advertising
282,500	Media General	4,545	12,289	1.3	Consumer cyclical	Publishing
	Total	$402,422	$911,564	96.4		
	All other common stocks	21,611	34,058	3.6		
	Total common stocks	$424,033	$945,622	100.0		

Source: Berkshire Hathaway 1982 Annual Report.
Note: Dollar amounts are in thousands.

Table A.7 Berkshire Hathaway 1983 Common Stock Portfolio

No. of Shares	Company	Cost	Market Value	Percentage of Portfolio	Industry	Business
6,850,000	GEICO Corporation	$ 47,138	$ 398,156	31.1	Finance	Insurance
5,618,661	R.J. Reynolds Industries	268,918	314,334	24.6	Consumer staples	Tobacco
4,451,544	General Foods	163,786	228,698	17.9	Consumer staples	Food
1,868,600	The Washington Post Company	10,628	136,875	10.7	Consumer cyclical	Publishing
901,788	Time, Inc.	27,732	56,860	4.4	Consumer cyclical	Publishing
2,379,200	Handy & Harman	27,318	42,231	3.3	Basic materials	Metals and mining
636,310	Interpublic Group of Companies	4,056	33,088	2.6	Consumer cyclical	Advertising
690,975	Affiliated Publications, Inc.	3,516	26,603	2.1	Consumer cyclical	Publishing
250,400	Ogilvy & Mather International	2,580	12,833	1.0	Consumer cyclical	Advertising
197,200	Media General	3,191	11,191	0.9	Consumer cyclical	Publishing
	Total	$558,863	$1,260,869	98.6		
	All other common stocks	7,485	18,044	1.4		
	Total common stocks	$566,348	$1,278,913	100.0		

Source: Berkshire Hathaway 1983 Annual Report.
Note: Dollar amounts are in thousands.

Table A.8 Berkshire Hathaway 1984 Common Stock Portfolio

No. of Shares	Company	Cost	Market Value	Percentage of Portfolio	Industry	Business
6,850,000	GEICO Corporation	$ 45,713	$ 397,300	31.3	Finance	Insurance
4,047,191	General Foods	149,870	226,137	17.8	Consumer staples	Food
3,895,710	Exxon Corporation	173,401	175,307	13.8	Energy	Oil
1,868,600	The Washington Post Company	10,628	149,955	11.8	Consumer cyclical	Publishing
2,553,488	Time, Inc.	89,237	109,162	8.6	Consumer cyclical	Publishing
740,400	American Broadcasting Companies	44,416	46,738	3.7	Consumer cyclical	Broadcasting
2,379,200	Handy & Harman	27,318	38,662	3.0	Basic materials	Metals and mining
690,975	Affiliated Publications, Inc.	3,516	32,908	2.6	Consumer cyclical	Publishing
818,872	Interpublic Group of Companies	2,570	28,149	2.2	Consumer cyclical	Advertising
555,949	Northwest Industries	26,581	27,242	2.1	Miscellaneous	Diversified
	Total	$573,340	$1,231,560	97.1		
	All other common stocks	11,634	37,326	2.9		
	Total common stocks	$584,974	$1,268,886	100.0		

Source: Berkshire Hathaway 1984 Annual Report.
Note: Dollar amounts are in thousands.

Table A.9 Berkshire Hathaway 1985 Common Stock Portfolio

No. of Shares	Company	Cost	Market Value	Percentage of Portfolio	Industry	Business
6,850,000	GEICO Corporation	$ 45,713	$ 595,950	49.7	Finance	Insurance
1,727,765	The Washington Post Company	9,731	205,172	17.1	Consumer cyclical	Publishing
900,800	American Broadcasting Companies	54,435	108,997	9.1	Consumer cyclical	Broadcasting
2,350,922	Beatrice Companies, Inc.	106,811	108,142	9.0	Consumer staples	Food
1,036,461	Affiliated Publications, Inc.	3,516	55,710	4.6	Consumer cyclical	Publishing
847,788	Time, Inc.	20,385	52,669	4.4	Consumer cyclical	Publishing
2,379,200	Handy & Harman	27,318	43,718	3.6	Basic materials	Metals and mining
	Total	$267,909	$1,170,358	97.7		
	All other common stocks	7,201	27,963	2.3		
	Total common stocks	$275,110	$1,198,321	100.0		

Source: Berkshire Hathaway 1985 Annual Report.
Note: Dollar amounts are in thousands.

Table A.10 Berkshire Hathaway 1986 Common Stock Portfolio

No. of Shares	Company	Cost	Market Value	Percentage of Portfolio	Industry	Business
2,990,000	Capital Cities/ABC, Inc.	$515,775	$ 801,694	42.8	Consumer cyclical	Broadcasting
6,850,000	GEICO Corporation	45,713	674,725	36.0	Finance	Insurance
1,727,765	The Washington Post Company	9,731	269,531	14.4	Consumer cyclical	Publishing
2,379,200	Handy & Harman	27,318	46,989	2.5	Basic materials	Metals and mining
489,300	Lear Siegler, Inc.	44,064	44,587	2.4	Capital Goods	Aerospace
	Total	$642,601	$1,837,526	98.1		
	All other common stocks	12,763	36,507	1.9		
	Total common stocks	$635,364	$1,874,033	100.0		

Source: Berkshire Hathaway 1986 Annual Report.
Note: Dollar amounts are in thousands.

Table A.11 Berkshire Hathaway 1987 Common Stock Portfolio

No. of Shares	Company	Cost	Market Value	Percentage of Portfolio	Industry	Business
3,000,000	Capital Cities/ABC, Inc.	$517,500	$1,035,000	48.9	Consumer cyclical	Broadcasting
6,850,000	GEICO Corporation	45,713	756,925	35.8	Finance	Insurance
1,727,765	The Washington Post Company	9,731	323,092	15.3	Consumer cyclical	Publishing
	Total common stocks	$572,944	$2,115,017	100.0		

Source: Berkshire Hathaway 1987 Annual Report.
Note: Dollar amounts are in thousands.

Table A.12 Berkshire Hathaway 1988 Common Stock Portfolio

No. of Shares	Company	Cost	Market Value	Percentage of Portfolio	Industry	Business
3,000,000	Capital Cities/ABC, Inc.	$ 517,500	$1,086,750	35.6	Consumer cyclical	Broadcasting
6,850,000	GEICO Corporation	45,713	849,400	27.8	Finance	Insurance
14,172,500	The Coca-Cola Company	592,540	632,448	20.7	Consumer staples	Beverage
1,727,765	The Washington Post Company	9,731	364,126	11.9	Consumer cyclical	Publishing
2,400,000	Federal Home Loan Mortgage Corp.	71,729	121,200	4.0	Finance	Financial services
	Total common stocks	$1,165,484	$3,053,924	100.0		

Source: Berkshire Hathaway 1988 Annual Report.
Note: Dollar amounts are in thousands.

Table A.13 Berkshire Hathaway 1989 Common Stock Portfolio

No. of Shares	Company	Cost	Market Value	Percentage of Portfolio	Industry	Business
23,350,000	The Coca-Cola Company	$1,023,920	$1,803,787	34.8	Consumer staples	Beverage
3,000,000	Capital Cities/ABC, Inc.	517,500	1,692,375	32.6	Consumer cyclical	Broadcasting
6,850,000	GEICO Corporation	45,713	1,044,625	20.1	Finance	Insurance
1,727,765	The Washington Post Company	9,731	486,366	9.4	Consumer cyclical	Publishing
2,400,000	Federal Home Loan Mortgage Corp.	71,729	161,100	3.1	Finance	Financial services
	Total common stocks	$1,668,593	$5,188,253	100.0		

Source: Berkshire Hathaway 1989 Annual Report.
Note: Dollar amounts are in thousands.

283

Table A.14 Berkshire Hathaway 1990 Common Stock Portfolio

No. of Shares	Company	Cost	Market Value	Percentage of Portfolio	Industry	Business
46,700,000	The Coca-Cola Company	$1,023,920	$2,171,550	40.2	Consumer staples	Beverage
3,000,000	Capital Cities/ABC, Inc.	517,500	1,377,375	25.5	Consumer cyclical	Broadcasting
6,850,000	GEICO Corporation	45,713	1,110,556	20.5	Finance	Insurance
1,727,765	The Washington Post Company	9,731	349,097	6.3	Consumer cyclical	Publishing
5,000,000	Wells Fargo & Company	289,431	289,375	5.4	Finance	Bank
2,400,000	Federal Home Loan Mortgage Corp.	71,729	117,000	2.2	Finance	Financial services
	Total common stocks	$1,958,024	$5,407,953	100.0		

Source: Berkshire Hathaway 1990 Annual Report.
Note: Dollar amounts are in thousands.

Table A.15 Berkshire Hathaway 1991 Common Stock Portfolio

No. of Shares	Company	Cost	Market Value	Percentage of Portfolio	Industry	Business
46,700,000	The Coca-Cola Company	$1,023,920	$3,747,675	41.5	Consumer staples	Beverage
6,850,000	GEICO Corporation	45,713	1,363,150	15.1	Finance	Insurance
24,000,000	The Gillette Company	600,000	1,347,000	14.9	Consumer staples	Toiletries
3,000,000	Capital Cities/ABC, Inc.	517,500	1,300,500	14.4	Consumer cyclical	Broadcasting
2,495,200	Federal Home Loan Mortgage Corp.	77,245	343,090	3.8	Finance	Financial services
1,727,765	The Washington Post Company	9,731	336,050	3.7	Consumer cyclical	Publishing
31,247,000	Guinness plc	264,782	296,755	3.3	Consumer staples	Beverage
5,000,000	Wells Fargo & Company	289,431	290,000	3.2	Finance	Bank
	Total common stocks	$2,828,322	$9,024,220	100.0		

Source: Berkshire Hathaway 1991 Annual Report.
Note: Dollar amounts are in thousands.

Table A.16 Berkshire Hathaway 1992 Common Stock Portfolio

No. of Shares	Company	Cost	Market Value	Percentage of Portfolio	Industry	Business
93,400,000	The Coca-Cola Company	$1,023,920	$ 3,911,125	34.2	Consumer staples	Beverage
34,250,000	GEICO Corporation	45,713	2,226,250	19.5	Finance	Insurance
3,000,000	Capital Cities/ABC, Inc.	517,500	1,523,500	13.3	Consumer cyclical	Broadcasting
24,000,000	The Gillette Company	600,000	1,365,000	11.9	Consumer staples	Toiletries
16,196,700	Federal Home Loan Mortgage Corp.	414,527	783,515	6.8	Finance	Financial services
6,358,418	Wells Fargo & Company	380,983	485,624	4.2	Finance	Bank
4,350,000	General Dynamics	312,438	450,769	3.9	Capital Goods	Aerospace
1,727,765	The Washington Post Company	9,731	396,954	3.5	Consumer cyclical	Publishing
38,335,000	Guinness plc	333,019	299,581	2.6	Consumer staples	Beverage
	Total common stocks	$3,637,831	$11,442,318	100.0		

Source: Berkshire Hathaway 1992 Annual Report.
Note: Dollar amounts are in thousands.

Table A.17 Berkshire Hathaway 1993 Common Stock Portfolio

No. of Shares	Company	Cost	Market Value	Percentage of Portfolio	Industry	Business
93,400,000	The Coca-Cola Company	$1,023,920	$ 4,167,975	37.0	Consumer staples	Beverage
34,250,000	GEICO Corporation	45,713	1,759,594	15.6	Finance	Insurance
24,000,000	The Gillette Company	600,000	1,431,000	12.7	Consumer staples	Toiletries
2,000,000	Capital Cities/ABC, Inc.	345,000	1,239,000	11.0	Consumer cyclical	Broadcasting
6,791,218	Wells Fargo & Company	423,680	878,614	7.8	Finance	Bank
13,654,600	Federal Home Loan Mortgage Corp.	307,505	681,023	6.0	Finance	Financial services
1,727,765	The Washington Post Company	9,731	440,148	3.9	Consumer cyclical	Publishing
4,350,000	General Dynamics	94,938	401,287	3.6	Capital goods	Aerospace
38,335,000	Guinness PLC	333,019	270,822	2.4	Consumer staples	Beverage
	Total common stocks	$3,183,506	$11,269,463	100.0		

Source: Berkshire Hathaway 1993 Annual Report.
Note: Dollar amounts are in thousands.

Table A.18 Berkshire Hathaway 1994 Common Stock Portfolio

No. of Shares	Company	Cost	Market Value	Percentage of Portfolio	Industry	Business
93,400,000	The Coca-Cola Company	$1,023,920	$ 5,150,000	36.9	Consumer staples	Beverage
24,000,000	The Gillette Company	600,000	1,797,000	12.9	Consumer staples	Toiletries
20,000,000	Capital Cities/ABC, Inc.	345,000	1,705,000	12.2	Consumer cyclical	Broadcasting
34,250,000	GEICO Corporation	45,713	1,678,250	12.0	Finance	Insurance
6,791,218	Wells Fargo & Company	423,680	984,272	7.0	Finance	Bank
27,759,941	American Express Company	723,919	818,918	5.9	Finance	Financial services
13,654,600	Federal Home Loan Mortgage Corp.	270,468	644,441	4.6	Finance	Financial services
1,727,765	The Washington Post Company	9,731	418,983	3.0	Consumer cyclical	Publishing
19,453,300	PNC Bank Corporation	503,046	410,951	2.9	Finance	Bank
6,854,500	Gannett Co., Inc.	335,216	365,002	2.6	Consumer cyclical	Publishing
	Total Common Stocks	$4,280,693	$13,972,817	100.0		

Source: Berkshire Hathaway 1994 Annual Report.
Note: Dollar amounts are in thousands.

288

Table A.19 Insurance Expense Ratios Corporate Expenses as Percentages of Premiums Written

	GEICO	Chubb	Continental	General Re	SAFECO	St. Paul	USF&G	Peer Group Average
1983	16.4	35.1	32.6	31.6	33.0	31.8	32.2	32.7
1984	15.6	34.9	32.1	31.2	31.9	30.9	31.4	32.1
1985	15.0	34.5	29.6	26.0	30.6	28.5	30.0	29.9
1986	14.7	28.4	28.6	23.7	30.0	27.9	29.1	27.9
1987	15.5	31.0	29.4	25.5	30.2	28.9	30.1	29.2
1988	18.6	33.7	31.9	29.1	28.8	30.0	31.1	30.8
1989	16.3	34.7	34.1	24.9	13.7	30.5	31.0	28.2
1990	15.2	34.4	33.7	31.2	28.8	30.0	29.9	31.3
1991	16.8	34.1	35.2	29.7	29.5	26.9	33.1	31.4
1992	15.3	34.4	32.7	29.6	28.2	32.2	34.9	32.0
Average	15.9	33.5	32.0	28.2	28.5	29.8	31.3	30.5

Table A.20 Insurance Industry Combined Ratio: Percentages of
Underwriting Loss and General Expenses

	GEICO	Insurance Industry[a]	GEICO's Combined Ratio Superiority[b]
1977	99.1	97.2	−1.9
1978	95.9	97.5	1.6
1979	96.3	100.6	4.3
1980	96.4	103.1	6.7
1981	96.2	106.0	9.8
1982	95.3	109.6	14.3
1983	95.5	112.0	16.5
1984	95.0	118.0	23.0
1985	102.9	116.0	13.1
1986	96.9	108.0	11.1
1987	96.7	104.6	7.9
1988	97.8	105.4	7.6
1989	97.4	109.2	11.8
1990	96.4	109.6	13.2
1991	96.4	108.8	12.4
1992	100.1	114.8	14.7
Average	97.1	107.5	10.4

[a]Data from AM Best Co.
[b]Compared to the industry average.

Table A.21 The Coca-Cola Company Discounted Owner Earnings Using a Two-Stage "Dividend" Discount Model (first stage is ten years)

	Year									
	1	2	3	4	5	6	7	8	9	10
Prior year owner earnings	$828	$952	$1,095	$1,259	$1,448	$1,665	$1,915	$2,202	$2,532	$2,912
Growth rate (add)	15%	15%	15%	15%	15%	15%	15%	15%	15%	15%
Owner earnings	$952	$1,095	$1,259	$1,448	$1,665	$1,915	$2,202	$2,532	$2,912	$3,349
Discount factor (multiply)	0.9174	0.8417	0.7722	0.7084	0.6499	0.5963	0.5470	0.5019	0.4604	0.4224
Discounted value per annum	$873	$922	$972	$1,026	$1,082	$1,142	$1,204	$1,271	$1,341	$1,415

Sum of present value of owner-earnings $11,248

Residual Value
Owner earnings in year 10	$3,349
Growth rate (g) (add)	5%
Owner earnings in year 11	$3,516
Capitalization rate (k – g)	4%
Value at end of year 10	$87,900
Discount factor at end of year 10 (multiply)	0.4224
Present Value of Residual	37,129
Intrinsic Value of Company	$48,377

Notes: Assumed first-stage growth rate = 15.0%; assumed second-stage growth rate = 5.0%; k = discount rate = 9.0%. Dollar amounts are in millions.

Table A.22 The Gillette Company

	Annual Sales	Annual Income	Depreciation	Capital Expenditures	Owner Earnings
1981	$2,334	$124.3	$ 76.7	$116.1	$ 84.9
1982	2,239	135.1	77.5	90.5	122.1
1983	2,183	145.9	78.2	90.1	134.0
1984	2,288	159.3	76.0	155.3	80.0
1985	2,400	159.9	77.7	158.1	79.5
1986	2,818	15.8	97.3	229.7	-116.6
1987	3,166	229.9	114.1	168.0	176.0
1988	3,581	268.5	127.4	189.0	206.9
1989	3,818	284.7	134.6	222.6	196.7
1990	4,344	367.9	162.1	255.2	274.8
1991	4,683	427.4	172.4	286.0	313.8
1992	5,162	513.4	188.0	321.4	380.0
Compounded Annual Growth Rates					
1981–1985	0.6%	5.2%	0.3%	6.4%	-1.3%
1987–1990	11.1%	17.0%	12.4%	15.0%	16.0%
1987–1992	10.3%	17.4%	10.5%	13.9%	16.6%

Note: Dollar amounts are in millions.

Table A.23 The Gillette Company Discounted Owner Earnings Using a Two-Stage "Dividend" Discount Model (first stage is ten years)

	Year									
	1	2	3	4	5	6	7	8	9	10
Prior year owner earnings	$275	$316	$363	$417	$480	$552	$635	$730	$840	$966
Growth rate (add)	15%	15%	15%	15%	15%	15%	15%	15%	15%	15%
Owner earnings	$316	$363	$417	$480	$552	$635	$730	$840	$966	$1,111
Discount factor (multiply)	0.9174	0.8417	0.7722	0.7084	0.6499	0.5963	0.5470	0.5019	0.4604	0.4224
Discounted value per annum	$290	$306	$322	$340	$359	$379	$399	$422	$445	$469

Sum of present value of owner-earnings $ 3,731

Residual Value
Owner earnings in year 10	$ 1,111	
Growth rate (g) (add)	5%	
Owner earnings in year 11	$ 1,167	
Capitalization rate (k − g)	4%	
Value at end of year 10	$29,175	
Discount factor at end of year 10 (multiply)	0.4224	
Present Value of Residual		$12,324
Intrinsic Value of Company		$16,055

Notes: Assumed first-stage growth rate = 15.0%; assumed second-stage growth rate = 5.0%; k = discount rate = 9.0%.
Dollar amounts are in millions.

Table A.24 Federal Home Loan Mortgage Corporation Discounted Owner Earnings Using a Two-Stage "Dividend" Discount Model (first stage is ten years)

	Year									
	1	2	3	4	5	6	7	8	9	10
Prior year owner earnings	$555	$638	$734	$844	$971	$1,117	$1,285	$1,478	$1,700	$1,955
Growth rate (add)	15%	15%	15%	15%	15%	15%	15%	15%	15%	15%
Owner earnings	$638	$734	$844	$971	$1,117	$1,285	$1,478	$1,700	$1,955	$2,248
Discount factor (multiply)	0.9174	0.8417	0.7722	0.7084	0.6499	0.5963	0.5470	0.5019	0.4604	0.4224
Discounted value per annum	$585	$618	$652	$688	$726	$766	$808	$853	$900	$950

Sum of present value of owner-earnings $ 7,546

Residual Value

Owner earnings in year 10	$ 2,248
Growth rate (g) (add)	5%
Owner earnings in year 11	$ 2,360
Capitalization rate (k − g)	4%
Value at end of year 10	$59,000
Discount factor at end of year 10 (multiply)	0.4224
Present Value of Residual	$24,922
Intrinsic Value of Company	$32,468

Notes: Assumed first-stage growth = 15.0%; assumed second-stage growth = 5.0%; k = discount rate = 9.0%. Dollar amounts are in millions.

294

Table A.25 Guinness plc Discounted Owner Earnings Using a Two-Stage "Dividend" Discount Model (first stage is ten years)

	Year									
	1	2	3	4	5	6	7	8	9	10
Prior year owner earnings	£534	£587	£646	£711	£782	£860	£ 946	£1,041	£1,145	£1,260
Growth rate (add)	10%	10%	10%	10%	10%	10%	10%	10%	10%	10%
Owner earnings	£587	£646	£711	£782	£860	£946	£1,041	£1,145	£1,260	£1,386
Discount factor (multiply)	0.9174	0.8417	0.7722	0.7084	0.6499	0.5963	0.5470	0.5019	0.4604	0.4224
Discounted value per annum	£539	£544	£549	£554	£559	£564	£ 569	£ 575	£ 580	£ 585

Sum of present value of owner-earnings   £ 5,618

Residual Value

Owner earnings in year 10		£ 1,386
Growth rate (g) (add)		5%
Owner earnings in year 11		£ 1,455
Capitalization rate ($k - g$)		4%
Value at end of year 10		£36,375
Discount factor at end of year 10 (multiply)		0.4224
Present Value of Residual	£15,365	
Intrinsic Value of Company	£20,983	

Notes: Assumed first-stage growth rate = 10.0%; assumed second-stage growth rate = 5.0%; k = discount rate = 9.0%. Cash amounts are in millions of British pounds.

Table A.26 The Gannett Company Discounted Owner Earnings Using a Two-Stage "Dividend" Discount Model (first stage is ten years)

					Year					
	1	2	3	4	5	6	7	8	9	10
Prior year owner earnings	$474	$531	$595	$666	$746	$836	$936	$1,048	$1,174	$1,315
Growth rate (add)	12.0%	12.0%	12.0%	12.0%	12.0%	12.0%	12.0%	12.0%	12.0%	12.0%
Owner earnings	$531	$595	$666	$746	$836	$936	$1,048	$1,174	$1,315	$1,473
Discount factor (multiply)	0.9091	0.8264	0.7513	0.6830	0.6209	0.5645	0.5132	0.4665	0.4241	0.3855
Discounted value per annum	$483	$492	$500	$510	$519	$528	$538	$548	$558	$568

Sum of present value of owner-earnings $5,244

Residual Value

Owner earnings in year 10	$1,473
Growth rate (g) (add)	5.0%
Owner earnings in year 11	$1,547
Capitalization rate ($k - g$)	5.0%
Value at end of year 10	$30,940
Discount factor at end of year 10 (multiply)	0.3855
Present Value of Residual	$11,927
Intrinsic Value of Company	$17,171
Intrinsic Value per Share	$122.65
(140 million shares outstanding)	

Notes: Assumed first-stage growth rate = 12.0%; assumed second-stage growth rate = 5.0%; k = discount rate = 10.0%. Dollars are in millions.

296

Table A.27 The American Express Company Discounted Owner Earnings Using a Two-Stage "Dividend" Discount Model (first stage is ten years)

	Year									
	1	2	3	4	5	6	7	8	9	10
Prior year owner earnings	$1,400	$1,540	$1,694	$1,863	$2,049	$2,254	$2,479	$2,727	$3,000	$3,300
Growth rate (add)	10.0%	10.0%	10.0%	10.0%	10.0%	10.0%	10.0%	10.0%	10.0%	10.0%
Owner earnings	$1,540	$1,694	$1,863	$2,049	$2,254	$2,479	$2,727	$3,000	$3,300	$3,630
Discount factor (multiply)	0.9091	0.8264	0.7513	0.6830	0.6209	0.5645	0.5132	0.4665	0.4241	0.3855
Discounted value per annum	$1,400	$1,400	$1,400	$1,399	$1,400	$1,399	$1,399	$1,400	$1,400	$1,399

Sum of present value of owner-earnings $13,996

Residual Value

Owner earnings in year 10	$3,630
Growth rate (g) (add)	5.0%
Owner earnings in year 11	$3,812
Capitalization rate (k – g)	5.0%
Value at end of year 10	$76,240
Discount factor at end of year 10 (multiply)	0.3855
Present Value of Residual	$29,391
Intrinsic Value of Company	$49,387
Intrinsic Value per Share	$86.77
(500 million shares outstanding)	

Notes: Assumed first-stage growth rate = 10.0%; assumed second-stage growth rate = 5.0%; k = discount rate = 10.0%. Dollars are in millions.

Table A.28 The Disney/Capital Cities Combined Discounted Owner Earnings Using a Two-Stage "Dividend" Discount Model (first stage is ten years)

	Year									
	1	2	3	4	5	6	7	8	9	10
Prior year owner earnings	$1,180	$1,357	$1,561	$1,795	$2,064	$2,374	$2,730	$3,140	$3,611	$4,153
Growth rate (add)	15.0%	15.0%	15.0%	15.0%	15.0%	15.0%	15.0%	15.0%	15.0%	15.0%
Owner earnings	$1,357	$1,561	$1,795	$2,064	$2,374	$2,730	$3,140	$3,611	$4,153	$4,776
Discount factor (multiply)	0.9091	0.8264	0.7513	0.6830	0.6209	0.5645	0.5132	0.4665	0.4241	0.3855
Discounted value per annum	$1,234	$1,290	$1,349	$1,410	$1,474	$1,541	$1,611	$1,685	$1,761	$1,841

Sum of present value of owner-earnings $15,196

Residual Value
Owner earnings in year 10	$4,776
Growth rate (g) (add)	5.0%
Owner earnings in year 11	$5,015
Capitalization rate ($k − g$)	5.0%
Value at end of year 10	$100,300
Discount factor at end of year 10 (multiply)	0.3855

Present Value of Residual	$38,666
Intrinsic Value of Company	$53,862
Intrinsic Value per Share	$79.80
(675 million shares outstanding)	

Notes: Assumed first-stage growth rate = 15.0%; assumed second-stage growth rate = 5.0%; k = discount rate = 10.0%. Dollars are in millions.

NOTES

ONE: Five-Sigma Event

1. Cited by Carol Loomis, "Inside Story on Warren Buffett," *Fortune*, April 11, 1988.
2. Warren Buffett, "The Superinvestors of Graham-and-Doddsville," *Hermes*, Fall 1984.
3. John Train, *The Money Masters* (New York: Penguin Books, 1981), 11.
4. Ibid., 12.
5. Berkshire Hathaway Annual Report, 1985, 8.
6. Linda J. Collins, "Berkshire's Buffett Sees More Competition Ahead," *Business Insurance*, May 7, 1990, 67.
7. Berkshire Hathaway Annual Report, 1987, 22.

TWO: The Two Wise Men

1. "The Money Men—How Omaha Beats Wall Street," *Forbes*, November 1, 1969, 82.
2. Warren Buffett, "What We Can Learn from Philip Fisher," *Forbes*, October 19, 1987, 40.
3. Adam Smith, *Supermoney* (New York: Random House, 1972), 178.
4. *New York Times*, December 2, 1934, 13D.
5. Benjamin Graham and David Dodd, *Security Analysis*, 3d ed. (New York: McGraw-Hill, 1951), 38.
6. Ibid., 13.

7. "Ben Graham: The Grandfather of Investment Value Is Still Concerned," *Institutional Investor*, April 1974, 62.

8. Ibid., 61.

9. John Train, *The Money Masters* (New York: Penguin Books, 1981), 60.

10. Philip Fisher, *Common Stocks and Uncommon Profits*, (New York: Harper & Brothers, 1958), 11.

11. Ibid., 16.

12. Ibid., 33.

13. Philip Fisher, *Developing an Investment Philosophy*, The Financial Analysts Research Foundation, Monograph Number 10, 1.

14. Fisher, *Common Stocks*, 13.

15. Fisher, "Developing an Investment Philosophy," 29.

16. Andrew Kilpatrick, *Warren Buffett: The Good Guy of Wall Street* (New York: Donald I. Fine, 1992), 38.

17. Robert Lenzner, "Warren Buffett's Idea of Heaven: I Don't Have to Work with People I Don't Like," *Forbes*, October 18, 1993, 43.

18. Berkshire Hathaway Annual Report, 1989, 21.

19. Ibid.

20. L. J. Davis, "Buffett Takes Stock," *The New York Times Magazine*, April 1, 1990, 61.

21. Berkshire Hathaway Annual Report, 1987, 15

22. Berkshire Hathaway Annual Report, 1990, 17.

23. Warren Buffett, "The Superinvestors of Graham-and-Doddsville," *Hermes*, Fall 1984.

24. Benjamin Graham, *The Intelligent Investor*, 4th ed. (New York: Harper & Row, 1973), 287.

THREE: Mr. Market and the Lemmings

1. Benjamin Graham, *The Intelligent Investor*, 4th ed. (New York: Harper & Row, 1973), 96.

2. Berkshire Hathaway Annual Report, 1992, 6.

3. Warren Buffett, "You Pay a Very High Price in the Stock Market for a Cheery Consensus," *Forbes*, August 6, 1979, 25–26.

4. Ibid.

5. Berkshire Hathaway Annual Report, 1986, 16.

6. Berkshire Hathaway Annual Report, 1990, 17.

7. Peter Lynch, *One Up on Wall Street* (New York: Penguin Books, 1990), 78.

8. Linda Grant, "Striking Out at Wall Street," *U.S. News & World Report*, June 20, 1994, 58.

9. Berkshire Hathaway Letters to Shareholders, 1977–1983, 19.

10. Warren Buffett, "How Inflation Swindles the Equity Investor," *Fortune*, May 5, 1977, 250–267.

11. Buffett makes a distinction between *book value*, an accounting concept, and *intrinsic value*, an economic concept. Intrinsic value is figured by estimating future cash flows and then discounting them back to present value. Intrinsic value is more meaningful, Buffett says, but it involves the very subjective exercise of estimating the future. That is why Berkshire's annual reports track the company's long-term performance by noting the growth in book value: It is easy to calculate, Buffett says, and avoids subjective opinions. In 1993, Berkshire's book value per share was $8,854 per share; its intrinsic value is considerably larger, although Buffett and Charlie may not agree on precisely what it is. The difference between the book value and intrinsic value is *economic goodwill.*

12. Berkshire Letters to Shareholders, 1977–1983, 81.

13. Berkshire Hathaway Annual Report, 1991, 10.

14. Linda Grant, "The $4 Billion Regular Guy," *Los Angeles Times*, April 7, 1991, magazine section, 36.

15. Berkshire Hathaway Annual Report, 1990, 15.

16. Mark Hulbert, "Be a Tiger Not a Hen," *Forbes*, May 25, 1992, 298.

17. Berkshire Hathaway Annual Report, 1991, 15.

18. Although Berkshire Hathaway owns 48 percent of GEICO Corporation, Buffett was ordered by the insurance supervisory authority to maintain an independent proxy arrangement for voting the shares of GEICO. Furthermore, the order, which dates back to the time of purchase, prohibits Berkshire from seeking to change this independent proxy. Since Berkshire does not have voting rights, it does not have influence over GEICO. Hence, accounting rules dictate that the GEICO investment should be treated as a less than 20 percent ownership.

19. Berkshire Hathaway Annual Report, 1990, 7.

20. Berkshire Hathaway Annual Report, 1984, 14.

FOUR: Buying a Business

1. Berkshire Hathaway Annual Report, 1987, 14.

2. Robert Lenzner, "Warren Buffett's Idea of Heaven: I Don't Have to Work with People I Don't Like," *Forbes*, October 18, 1993, 43.

3. *Fortune*, November 29, 1993, 11.

4. Berkshire Hathaway Annual Report, 1992, 15.

5. Berkshire Hathaway Annual Report, 1987, 7.

6. Berkshire Hathaway Annual Report, 1989, 22.

7. Berkshire Letters to Shareholders, 1977–1983, 57.

8. Lenzner, "Warren Buffett's Idea of Heaven."
9. Berkshire Hathaway Annual Report, 1991, 8.
10. Carol Loomis, "Inside Story on Warren Buffett," *Fortune*, April 11, 1988, 32.
11. Berkshire Hathaway Annual Report, 1988, 5.
12. Berkshire Hathaway Annual Report, 1986, 5.
13. Berkshire Hathaway Annual Report, 1989, 22.
14. Ibid.
15. Linda Grant, "The $4 Billion Regular Guy," *Los Angeles Times*, April 7, 1991, magazine section, 36.
16. Lenzner, "Warren Buffett's Idea of Heaven," 43.
17. Berkshire Hathaway Annual Report, 1985, 9.
18. Berkshire Letters to Shareholders, 1977–1983, 17.
19. Berkshire Hathaway Annual Report, 1987, 20.
20. Ibid., 21.
21. Berkshire Hathaway Annual Report, 1984, 15.
22. Berkshire Hathaway Annual Report, 1986, 25.
23. Loomis, "Inside Story on Warren Buffett," 34.
24. Berkshire Hathaway Annual Report, 1990, 16.
25. Berkshire Letters to Shareholders, 1977–1983, 52.
26. Berkshire Hathaway Annual Report, 1989, 5.
27. Jim Rasmussen, "Buffett Talks Strategy With Students," *Omaha World-Herald*, January 2, 1994, 26.
28. Berkshire Hathaway Annual Report, 1992, 14.
29. Berkshire Letters to Shareholders, 1977–1983, 53.
30. Lenzner, "Warren Buffett's Idea of Heaven," 43.
31. Berkshire Letters to Shareholders, 1977–1983, 82.

FIVE: Permanent Holdings

1. Berkshire Hathaway Annual Report, 1987, 15.
2. Ibid.
3. Mary Rowland, "Mastermind of a Media Empire," *Working Woman*, November 11, 1989, 115.
4. The Washington Post Company Annual Report, 1991, 2.
5. Berkshire Hathaway Annual Report, 1984, 8.
6. Berkshire Hathaway Annual Report, 1985, 19.
7. Chalmers M. Roberts, *The Washington Post, The First 100 Years* (Boston: Houghton Mifflin Company, 1977), 449.
8. The Washington Post Company Annual Report, 1992, 5.
9. Berkshire Hathaway Annual Report, 1991, 8.
10. Ibid., 9.
11. Berkshire Hathaway Annual Report, 1985, 19.

Notes

12. Carol Loomis, "An Accident Report on GEICO," *Fortune*, June 1976, 120.
13. Although the 1973–1974 bear market might have contributed to part of GEICO's earlier fall, its decline in 1975 and 1976 was all of its own making. In 1975, the Standard & Poor's 500 Index began at 70.23 and ended the year at 90.9. The next year, the stock market was equally as strong. In 1976, the stock market rose and interest rates fell. GEICO's share price decline had nothing to do with the financial markets.
14. Beth Brophy, "After the Fall and Rise," *Forbes*, February 2, 1981, 86.
15. Lynn Dodds, "Handling the Naysayers," *Financial World*, August 17, 1985, 42.
16. Stan Hinden, "Annual Reports: Standing Out in a Crowded Field," *The Washington Post*, April 29, 1991.
17. Solveig Jansson, "GEICO Sticks to Its Last," *Institutional Investor*, July 1986, 130.
18. GEICO Annual Report, 1991, 5.
19. David Vise, "GEICO's Top Market Strategist Churning Out Profits," *The Washington Post*, May 11, 1987.
20. GEICO Annual Report, 1990, 5.
21. Berkshire Letters to Shareholders, 1977–1983, 58.
22. "Why GEICO Is Acquiring More of Itself," *Business Week*, September 12, 1983, 45.
23. Buying back its own shares was not only a rational strategy for GEICO but a financial bonanza for Berkshire Hathaway as well. Since Berkshire owned one-third of the shares outstanding, Buffett agreed to tender one share of stock for every two shares of publicly tendered stock. By maintaining its one-third ownership in the company, Berkshire was entitled to special tax treatment. Under Section 302 of the Tax Code, because Berkshire's percentage of ownership of GEICO did not change, the proceeds from the tender were treated as a dividend, not a capital gain. Hence, Berkshire's $18.6 million profit on GEICO's stock qualified for an 85 percent corporate deduction on dividends, thereby reducing its effective tax rate to 6.9 percent versus 28 percent for capital gains.
24. Berkshire Letters to Shareholders, 1977–1983, 33.
25. "Annual Report on American Industry," *Forbes*, January 8, 1990, 119.
26. Andrew Kilpatrick, *Warren Buffett: The Good Guy of Wall Street* (New York: Donald Fine Inc., 1992), 102.
27. Anthony Bianco, "Why Warren Buffett Is Breaking His Own Rules," *Business Week*, April 15, 1985, 34.
28. Berkshire Hathaway Annual Report, 1991, 8.
29. Bianco, "Why Warren Buffett Is Breaking His Own Rules."
30. Dennis Kneale, "Murphy & Burke," *The Wall Street Journal*, February 2, 1990, 1.
31. Capital Cities/ABC Inc. Annual Report, 1992.

32. "A Star Is Born," *Business Week*, April 1, 1985, 77.

33. Anthony Baldo, "CEO of the Year Daniel B. Burke," *Financial World*, April 2, 1991, 38.

34. Berkshire Hathaway Annual Report, 1985, 20.

35. R. Hutchings Vernon, "Mother of All Annual Meetings," *Barron's*, May 6, 1991, 32.

36. Robert Lenzner, "Warren Buffett's Idea of Heaven: I Don't Have to Work with People I Don't Like," *Forbes*, October 18, 1993, 44.

37. Berkshire Hathaway Annual Report, 1991, 9.

38. Kilpatrick, *Warren Buffett: The Good Guy of Wall Street*, 123.

39. Ibid.

40. Mark Pendergrast, *For God, Country and Coca-Cola* (New York: Charles Scribner's Sons, 1993).

41. Art Harris, "The Man Who Changed the Real Thing," *The Washington Post*, July 22, 1985, B1.

42. "Strategy for the 1980s," The Coca Cola Company.

43. Ibid.

44. The first stage applies 15 percent annual growth for ten years. In year one, 1989, owner earnings would equal $952 million; by year ten, they will be $3.349 billion. Starting with year eleven, growth will slow to 5 percent per year, the second stage. In year eleven, owner earnings will equal $3.516 billion ($3.349 billion × 5% + $3.349 billion). Now, we can subtract this 5 percent growth rate from the risk-free rate of return (9 percent) and reach a capitalization rate of 4 percent. The discounted value of a company with $3.516 billion in owner earnings capitalized at 4 percent is $87.9 billion. Since this value, $87.9 billion, is the discounted value of Coca-Cola's owner earnings in year eleven, we next have to discount this future value by the discount factor at the end of year ten $1/(1 + .09)^{10} = .4224$. The present value of the residual value of Coca-Cola in year ten is $37.129 billion. The value of Coca-Cola then equals its residual value ($37.129 billion) plus the sum of the present value of cash flows during this period ($11.248 billion), for a total of $48.377 billion.

SIX: Fixed-Income Marketable Securities

1. Berkshire Hathaway Annual Report, 1988, 14.

2. Berkshire Hathaway Annual Report, 1990, 18.

3. Ibid.

4. Berkshire Hathaway Annual Report, 1988, 15.

5. Ibid., 14.

6. Ibid., 16.

7. Beth McGoldrick and Beth Selby, "Salomon's John Gutfreund," *Institutional Investor*, February 1991, 53.
8. Berkshire Hathaway Annual Report, 1987, 19.
9. Jim Rasmussen, "Buffett Talks Strategy with Students," *Omaha World-Herald*, January 2, 1994, 26.
10. Ibid.
11. Nightly Business Report, interview with Linda O'Bryon, April 28, 1994.
12. Berkshire Hathaway Annual Report, 1990, 18.
13. Berkshire Hathaway Annual Report, 1989, 17.
14. Berkshire Hathaway Annual Report, 1990, 19.
15. Berkshire Hathaway Annual Report, 1991, 17.
16. Rasmussen, "Buffett Talks Strategy with Students," 26.
17. Richard Phalon and Gilbert Steedly, "Paper Chase," *Forbes*, February 14, 1994, 184.
18. "Why AMEX Wooed Warren Buffett," *Business Week*, August 19, 1991, 97.
19. Ibid.
20. Berkshire Hathaway Annual Report, 1990, 19.
21. Berkshire Hathaway Annual Report, 1989, 17.

SEVEN: Equity Marketable Securities

1. Berkshire Hathaway Annual Report, 1987, 15.
2. Berkshire Hathaway Annual Report, 1989, 17.
3. Berkshire Hathaway Annual Report, 1991, 5.
4. Robert Lenzner, "Warren Buffett's Idea of Heaven: I Don't Have to Work with People I Don't Like," *Forbes*, October 18, 1993, 43.
5. Berkshire Hathaway Annual Report, 1992, 13.
6. Ibid.
7. Brett Duval Fromson, "A Warm Tip from Warren Buffett: It's Time to Buy Freddie Macs," *Fortune*, December 19, 1988, 33.
8. Ibid.
9. Berkshire Hathaway Annual Report, 1991, 15.
10. Bill Saporito, "Liquor Profits," *Fortune*, November 4, 1991, 176.
11. R. Hutchings Vernon, "The Warren and Charlie Show," *Barron's*, May 11, 1992, 14.
12. Saporito, "Liquor Profits," 176.
13. John Dorfman, "Wells Fargo Has Bulls and Bears; So Who's Right?" *The Wall Street Journal*, November 1, 1990, C1.
14. Ibid.
15. John Liscio, "Trading Points," *Barron's*, October 29, 1990, 51.

16. Berkshire Letters to Shareholders, 1977–1983, 15.
17. Berkshire Hathaway Annual Report, 1990, 16.
18. Reid Nagle, "Interpreting the Banking Numbers," in *The Financial Ser vices Industry—Banks, Thrifts, Insurance Companies, and Securities Firms* Association of Investment Management and Research, 1991.
19. "CEO Silver Award," *Financial World*, April 5, 1988, 92.
20. Gary Hector, "Warren Buffett's Favorite Banker," *Forbes*, October 18, 1993, 46.
21. Berkshire Hathaway Annual Report, 1990, 16.
22. Ibid.
23. Ibid.
24. R. Hutchings Vernon, "Mother of All Annual Meetings," *Barron's*, May 6, 1991.
25. John Taylor, "A Leveraged Bet," *Forbes*, April 15, 1991, 42.
26. Susan Pulliam, "Wells Fargo's Loan-Loss Reserves May Prove Far Too Large, Boosting Profit and Stock in '94," *The Wall Street Journal*, November 11, 1993, C2.
27. Hector, "Warren Buffett's Favorite Banker," 46.

EIGHT: A Few More Good Stocks

1. Gannett Annual Report, 1994, 4.
2. Berkshire Hathaway Annual Report, 1994, 1.
3. Berkshire Hathaway Annual Report, 1994, 17.
4. Tony Jackson, "Disney in $19bn TV Takeover," *Financial Times*, August 1, 1995, 1.
5. Ibid.
6. Maggie Mahar, "Magic Kingdom?" *Barron's*, August 7, 1995, 14.
7. Bill Carter and Richard Sandomir, "The Trophy in Eisner's Big Deal," *The New York Times*, August 6, 1995, 3-1.
8. Bill Carter, "Suddenly at ABC, The Future Is Now," *The New York Times*, August 1, 1995, D1.
9. Jackson, "Disney."

NINE: An Unreasonable Man

1. This quote was used to describe Warren Buffett in V. Eugene Shahan's article, "Are Short-Term Performance and Value Investing Mutually Exclusive?" *Hermes*, Spring 1986.
2. Carol Loomis, "Inside Story on Warren Buffett," *Fortune*, April 11, 1988, 34.
3. Warren Buffett, "Oil Discovered in Hell," *Investment Decision*, May 1985, 22.

4. Loomis, "Inside Story of Warren Buffett," 28.
5. Linda Grant, "The $4 Billion Regular Guy," *Los Angeles Times*, April 7, 1991, Magazine Section, 36.
6. Berkshire Hathaway Annual Report, 1993, 15.
7. Ibid., 16.
8. Ibid.
9. Ibid., 14.
10. Ibid.
11. Berkshire Hathaway Annual Report, 1987, 15.
12. Robert Lenzner, "Warren Buffett's Idea of Heaven: I Don't Have to Work with People I Don't Like," *Forbes*, October 18, 1993, 40.
13. Berkshire Hathaway Annual Report, 1992, 6.

INDEX

Index